RED SONJA

VULTURE'S CIRCLE

RED SONJA

VULTURE'S CIRCLE

written by
NANCY A. COLLINS
LUKE LIEBERMAN
art by
FRITZ CASAS
colors by
ADRIANO AUGUSTO
letters by
JOSHUA COZINE
cover by
JAY ANACLETO
IVAN NUNES

based on the heroine created by ROBERT E. HOWARD
executive editor - Red Sonja, LUKE LIEBERMAN
in memory of ARTHUR LIEBERMAN

DYNAMITE.

Nick Barrucci, CEO / Publisher
Juan Collado, President / COO

Joe Rybandt, Senior Editor
Rachel Pinnelas, Associate Editor

Jason Ullmeyer, Design Director
Katie Hidalgo, Graphic Designer
Geoff Harkins, Graphic Designer
Chris Caniano, Digital Associate
Rachel Kilbury, Digital Assistant

Rich Young, Director Business Development
Keith Davidsen, Marketing Manager
Kevin Pearl, Sales Associate

Online at www.DYNAMITE.com
On Twitter @dynamitecomics
On Facebook /Dynamitecomics
On YouTube /Dynamitecomics
On Tumblr dynamitecomics.tumblr.com

Online at www.REDSONJA.com
On Twitter @therealredsonja
On Facebook /Redsonja
On Instagram /redsonjaofficial

ISBN-10: 1-60690-802-2   ISBN-13: 978-1-60690-802-0   First Printing   10 9 8 7 6 5 4 3 2 1

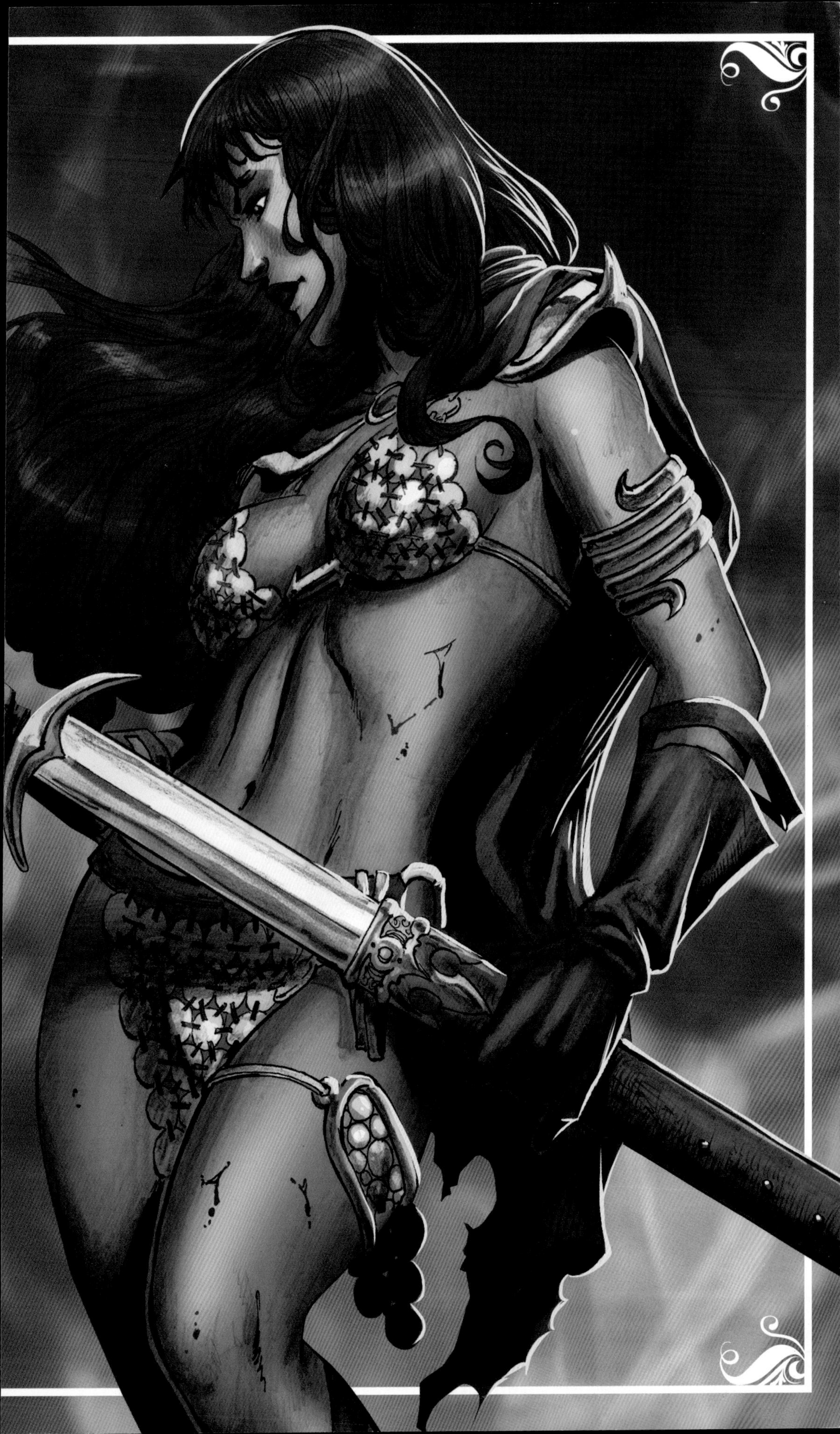

ISSUE ONE
cover art by Jay Anacleto and Ivan Nunes

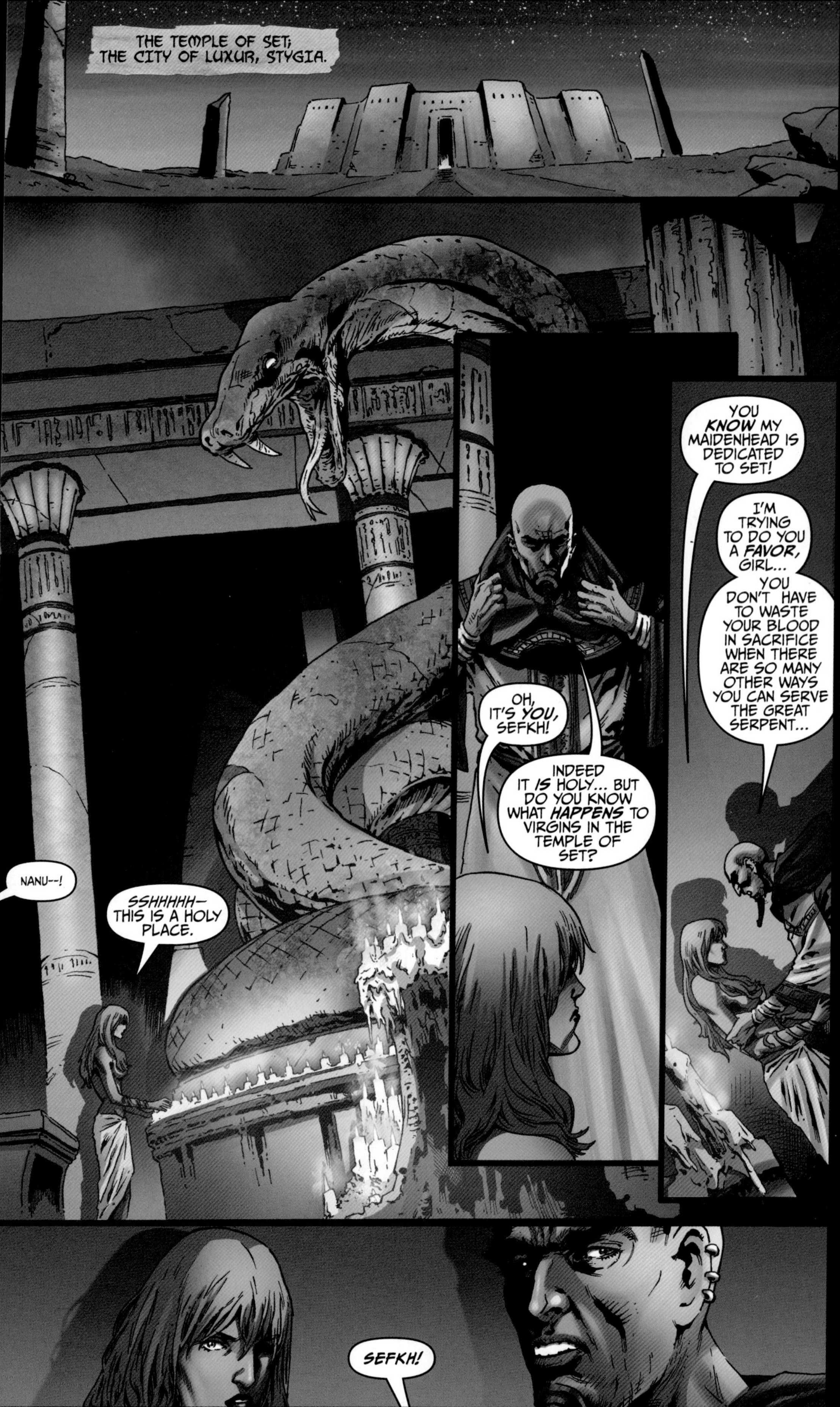
THE TEMPLE OF SET; THE CITY OF LUXUR, STYGIA.
NANU--!
SSHHHHH— THIS IS A HOLY PLACE.
OH, IT'S YOU, SEFKH!
INDEED IT IS HOLY... BUT DO YOU KNOW WHAT HAPPENS TO VIRGINS IN THE TEMPLE OF SET?
YOU KNOW MY MAIDENHEAD IS DEDICATED TO SET!
I'M TRYING TO DO YOU A FAVOR, GIRL...
YOU DON'T HAVE TO WASTE YOUR BLOOD IN SACRIFICE WHEN THERE ARE SO MANY OTHER WAYS YOU CAN SERVE THE GREAT SERPENT...
SEFKH!

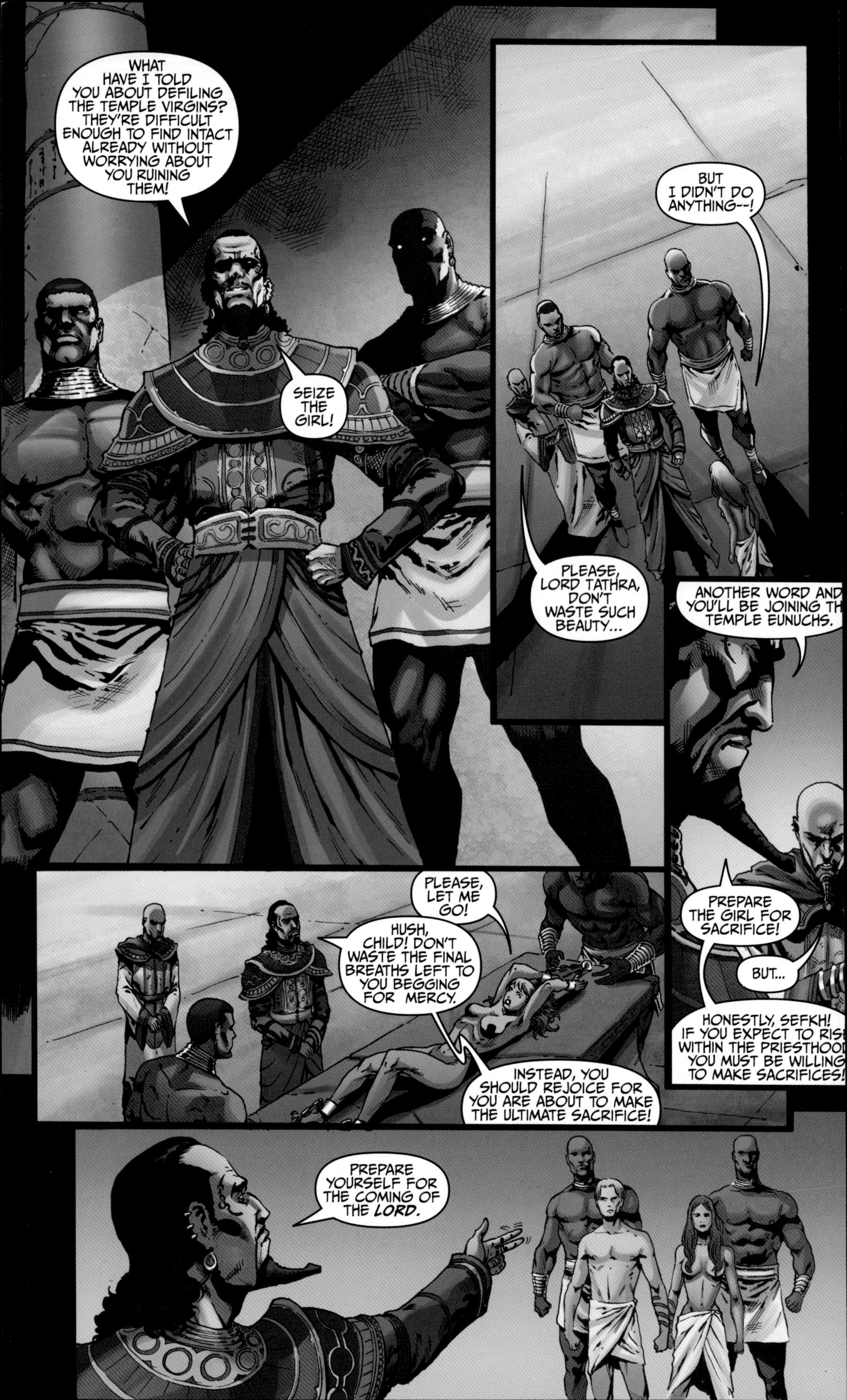
WHAT HAVE I TOLD YOU ABOUT DEFILING THE TEMPLE VIRGINS? THEY'RE DIFFICULT ENOUGH TO FIND INTACT ALREADY WITHOUT WORRYING ABOUT YOU RUINING THEM!
SEIZE THE GIRL!
BUT I DIDN'T DO ANYTHING--!
PLEASE, LORD TATHRA, DON'T WASTE SUCH BEAUTY...
ANOTHER WORD AND YOU'LL BE JOINING TH TEMPLE EUNUCHS.
PREPARE THE GIRL FOR SACRIFICE!
BUT...
HONESTLY, SEFKH! IF YOU EXPECT TO RIS WITHIN THE PRIESTHOOD YOU MUST BE WILLING TO MAKE SACRIFICES!
PLEASE, LET ME GO!
HUSH, CHILD! DON'T WASTE THE FINAL BREATHS LEFT TO YOU BEGGING FOR MERCY.
INSTEAD, YOU SHOULD REJOICE FOR YOU ARE ABOUT TO MAKE THE ULTIMATE SACRIFICE!
PREPARE YOURSELF FOR THE COMING OF THE LORD.

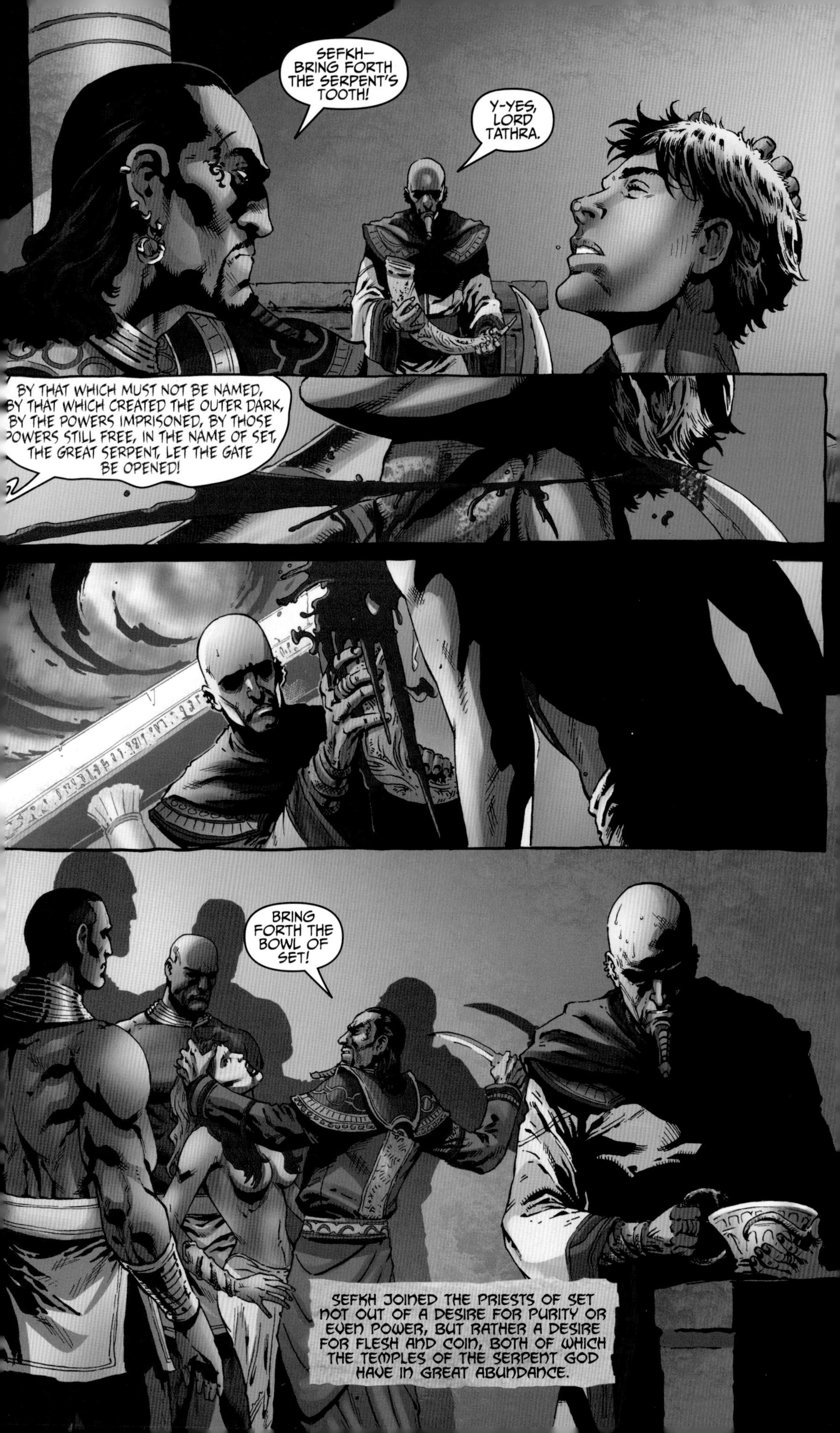
SEFKH– BRING FORTH THE SERPENT'S TOOTH!
Y-YES, LORD TATHRA.
BY THAT WHICH MUST NOT BE NAMED, BY THAT WHICH CREATED THE OUTER DARK, BY THE POWERS IMPRISONED, BY THOSE POWERS STILL FREE, IN THE NAME OF SET, THE GREAT SERPENT, LET THE GATE BE OPENED!
BRING FORTH THE BOWL OF SET!
SEFKH JOINED THE PRIESTS OF SET NOT OUT OF A DESIRE FOR PURITY OR EVEN POWER, BUT RATHER A DESIRE FOR FLESH AND COIN, BOTH OF WHICH THE TEMPLES OF THE SERPENT GOD HAVE IN GREAT ABUNDANCE.

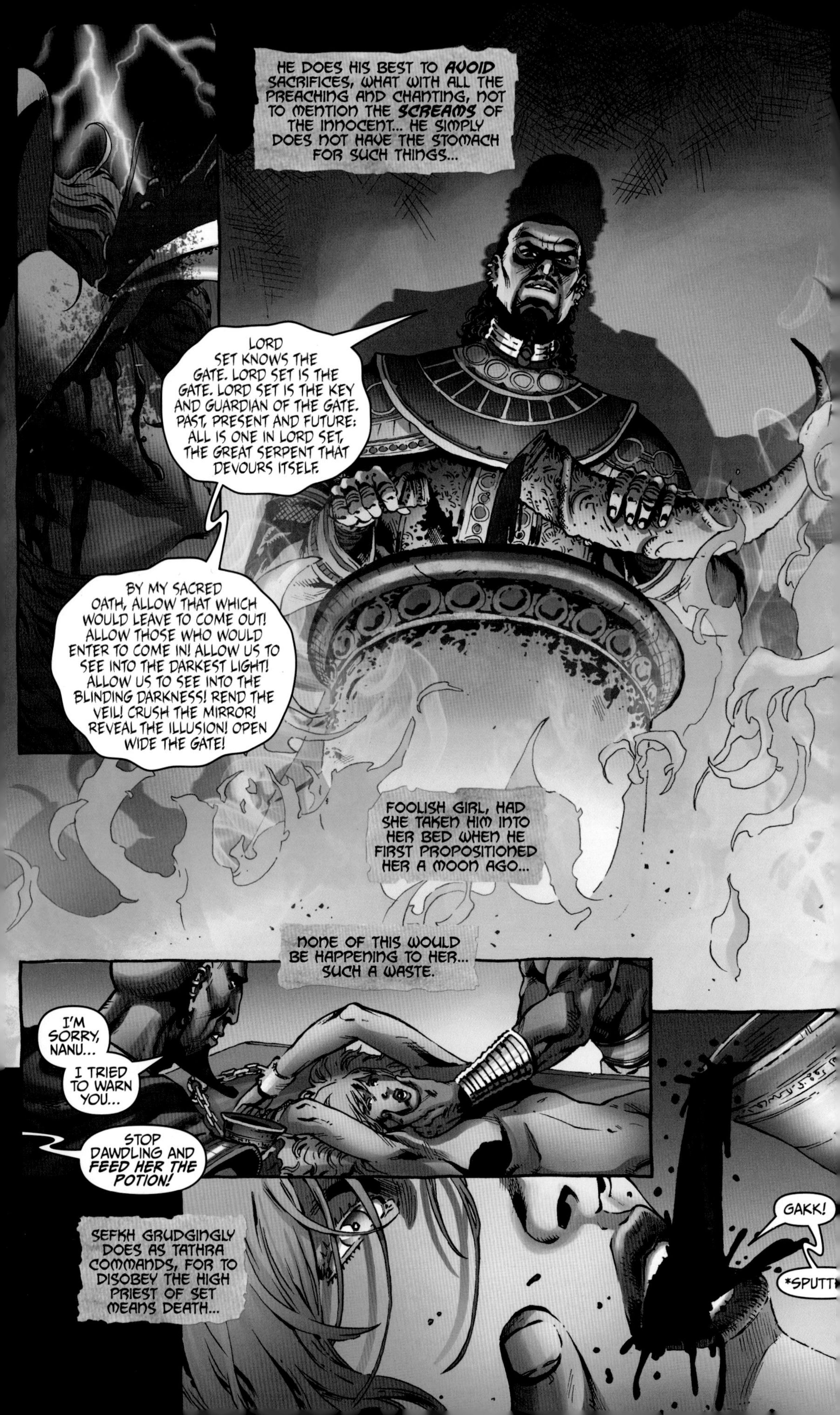
HE DOES HIS BEST TO AVOID SACRIFICES, WHAT WITH ALL THE PREACHING AND CHANTING, NOT TO MENTION THE SCREAMS OF THE INNOCENT... HE SIMPLY DOES NOT HAVE THE STOMACH FOR SUCH THINGS...
LORD SET KNOWS THE GATE. LORD SET IS THE GATE. LORD SET IS THE KEY AND GUARDIAN OF THE GATE. PAST, PRESENT AND FUTURE: ALL IS ONE IN LORD SET, THE GREAT SERPENT THAT DEVOURS ITSELF.
BY MY SACRED OATH, ALLOW THAT WHICH WOULD LEAVE TO COME OUT! ALLOW THOSE WHO WOULD ENTER TO COME IN! ALLOW US TO SEE INTO THE DARKEST LIGHT! ALLOW US TO SEE INTO THE BLINDING DARKNESS! REND THE VEIL! CRUSH THE MIRROR! REVEAL THE ILLUSION! OPEN WIDE THE GATE!
FOOLISH GIRL, HAD SHE TAKEN HIM INTO HER BED WHEN HE FIRST PROPOSITIONED HER A MOON AGO...
NONE OF THIS WOULD BE HAPPENING TO HER... SUCH A WASTE.
I'M SORRY, NANU...
I TRIED TO WARN YOU...
STOP DAWDLING AND FEED HER THE POTION!
SEFKH GRUDGINGLY DOES AS TATHRA COMMANDS, FOR TO DISOBEY THE HIGH PRIEST OF SET MEANS DEATH...
GAKK!
SPUTT

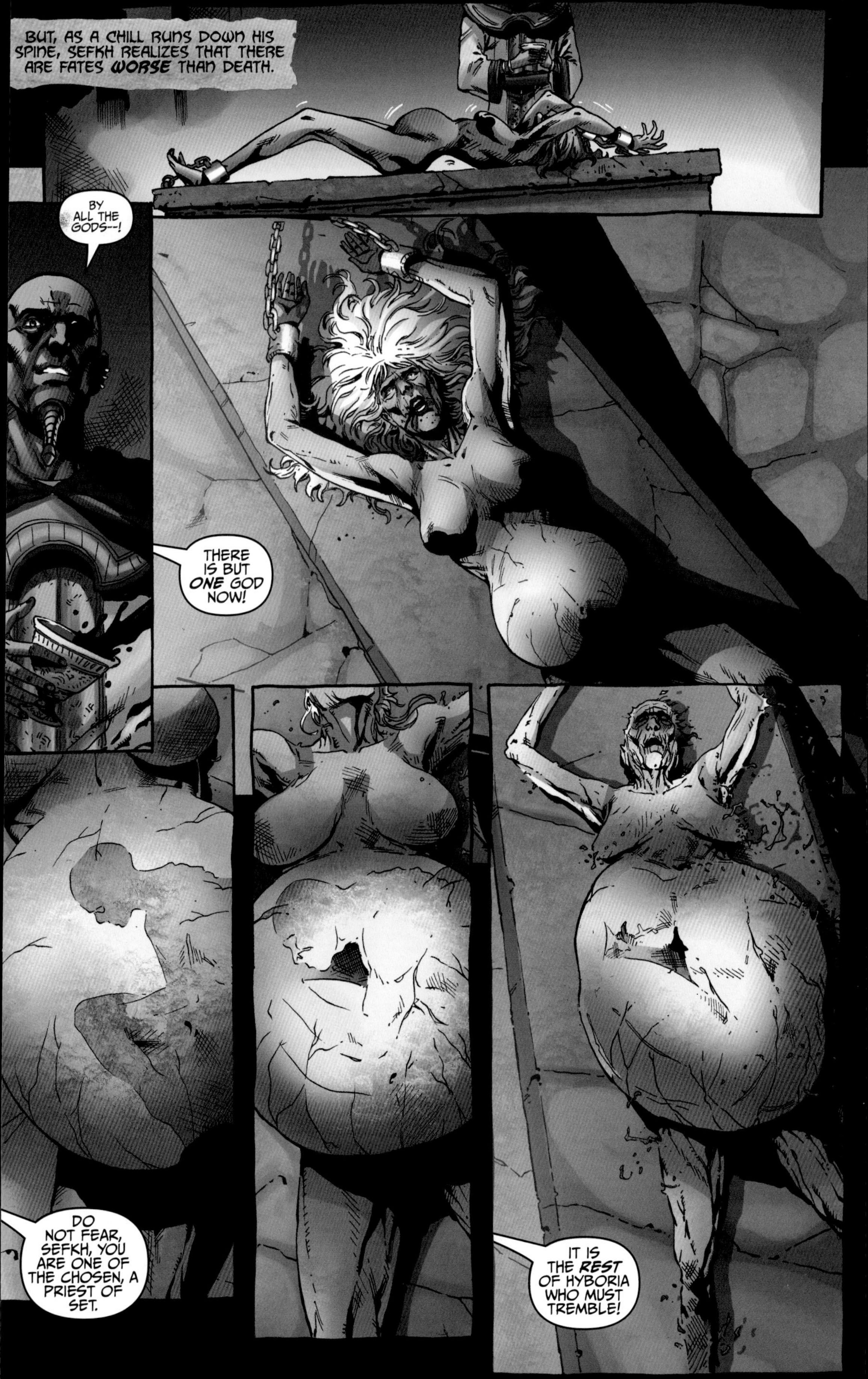

BUT, AS A CHILL RUNS DOWN HIS SPINE, SEFKH REALIZES THAT THERE ARE FATES WORSE THAN DEATH.
BY ALL THE GODS--!
THERE IS BUT ONE GOD NOW!
DO NOT FEAR, SEFKH, YOU ARE ONE OF THE CHOSEN, A PRIEST OF SET.
IT IS THE REST OF HYBORIA WHO MUST TREMBLE!

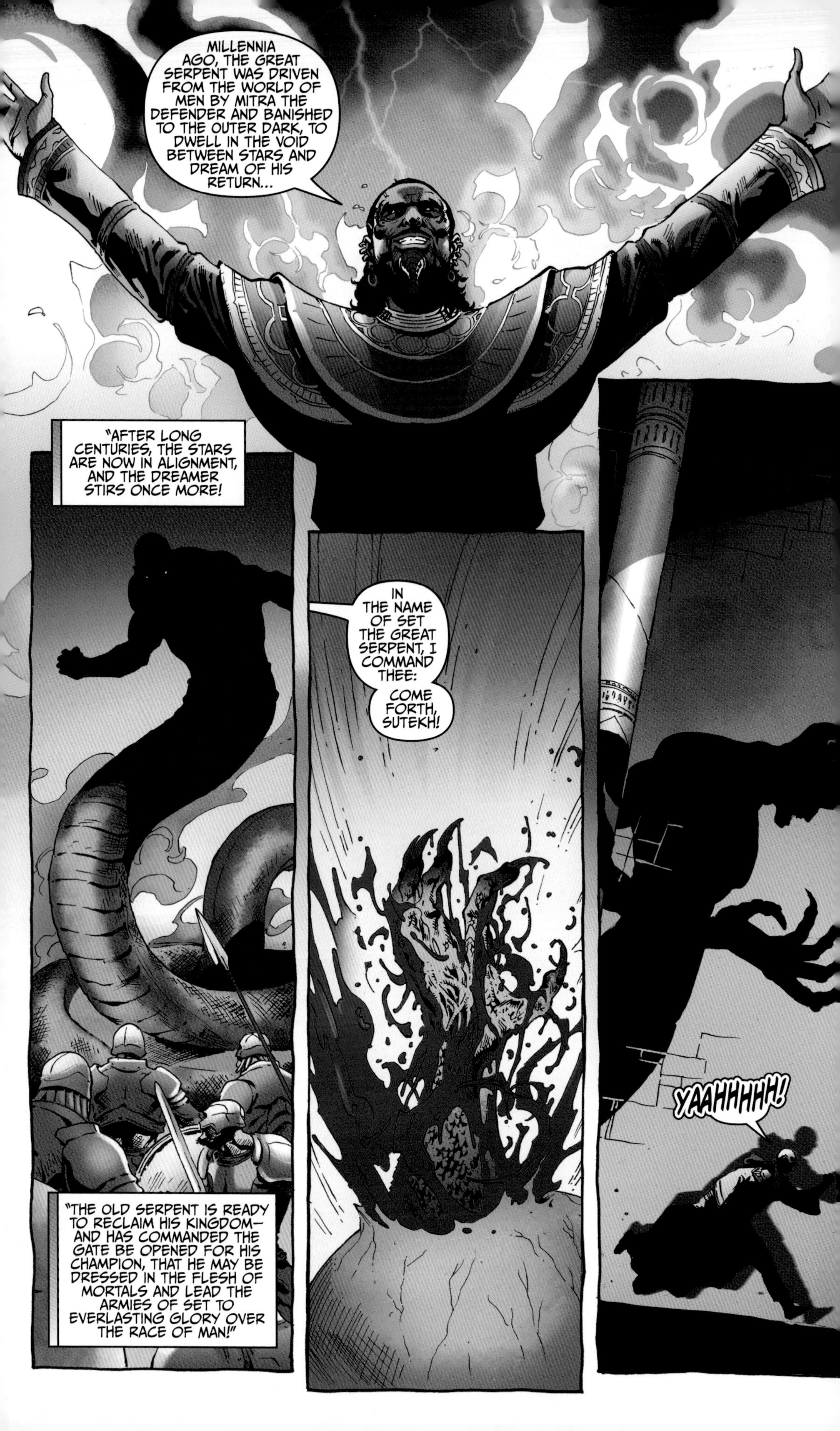
MILLENNIA AGO, THE GREAT SERPENT WAS DRIVEN FROM THE WORLD OF MEN BY MITRA THE DEFENDER AND BANISHED TO THE OUTER DARK, TO DWELL IN THE VOID BETWEEN STARS AND DREAM OF HIS RETURN...
"AFTER LONG CENTURIES, THE STARS ARE NOW IN ALIGNMENT, AND THE DREAMER STIRS ONCE MORE!
"THE OLD SERPENT IS READY TO RECLAIM HIS KINGDOM—AND HAS COMMANDED THE GATE BE OPENED FOR HIS CHAMPION, THAT HE MAY BE DRESSED IN THE FLESH OF MORTALS AND LEAD THE ARMIES OF SET TO EVERLASTING GLORY OVER THE RACE OF MAN!"
IN THE NAME OF SET THE GREAT SERPENT, I COMMAND THEE:
COME FORTH, SUTEKH!
YAAHHHHH!

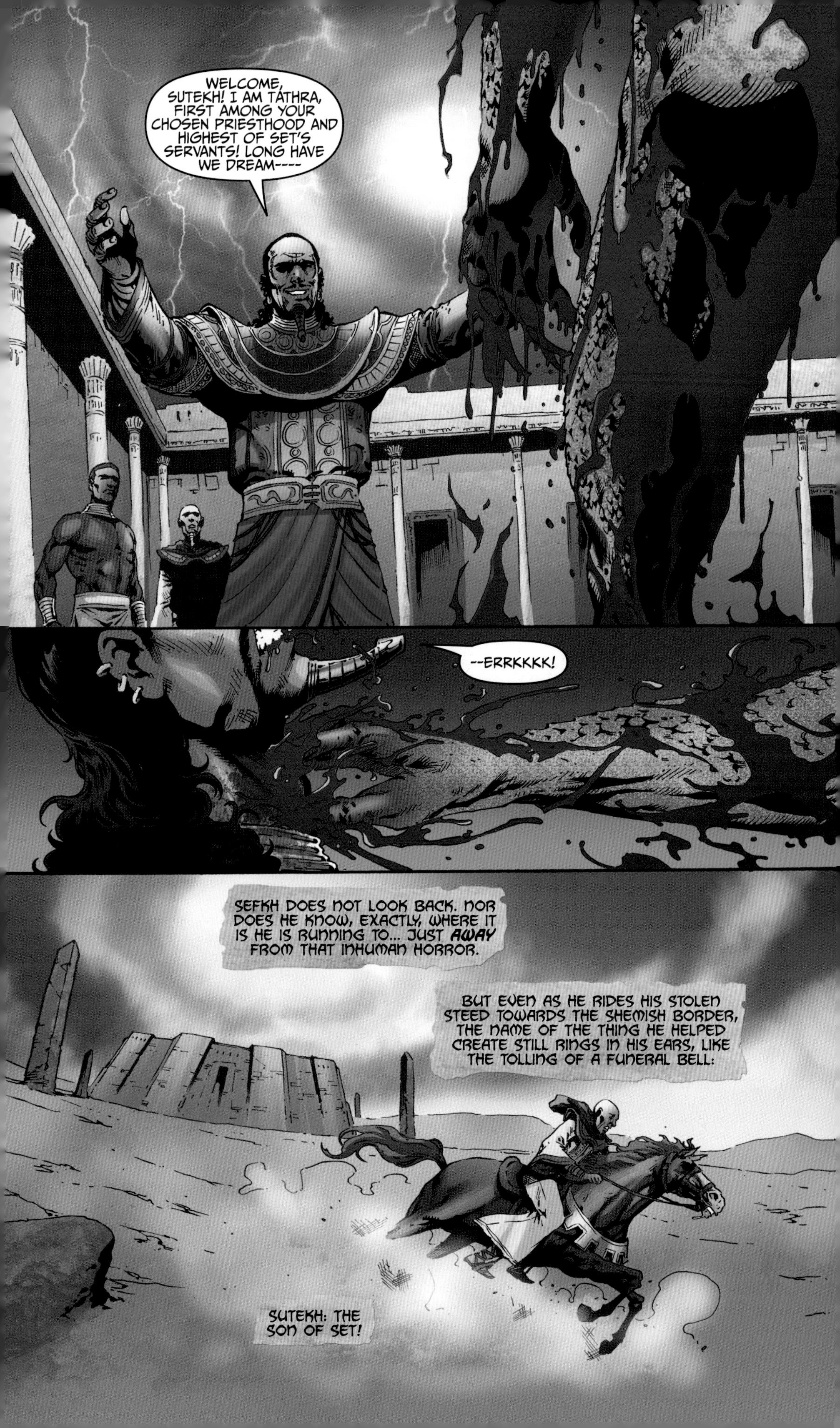
WELCOME, SUTEKH! I AM TATHRA, FIRST AMONG YOUR CHOSEN PRIESTHOOD AND HIGHEST OF SET'S SERVANTS! LONG HAVE WE DREAM----
--ERRKKKK!
SEFKH DOES NOT LOOK BACK. NOR DOES HE KNOW, EXACTLY, WHERE IT IS HE IS RUNNING TO... JUST AWAY FROM THAT INHUMAN HORROR.
BUT EVEN AS HE RIDES HIS STOLEN STEED TOWARDS THE SHEMISH BORDER, THE NAME OF THE THING HE HELPED CREATE STILL RINGS IN HIS EARS, LIKE THE TOLLING OF A FUNERAL BELL:
SUTEKH: THE SON OF SET!

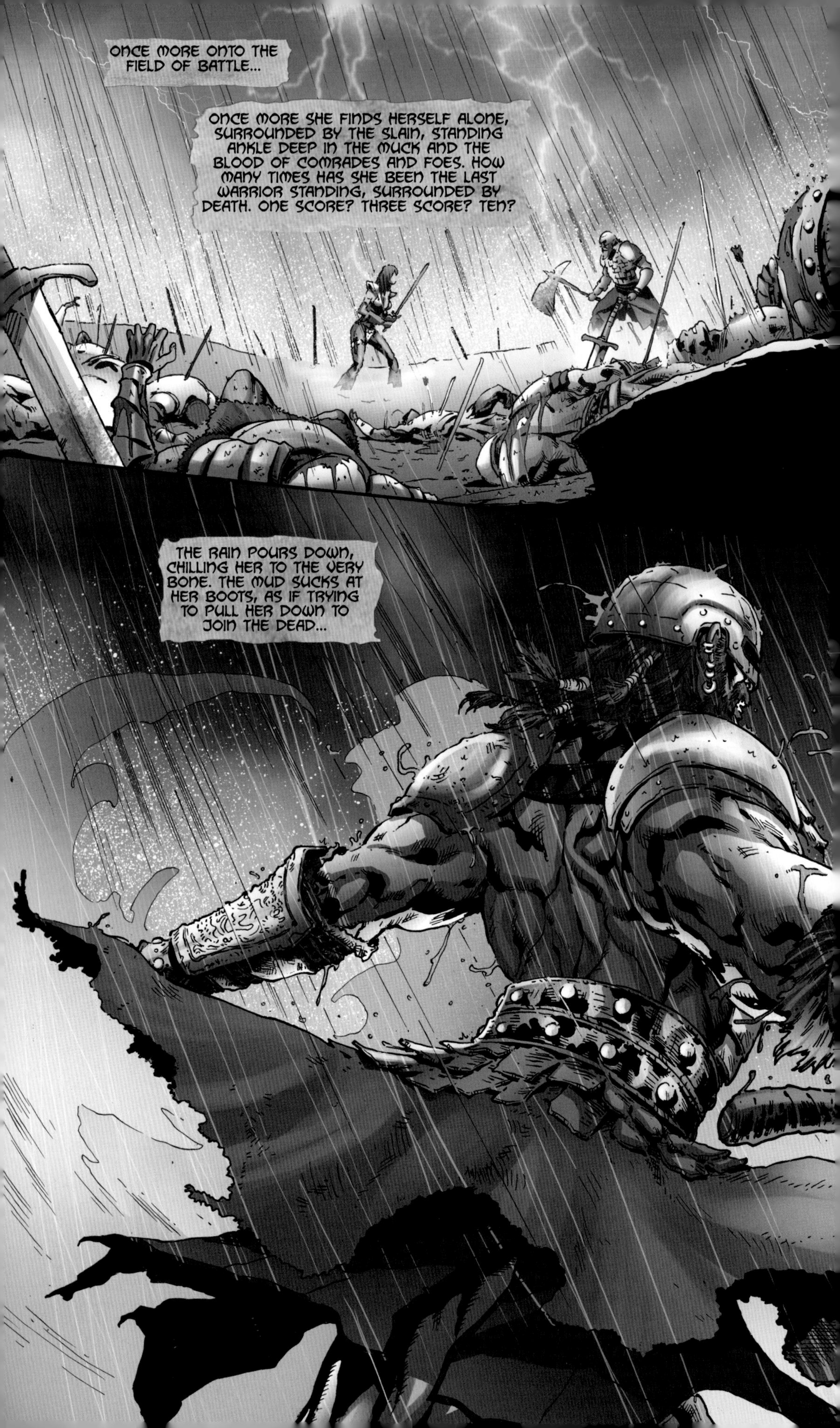
ONCE MORE ONTO THE FIELD OF BATTLE...
ONCE MORE SHE FINDS HERSELF ALONE, SURROUNDED BY THE SLAIN, STANDING ANKLE DEEP IN THE MUCK AND THE BLOOD OF COMRADES AND FOES. HOW MANY TIMES HAS SHE BEEN THE LAST WARRIOR STANDING, SURROUNDED BY DEATH. ONE SCORE? THREE SCORE? TEN?
THE RAIN POURS DOWN, CHILLING HER TO THE VERY BONE. THE MUD SUCKS AT HER BOOTS, AS IF TRYING TO PULL HER DOWN TO JOIN THE DEAD...

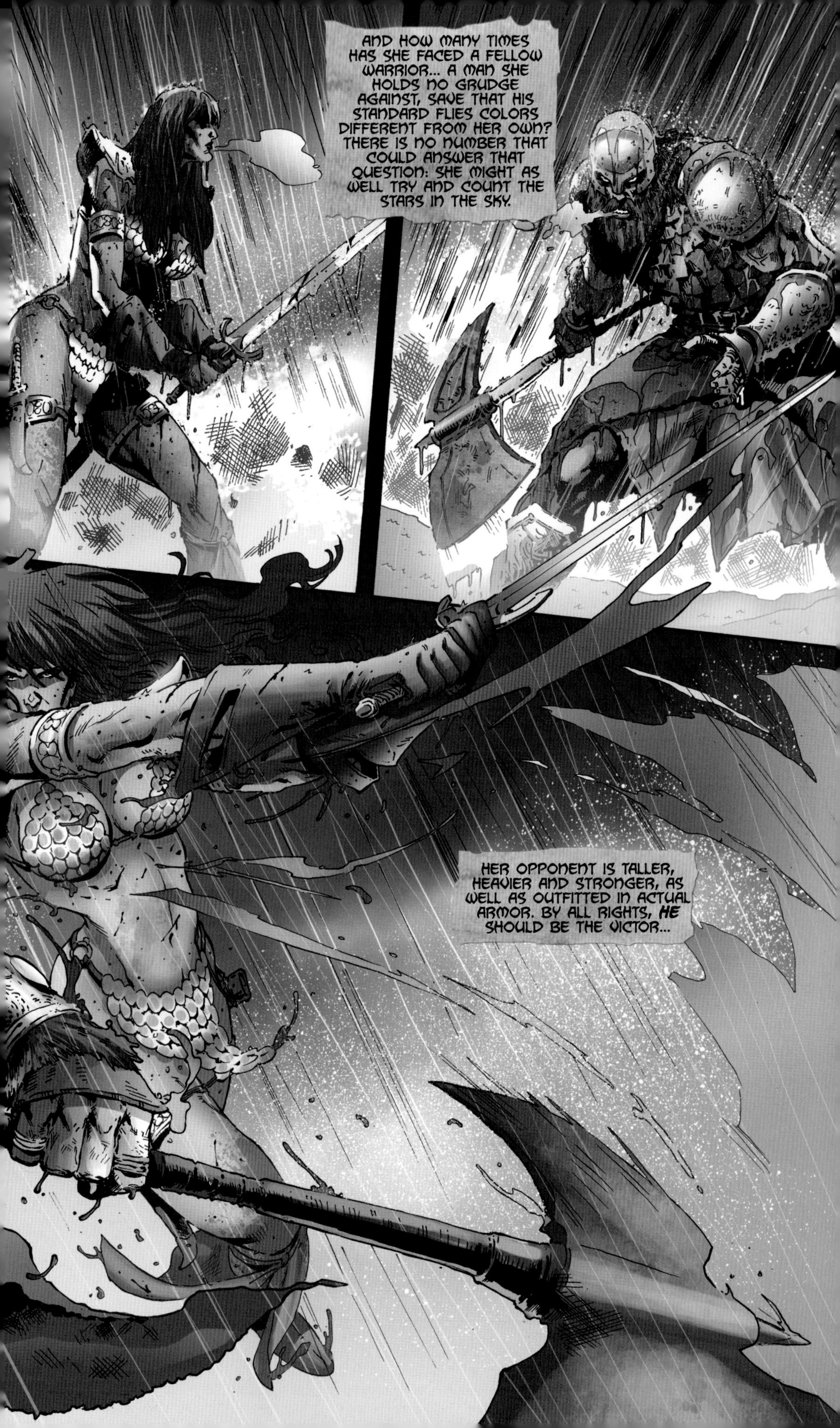
AND HOW MANY TIMES HAS SHE FACED A FELLOW WARRIOR... A MAN SHE HOLDS NO GRUDGE AGAINST, SAVE THAT HIS STANDARD FLIES COLORS DIFFERENT FROM HER OWN? THERE IS NO NUMBER THAT COULD ANSWER THAT QUESTION: SHE MIGHT AS WELL TRY AND COUNT THE STARS IN THE SKY.
HER OPPONENT IS TALLER, HEAVIER AND STRONGER, AS WELL AS OUTFITTED IN ACTUAL ARMOR. BY ALL RIGHTS, HE SHOULD BE THE VICTOR...

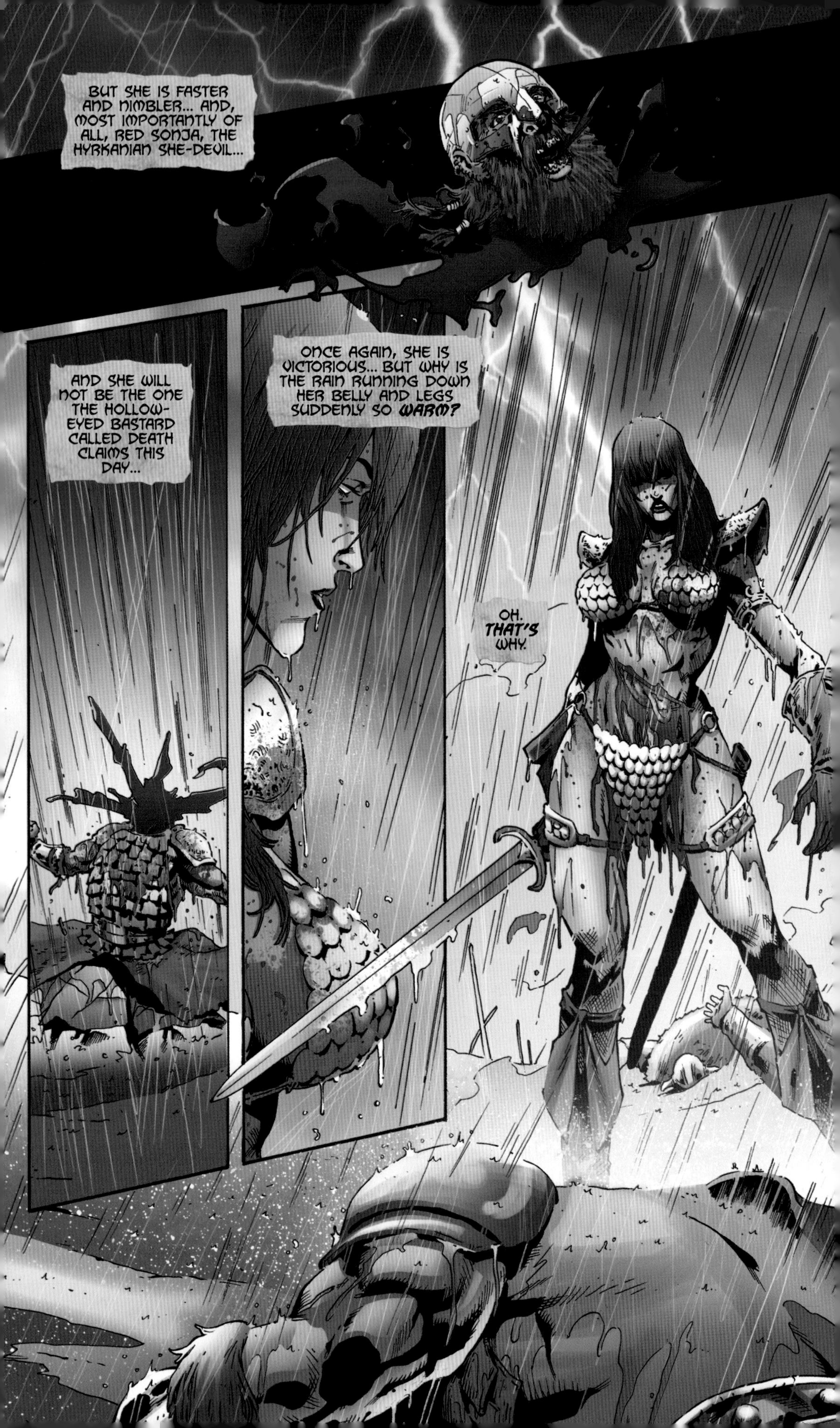
BUT SHE IS FASTER AND NIMBLER... AND, MOST IMPORTANTLY OF ALL, RED SONJA, THE HYRKANIAN SHE-DEVIL...
AND SHE WILL NOT BE THE ONE THE HOLLOW-EYED BASTARD CALLED DEATH CLAIMS THIS DAY...
ONCE AGAIN, SHE IS VICTORIOUS... BUT WHY IS THE RAIN RUNNING DOWN HER BELLY AND LEGS SUDDENLY SO WARM?
OH. THAT'S WHY.

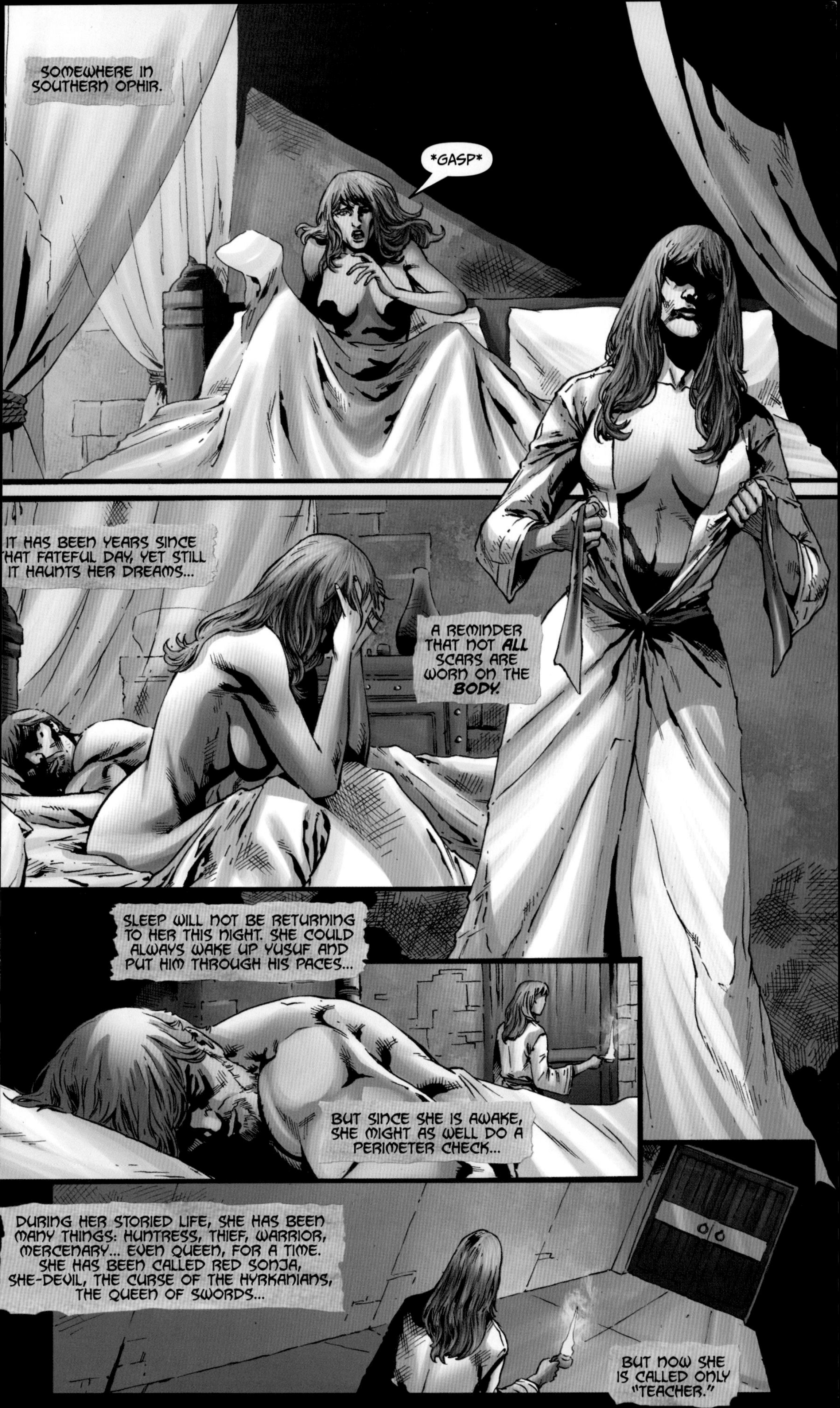
SOMEWHERE IN SOUTHERN OPHIR.
GASP
IT HAS BEEN YEARS SINCE THAT FATEFUL DAY, YET STILL IT HAUNTS HER DREAMS...
A REMINDER THAT NOT ALL SCARS ARE WORN ON THE BODY.
SLEEP WILL NOT BE RETURNING TO HER THIS NIGHT. SHE COULD ALWAYS WAKE UP YUSUF AND PUT HIM THROUGH HIS PACES...
BUT SINCE SHE IS AWAKE, SHE MIGHT AS WELL DO A PERIMETER CHECK...
DURING HER STORIED LIFE, SHE HAS BEEN MANY THINGS: HUNTRESS, THIEF, WARRIOR, MERCENARY... EVEN QUEEN, FOR A TIME. SHE HAS BEEN CALLED RED SONJA, SHE-DEVIL, THE CURSE OF THE HYRKANIANS, THE QUEEN OF SWORDS...
BUT NOW SHE IS CALLED ONLY "TEACHER."

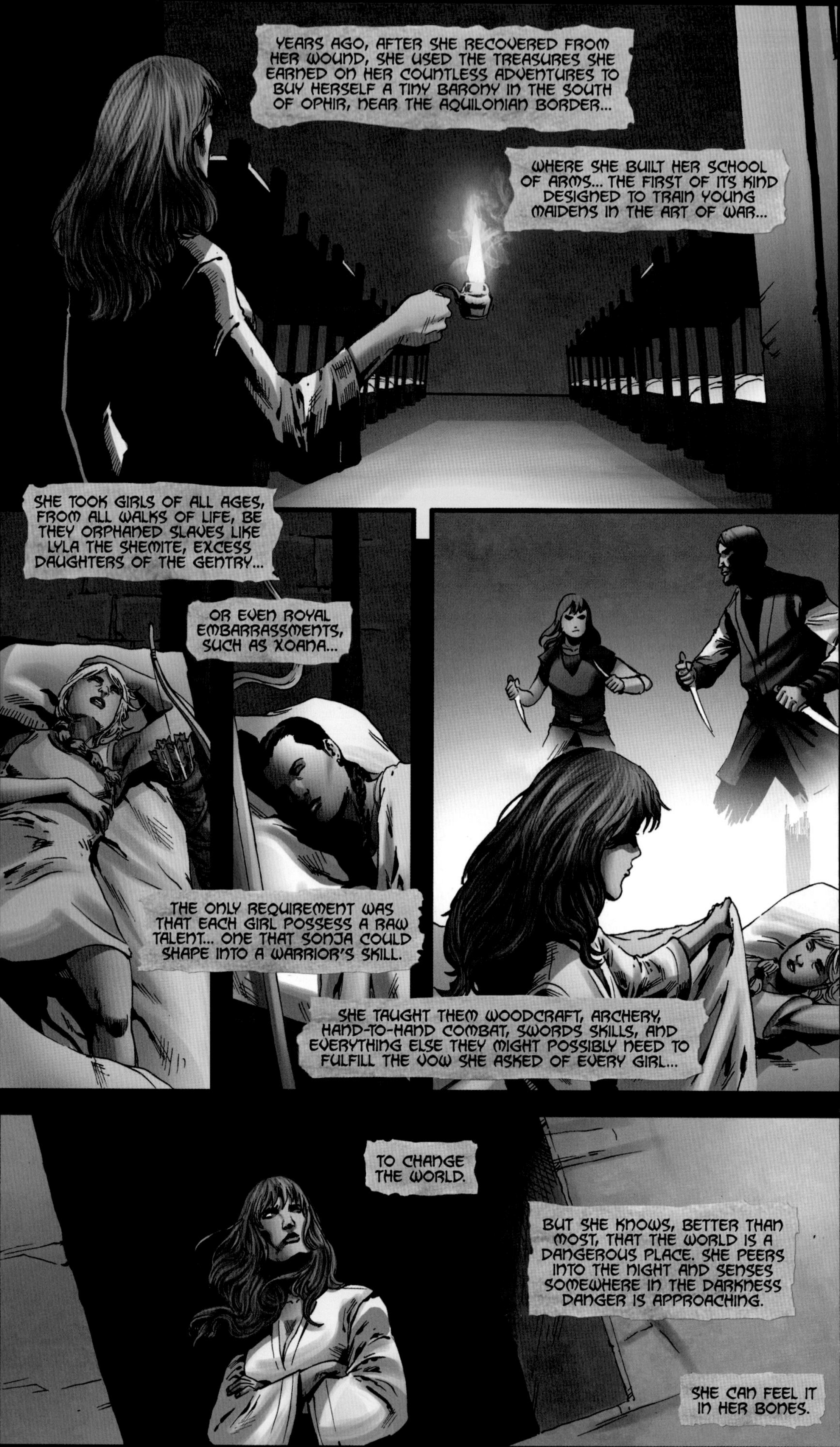
YEARS AGO, AFTER SHE RECOVERED FROM HER WOUND, SHE USED THE TREASURES SHE EARNED ON HER COUNTLESS ADVENTURES TO BUY HERSELF A TINY BARONY IN THE SOUTH OF OPHIR, NEAR THE AQUILONIAN BORDER...
WHERE SHE BUILT HER SCHOOL OF ARMS... THE FIRST OF ITS KIND DESIGNED TO TRAIN YOUNG MAIDENS IN THE ART OF WAR...
SHE TOOK GIRLS OF ALL AGES, FROM ALL WALKS OF LIFE, BE THEY ORPHANED SLAVES LIKE LYLA THE SHEMITE, EXCESS DAUGHTERS OF THE GENTRY...
OR EVEN ROYAL EMBARRASSMENTS, SUCH AS XOANA...
THE ONLY REQUIREMENT WAS THAT EACH GIRL POSSESS A RAW TALENT... ONE THAT SONJA COULD SHAPE INTO A WARRIOR'S SKILL.
SHE TAUGHT THEM WOODCRAFT, ARCHERY, HAND-TO-HAND COMBAT, SWORDS SKILLS, AND EVERYTHING ELSE THEY MIGHT POSSIBLY NEED TO FULFILL THE VOW SHE ASKED OF EVERY GIRL...
TO CHANGE THE WORLD.
BUT SHE KNOWS, BETTER THAN MOST, THAT THE WORLD IS A DANGEROUS PLACE. SHE PEERS INTO THE NIGHT AND SENSES SOMEWHERE IN THE DARKNESS DANGER IS APPROACHING.
SHE CAN FEEL IT IN HER BONES.

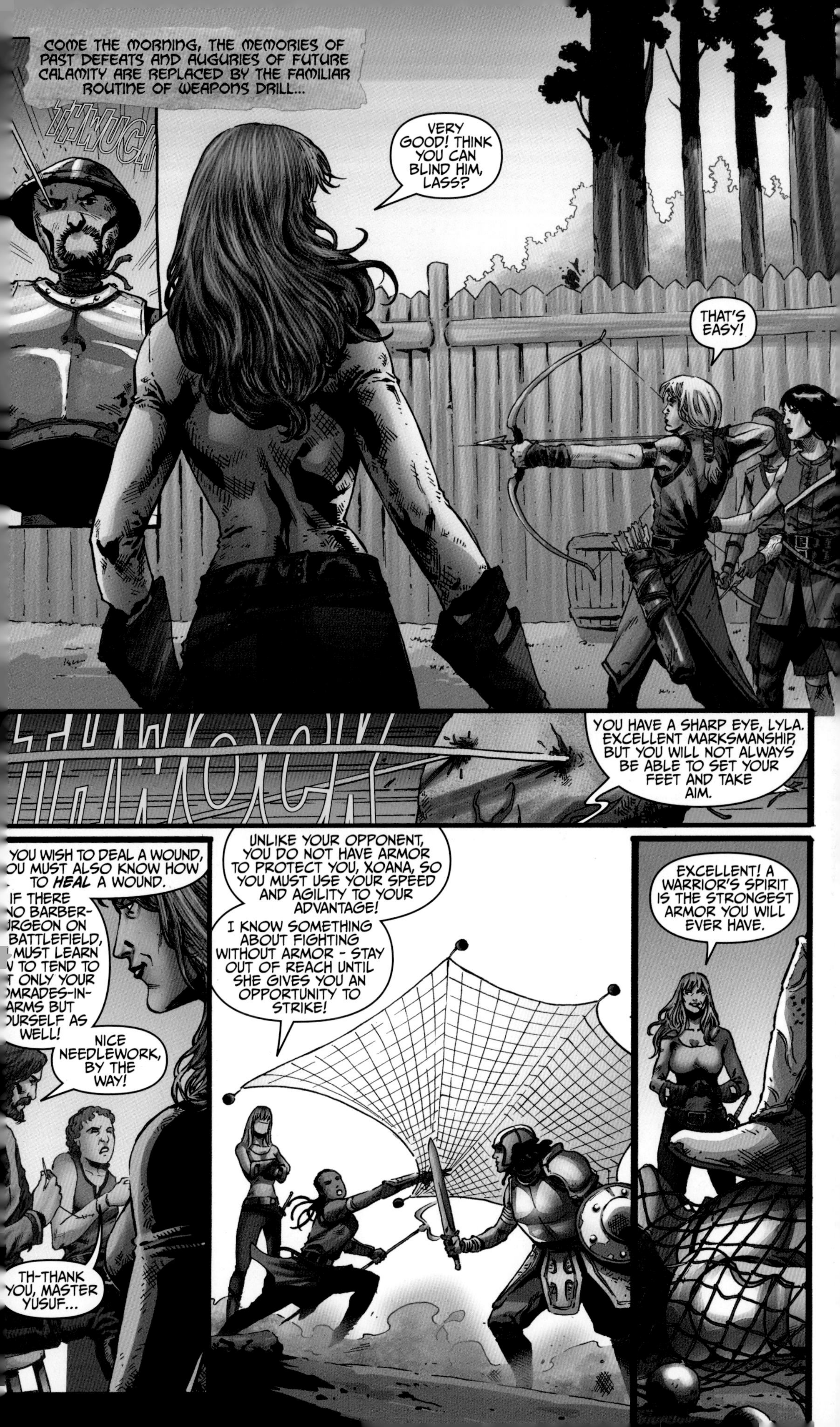
COME THE MORNING, THE MEMORIES OF PAST DEFEATS AND AUGURIES OF FUTURE CALAMITY ARE REPLACED BY THE FAMILIAR ROUTINE OF WEAPONS DRILL...
THWUCK
VERY GOOD! THINK YOU CAN BLIND HIM, LASS?
THAT'S EASY!
YOU HAVE A SHARP EYE, LYLA. EXCELLENT MARKSMANSHIP, BUT YOU WILL NOT ALWAYS BE ABLE TO SET YOUR FEET AND TAKE AIM.
YOU WISH TO DEAL A WOUND, OU MUST ALSO KNOW HOW TO HEAL A WOUND.
IF THERE NO BARBER- URGEON ON BATTLEFIELD, MUST LEARN TO TEND TO T ONLY YOUR OMRADES-IN- ARMS BUT OURSELF AS WELL!
NICE NEEDLEWORK, BY THE WAY!
TH-THANK YOU, MASTER YUSUF...
UNLIKE YOUR OPPONENT, YOU DO NOT HAVE ARMOR TO PROTECT YOU, XOANA, SO YOU MUST USE YOUR SPEED AND AGILITY TO YOUR ADVANTAGE!
I KNOW SOMETHING ABOUT FIGHTING WITHOUT ARMOR - STAY OUT OF REACH UNTIL SHE GIVES YOU AN OPPORTUNITY TO STRIKE!
EXCELLENT! A WARRIOR'S SPIRIT IS THE STRONGEST ARMOR YOU WILL EVER HAVE.

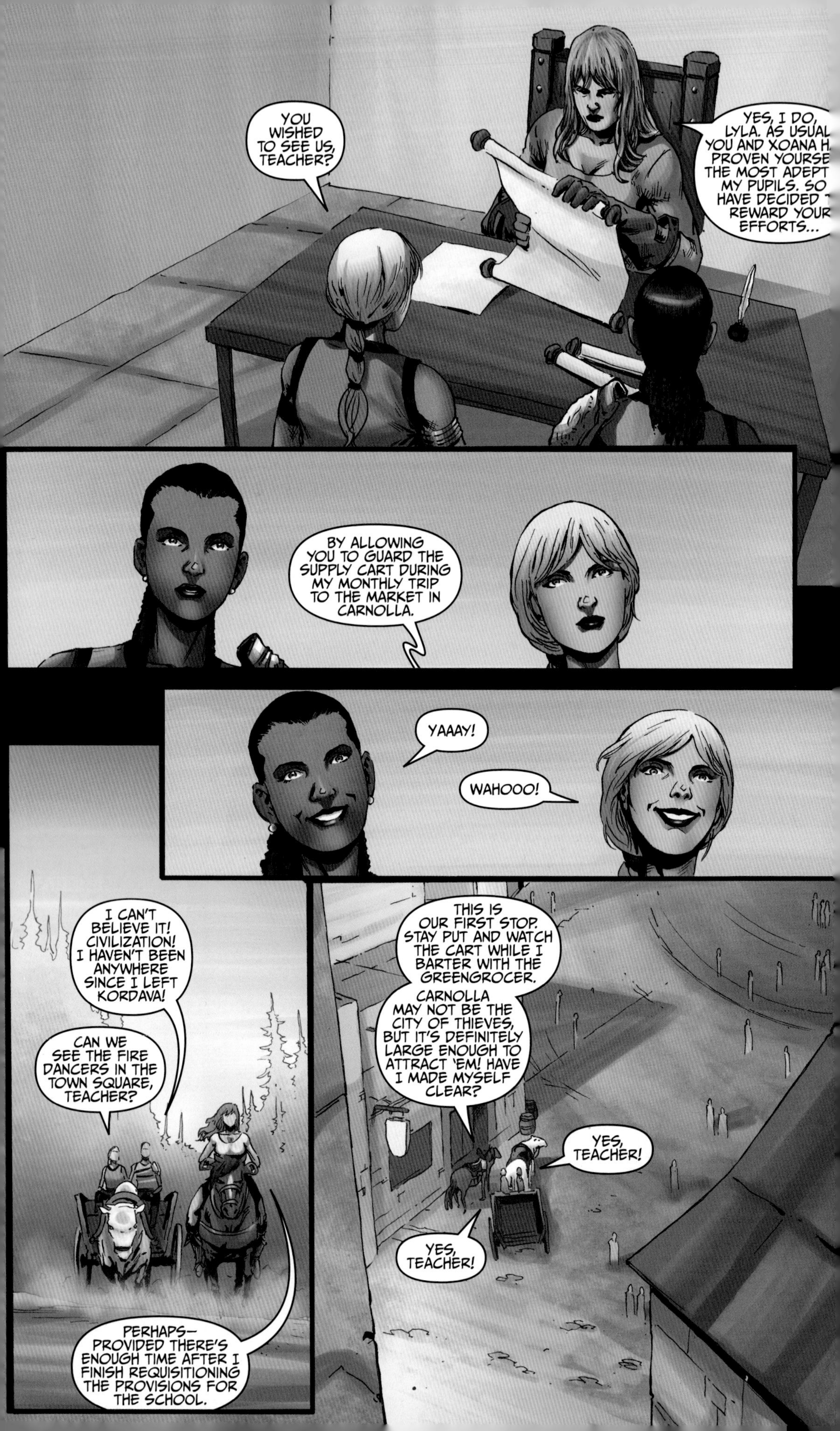
YOU WISHED TO SEE US, TEACHER?
YES, I DO, LYLA. AS USUAL YOU AND XOANA HA PROVEN YOURSE THE MOST ADEPT MY PUPILS. SO HAVE DECIDED T REWARD YOUR EFFORTS...
BY ALLOWING YOU TO GUARD THE SUPPLY CART DURING MY MONTHLY TRIP TO THE MARKET IN CARNOLLA.
YAAAY!
WAHOOO!
I CAN'T BELIEVE IT! CIVILIZATION! I HAVEN'T BEEN ANYWHERE SINCE I LEFT KORDAVA!
CAN WE SEE THE FIRE DANCERS IN THE TOWN SQUARE, TEACHER?
PERHAPS— PROVIDED THERE'S ENOUGH TIME AFTER I FINISH REQUISITIONING THE PROVISIONS FOR THE SCHOOL.
THIS IS OUR FIRST STOP. STAY PUT AND WATCH THE CART WHILE I BARTER WITH THE GREENGROCER.
CARNOLLA MAY NOT BE THE CITY OF THIEVES, BUT IT'S DEFINITELY LARGE ENOUGH TO ATTRACT 'EM! HAVE I MADE MYSELF CLEAR?
YES, TEACHER!
YES, TEACHER!

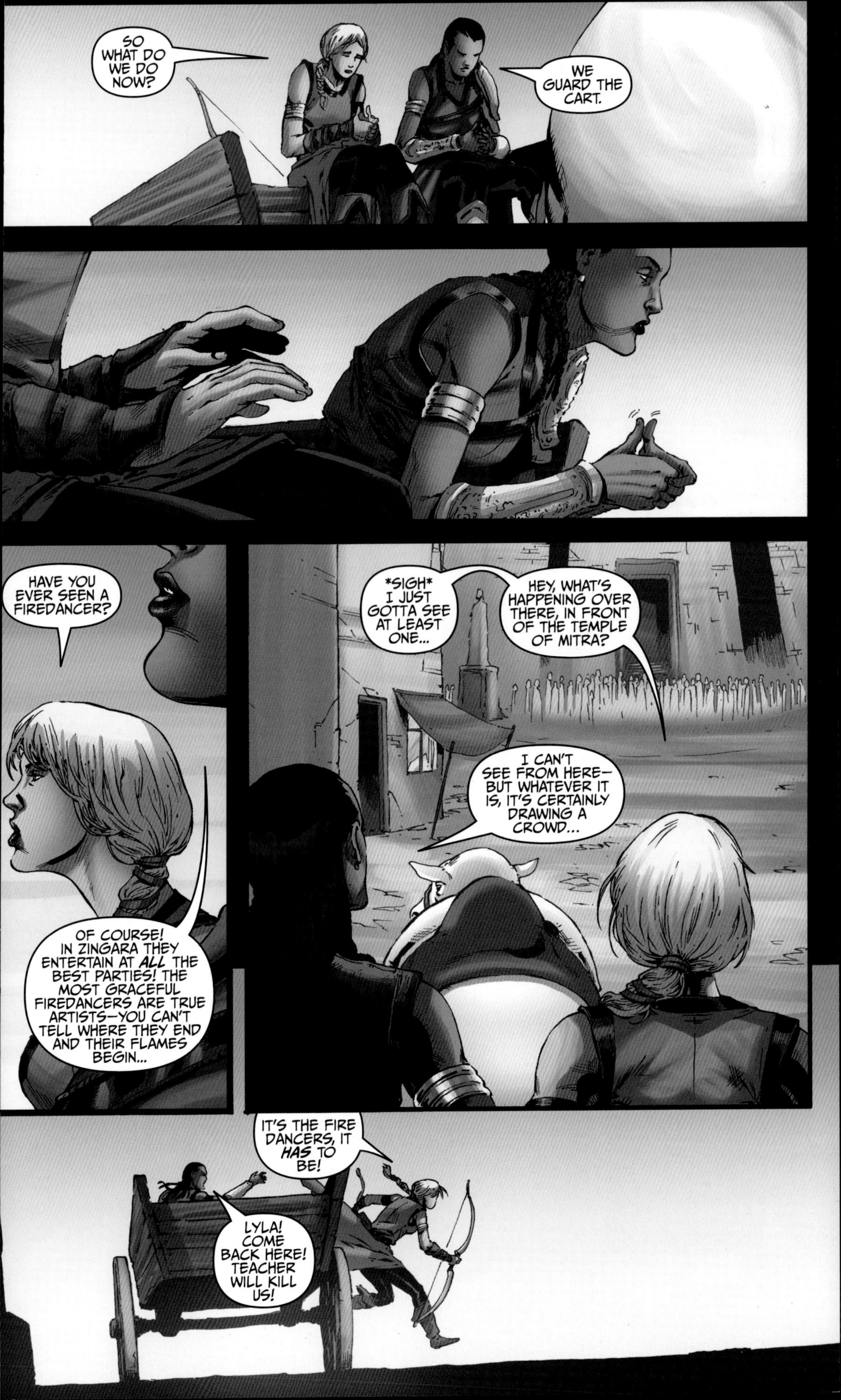
SO WHAT DO WE DO NOW?
WE GUARD THE CART.
HAVE YOU EVER SEEN A FIREDANCER?
OF COURSE! IN ZINGARA THEY ENTERTAIN AT ***ALL*** THE BEST PARTIES! THE MOST GRACEFUL FIREDANCERS ARE TRUE ARTISTS—YOU CAN'T TELL WHERE THEY END AND THEIR FLAMES BEGIN...
SIGH I JUST GOTTA SEE AT LEAST ONE...
HEY, WHAT'S HAPPENING OVER THERE, IN FRONT OF THE TEMPLE OF MITRA?
I CAN'T SEE FROM HERE—BUT WHATEVER IT IS, IT'S CERTAINLY DRAWING A CROWD...
IT'S THE FIRE DANCERS, IT ***HAS*** TO BE!
LYLA! COME BACK HERE! TEACHER WILL KILL US!

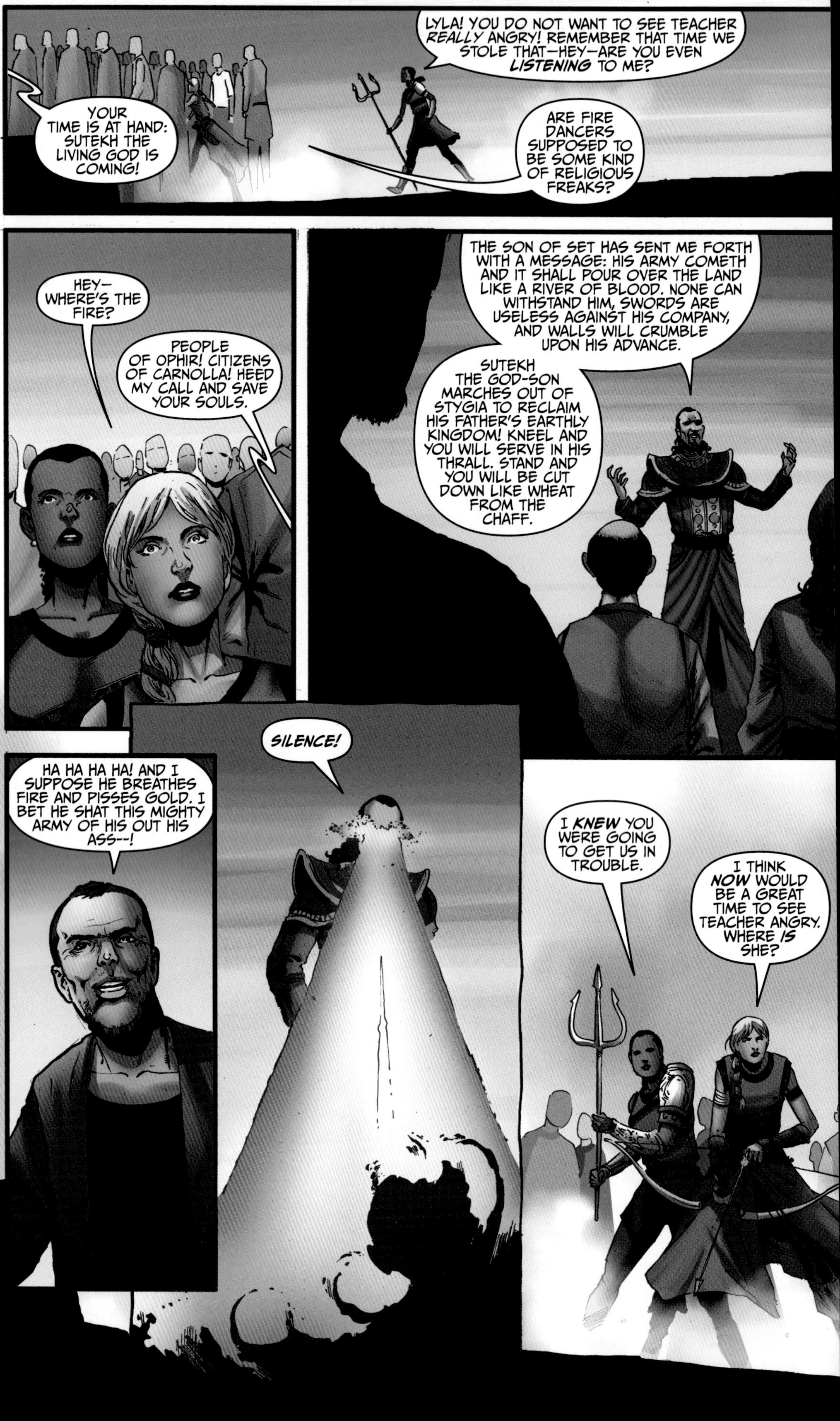
YOUR TIME IS AT HAND: SUTEKH THE LIVING GOD IS COMING!
LYLA! YOU DO NOT WANT TO SEE TEACHER *REALLY* ANGRY! REMEMBER THAT TIME WE STOLE THAT—HEY—ARE YOU EVEN ***LISTENING*** TO ME?
ARE FIRE DANCERS SUPPOSED TO BE SOME KIND OF RELIGIOUS FREAKS?
HEY— WHERE'S THE FIRE?
PEOPLE OF OPHIR! CITIZENS OF CARNOLLA! HEED MY CALL AND SAVE YOUR SOULS.
THE SON OF SET HAS SENT ME FORTH WITH A MESSAGE: HIS ARMY COMETH AND IT SHALL POUR OVER THE LAND LIKE A RIVER OF BLOOD. NONE CAN WITHSTAND HIM, SWORDS ARE USELESS AGAINST HIS COMPANY, AND WALLS WILL CRUMBLE UPON HIS ADVANCE.
SUTEKH THE GOD-SON MARCHES OUT OF STYGIA TO RECLAIM HIS FATHER'S EARTHLY KINGDOM! KNEEL AND YOU WILL SERVE IN HIS THRALL. STAND AND YOU WILL BE CUT DOWN LIKE WHEAT FROM THE CHAFF.
HA HA HA HA! AND I SUPPOSE HE BREATHES FIRE AND PISSES GOLD. I BET HE SHAT THIS MIGHTY ARMY OF HIS OUT HIS ASS--!
SILENCE!
I ***KNEW*** YOU WERE GOING TO GET US IN TROUBLE.
I THINK ***NOW*** WOULD BE A GREAT TIME TO SEE TEACHER ANGRY. WHERE ***IS*** SHE?

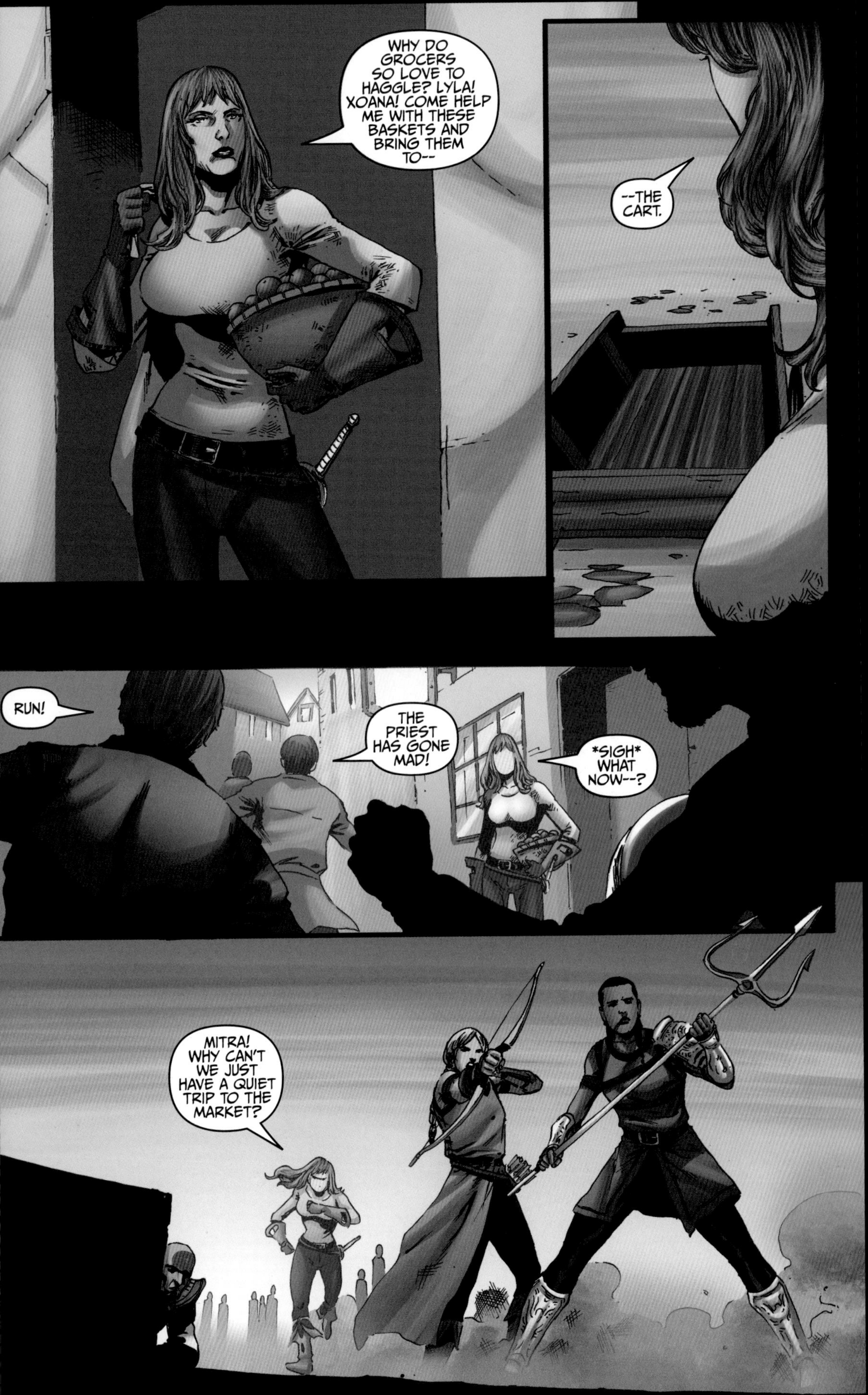
WHY DO GROCERS SO LOVE TO HAGGLE? LYLA! XOANA! COME HELP ME WITH THESE BASKETS AND BRING THEM TO--
--THE CART.
RUN!
THE PRIEST HAS GONE MAD!
SIGH WHAT NOW--?
MITRA! WHY CAN'T WE JUST HAVE A QUIET TRIP TO THE MARKET?

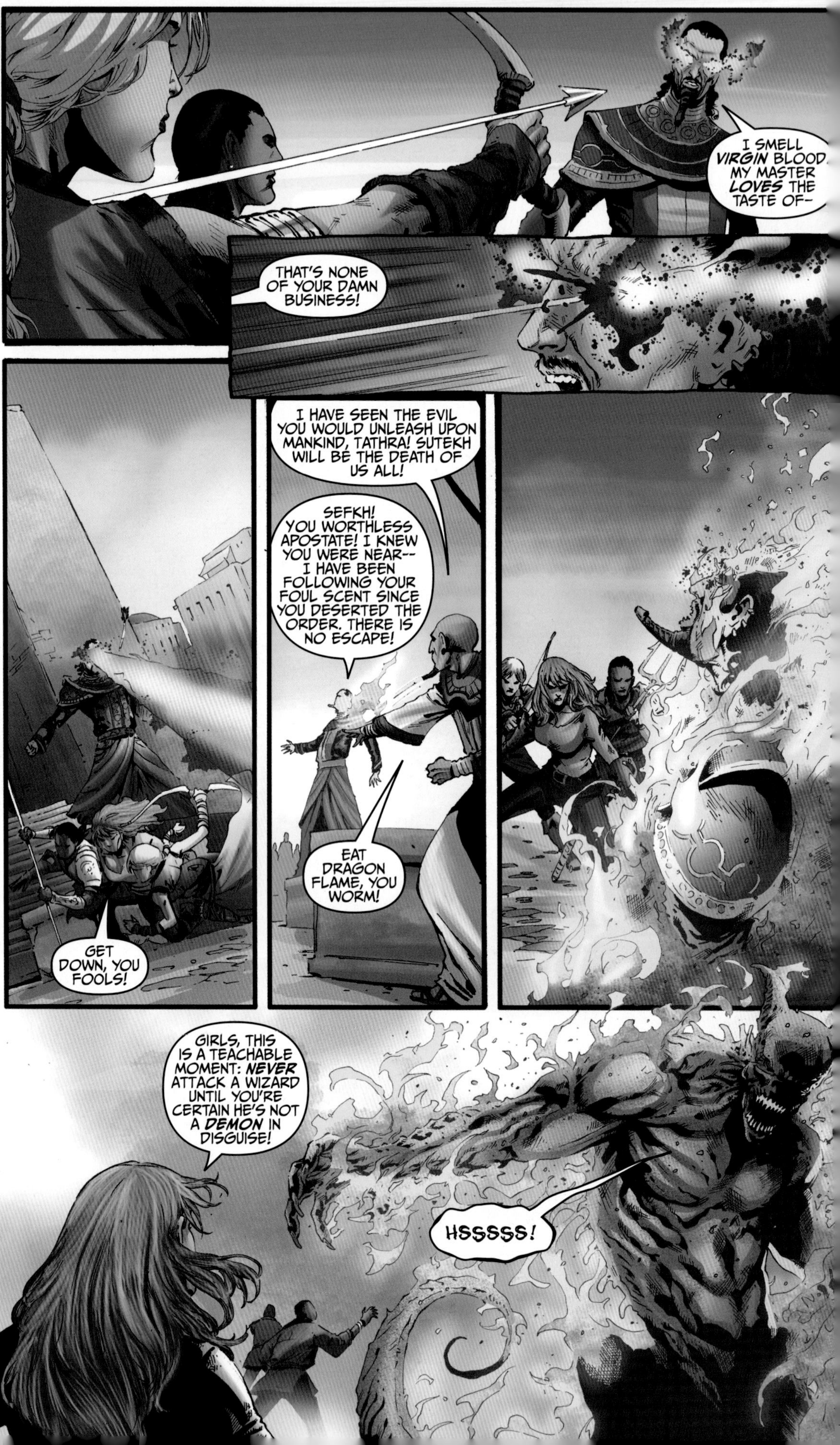
I SMELL VIRGIN BLOOD. MY MASTER LOVES THE TASTE OF-
THAT'S NONE OF YOUR DAMN BUSINESS!
I HAVE SEEN THE EVIL YOU WOULD UNLEASH UPON MANKIND, TATHRA! SUTEKH WILL BE THE DEATH OF US ALL!
SEFKH! YOU WORTHLESS APOSTATE! I KNEW YOU WERE NEAR-- I HAVE BEEN FOLLOWING YOUR FOUL SCENT SINCE YOU DESERTED THE ORDER. THERE IS NO ESCAPE!
EAT DRAGON FLAME, YOU WORM!
GET DOWN, YOU FOOLS!
GIRLS, THIS IS A TEACHABLE MOMENT: NEVER ATTACK A WIZARD UNTIL YOU'RE CERTAIN HE'S NOT A DEMON IN DISGUISE!
HSSSSS!

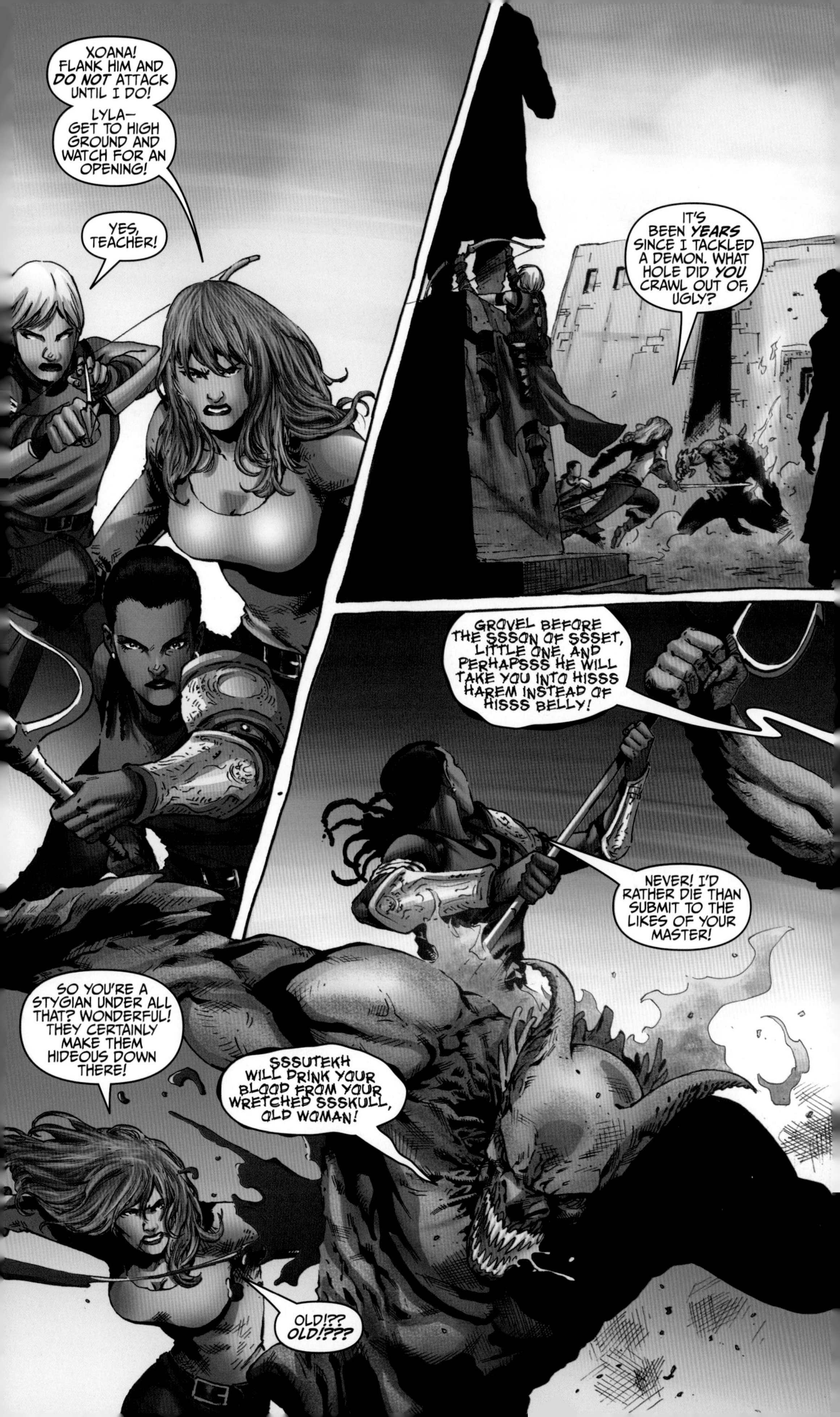
XOANA! FLANK HIM AND *DO NOT* ATTACK UNTIL I DO!
LYLA— GET TO HIGH GROUND AND WATCH FOR AN OPENING!
YES, TEACHER!
IT'S BEEN *YEARS* SINCE I TACKLED A DEMON. WHAT HOLE DID *YOU* CRAWL OUT OF, UGLY?
GROVEL BEFORE THE SSSON OF SSSET, LITTLE ONE, AND PERHAPSSS HE WILL TAKE YOU INTO HISSS HAREM INSTEAD OF HISSS BELLY!
NEVER! I'D RATHER DIE THAN SUBMIT TO THE LIKES OF YOUR MASTER!
SO YOU'RE A STYGIAN UNDER ALL THAT? WONDERFUL! THEY CERTAINLY MAKE THEM HIDEOUS DOWN THERE!
SSSUTEKH WILL DRINK YOUR BLOOD FROM YOUR WRETCHED SSSKULL, OLD WOMAN!
OLD!?? *OLD!???*

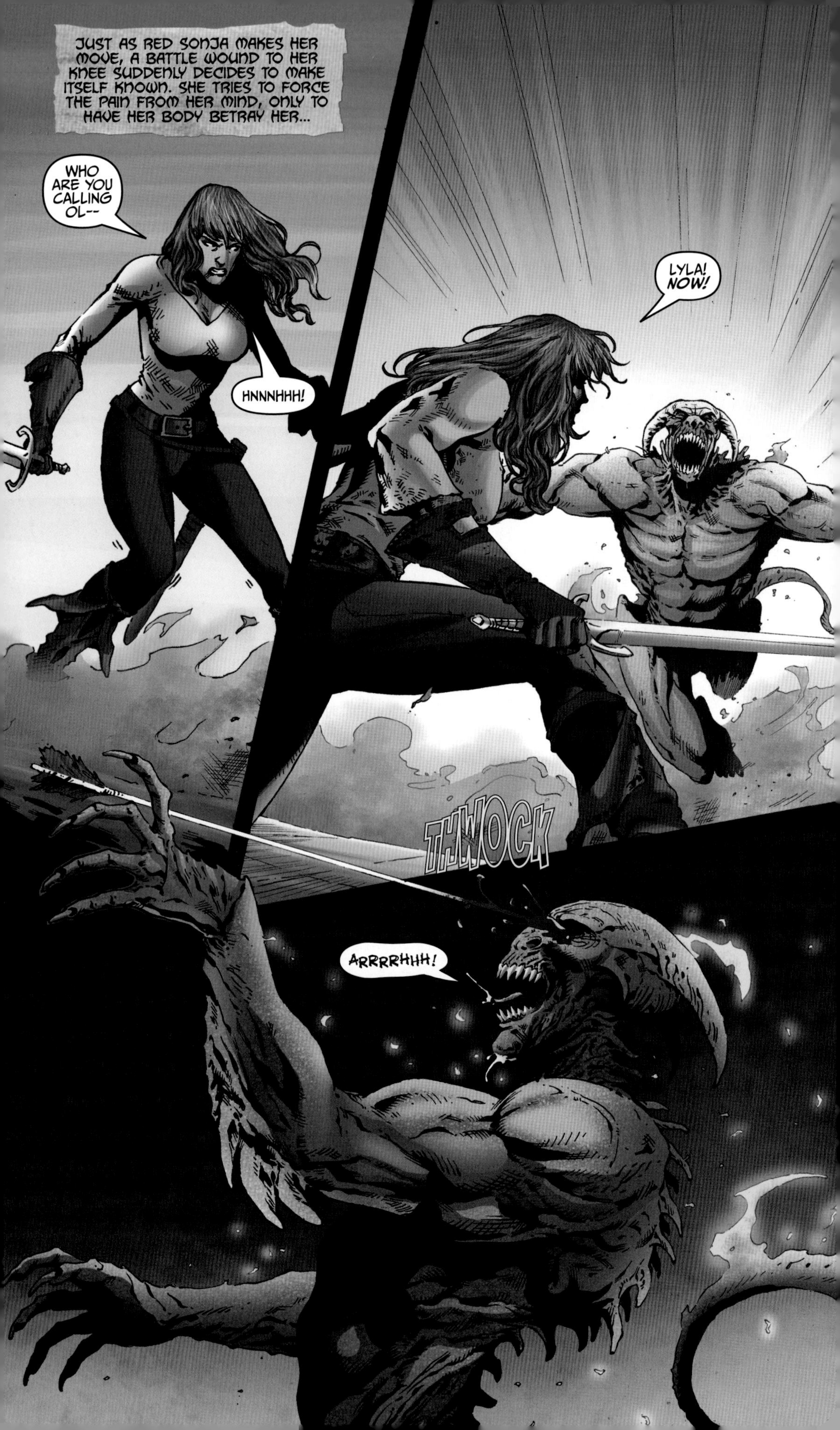
JUST AS RED SONJA MAKES HER MOVE, A BATTLE WOUND TO HER KNEE SUDDENLY DECIDES TO MAKE ITSELF KNOWN. SHE TRIES TO FORCE THE PAIN FROM HER MIND, ONLY TO HAVE HER BODY BETRAY HER...
WHO ARE YOU CALLING OL--
HNNNHHH!
LYLA! NOW!
THWOCK
ARRRRHHH!

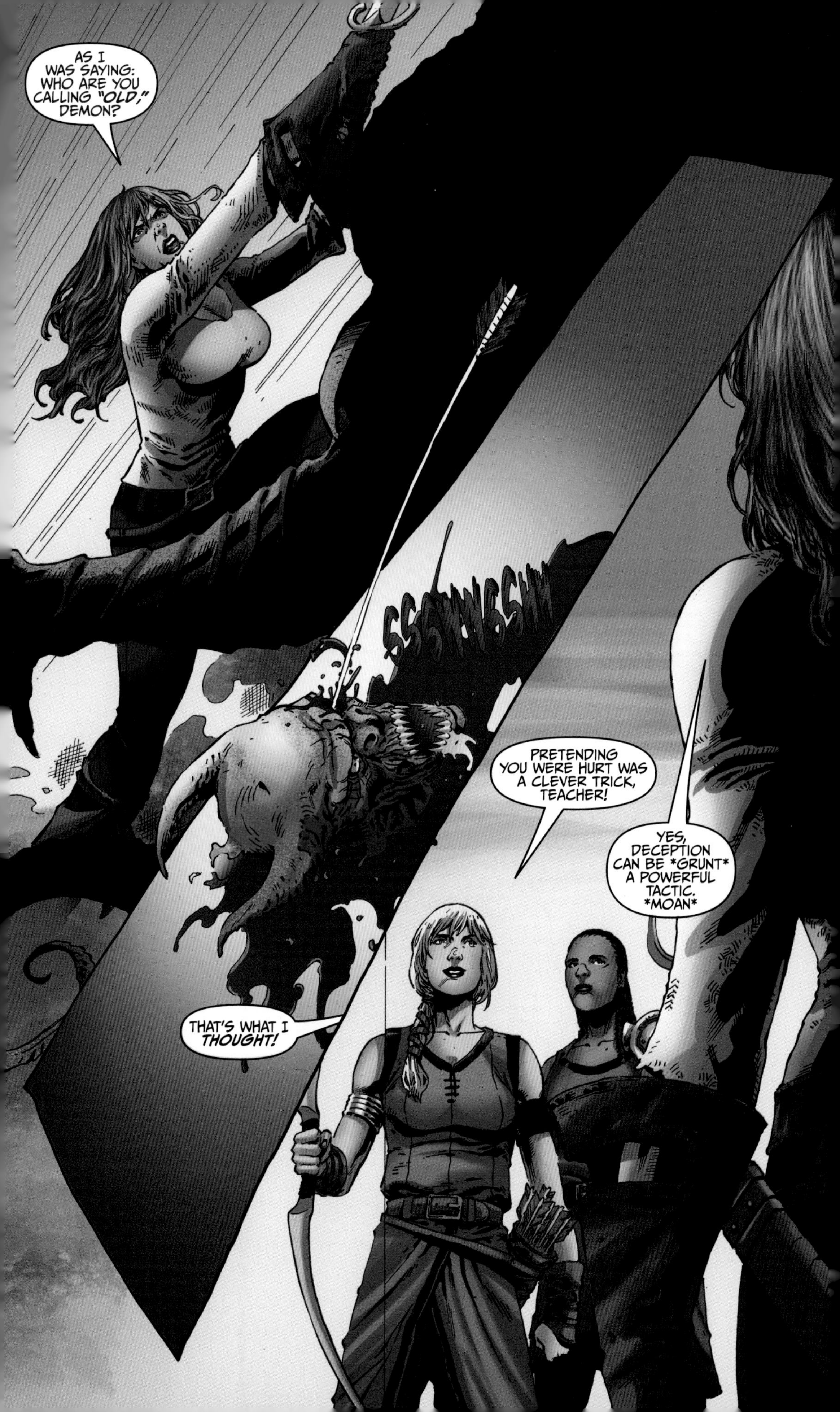
AS I WAS SAYING: WHO ARE YOU CALLING "OLD," DEMON?
SSSWWSSHH
THAT'S WHAT I THOUGHT!
PRETENDING YOU WERE HURT WAS A CLEVER TRICK, TEACHER!
YES, DECEPTION CAN BE *GRUNT* A POWERFUL TACTIC. *MOAN*

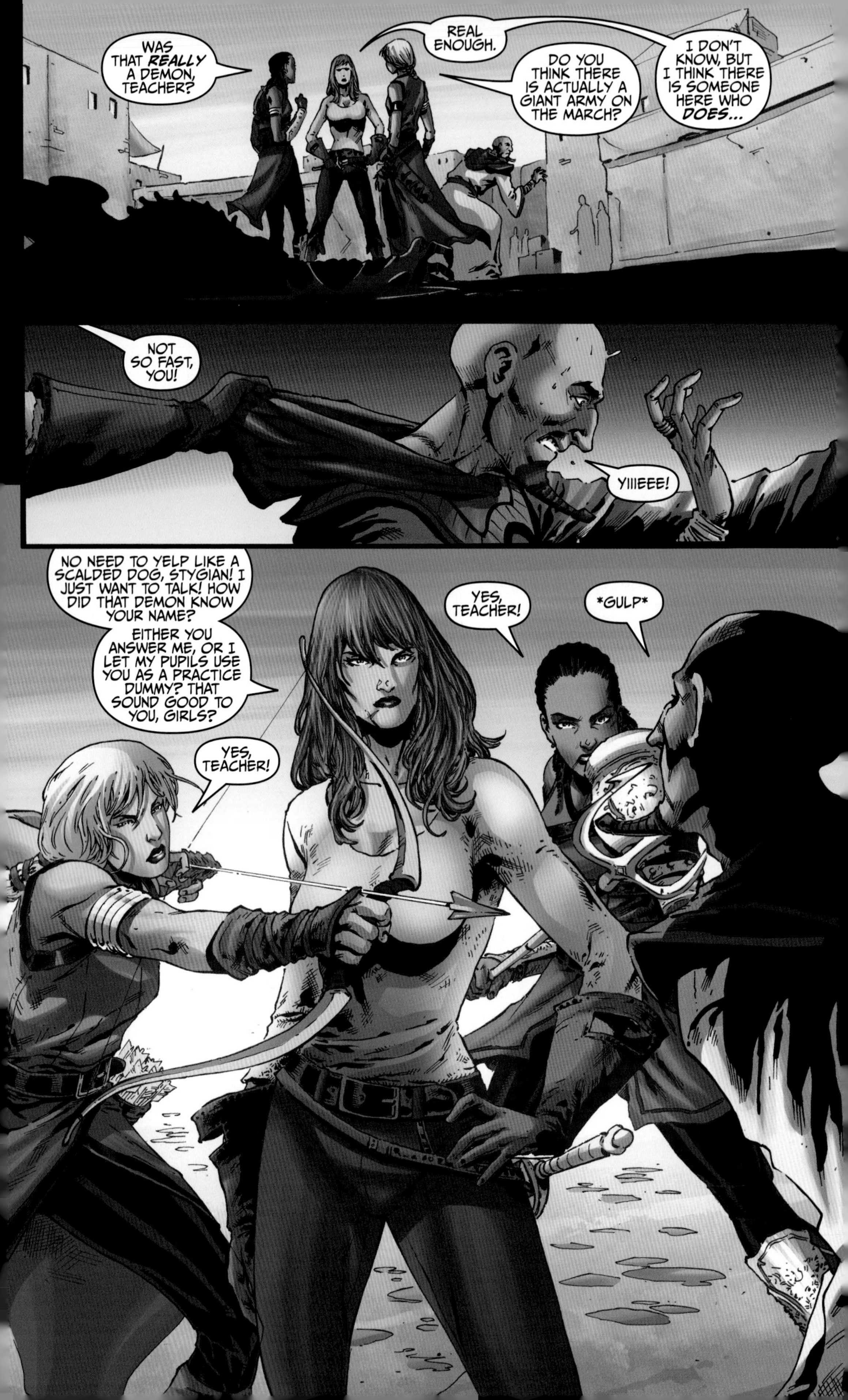

WAS THAT REALLY A DEMON, TEACHER?
REAL ENOUGH.
DO YOU THINK THERE IS ACTUALLY A GIANT ARMY ON THE MARCH?
I DON'T KNOW, BUT I THINK THERE IS SOMEONE HERE WHO DOES...
NOT SO FAST, YOU!
YIIIEEE!
NO NEED TO YELP LIKE A SCALDED DOG, STYGIAN! I JUST WANT TO TALK! HOW DID THAT DEMON KNOW YOUR NAME?
EITHER YOU ANSWER ME, OR I LET MY PUPILS USE YOU AS A PRACTICE DUMMY? THAT SOUND GOOD TO YOU, GIRLS?
YES, TEACHER!
GULP
YES, TEACHER!

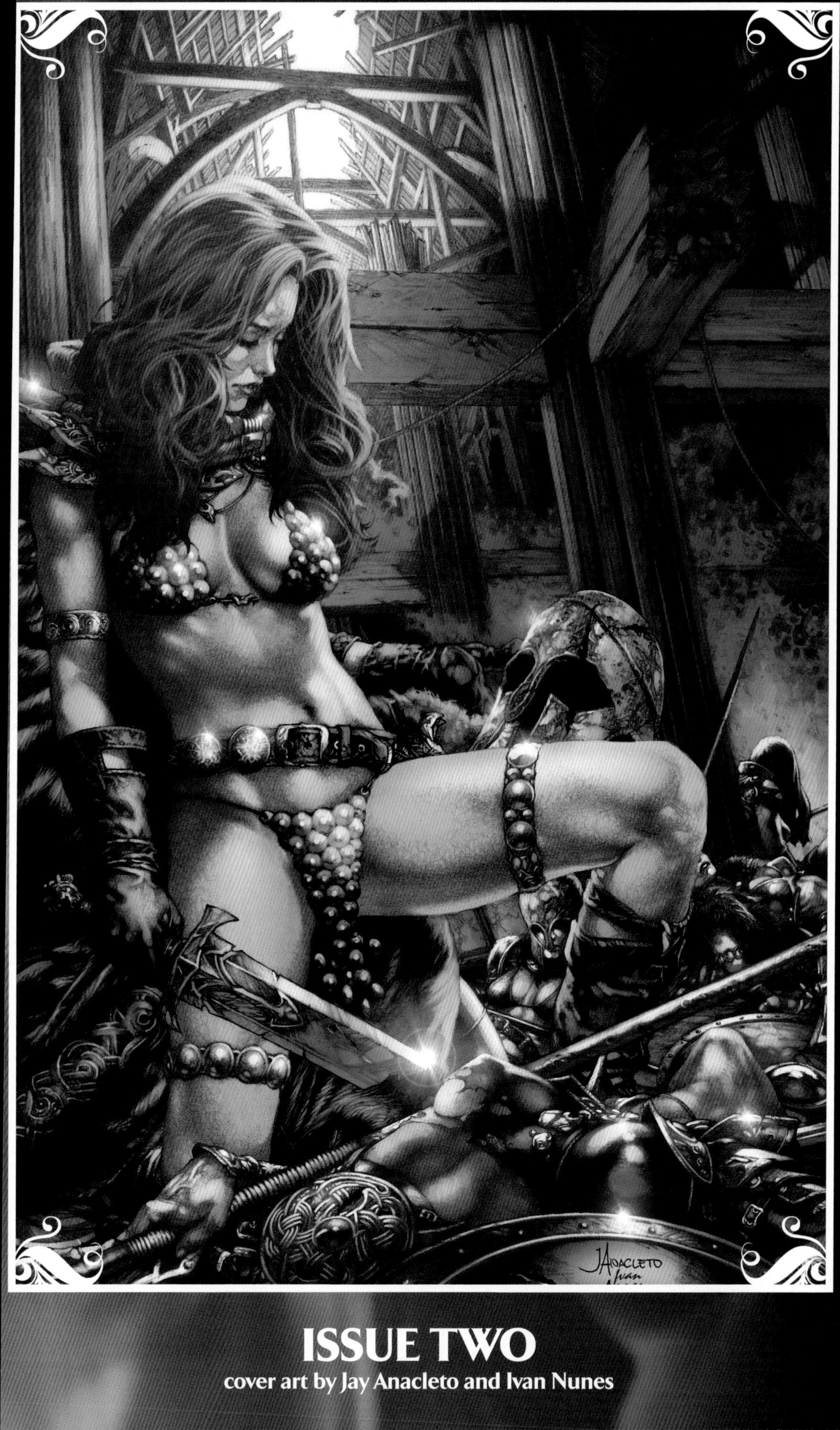

ISSUE TWO

cover art by Jay Anacleto and Ivan Nunes

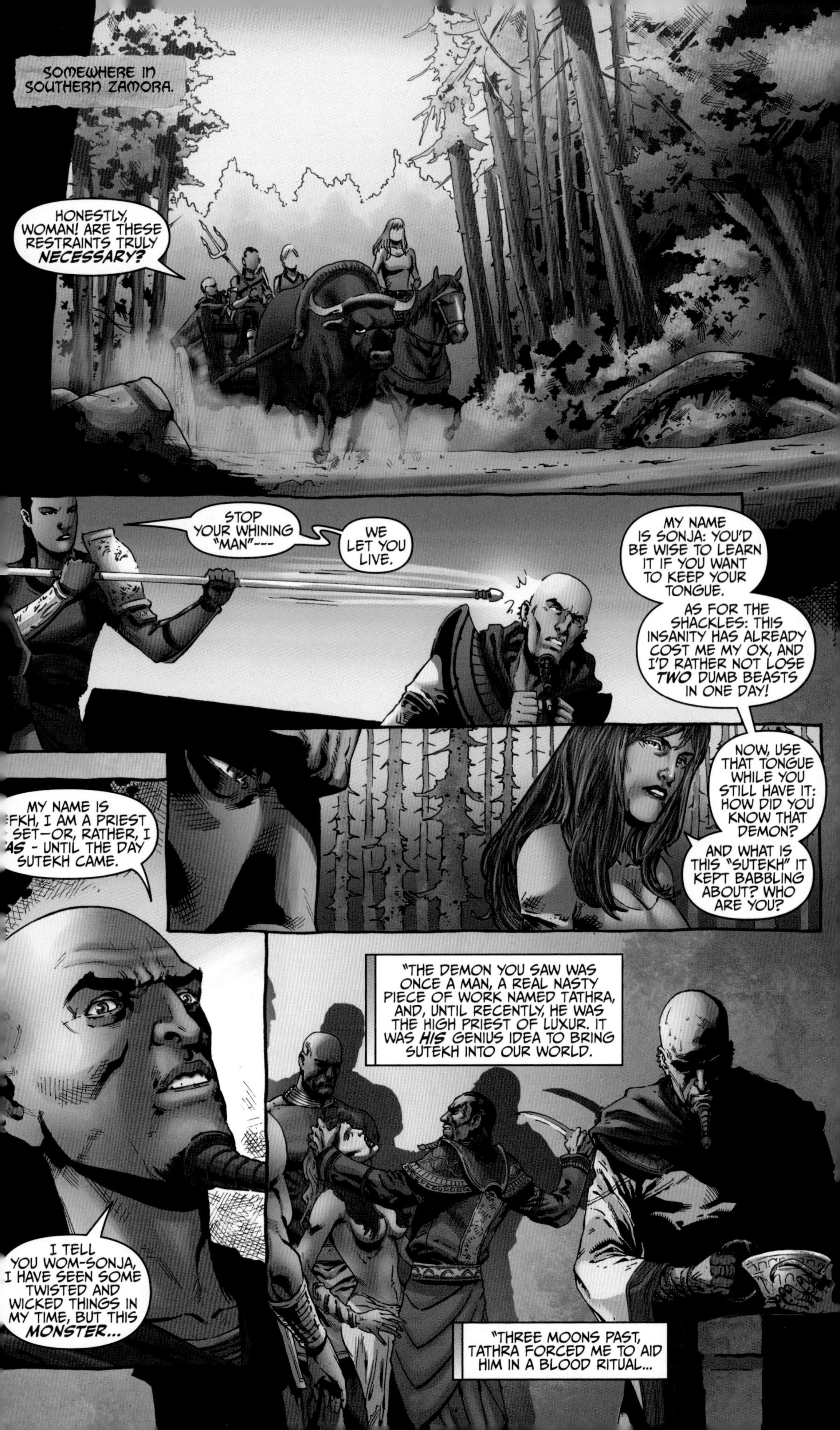
SOMEWHERE IN SOUTHERN ZAMORA.
HONESTLY, WOMAN! ARE THESE RESTRAINTS TRULY NECESSARY?
STOP YOUR WHINING "MAN"---
WE LET YOU LIVE.
MY NAME IS SONJA: YOU'D BE WISE TO LEARN IT IF YOU WANT TO KEEP YOUR TONGUE.
AS FOR THE SHACKLES: THIS INSANITY HAS ALREADY COST ME MY OX, AND I'D RATHER NOT LOSE TWO DUMB BEASTS IN ONE DAY!
NOW, USE THAT TONGUE WHILE YOU STILL HAVE IT: HOW DID YOU KNOW THAT DEMON?
AND WHAT IS THIS "SUTEKH" IT KEPT BABBLING ABOUT? WHO ARE YOU?
MY NAME IS EFKH, I AM A PRIEST SET--OR, RATHER, I AS - UNTIL THE DAY SUTEKH CAME.
I TELL YOU WOM-SONJA, I HAVE SEEN SOME TWISTED AND WICKED THINGS IN MY TIME, BUT THIS MONSTER...
"THE DEMON YOU SAW WAS ONCE A MAN, A REAL NASTY PIECE OF WORK NAMED TATHRA, AND, UNTIL RECENTLY, HE WAS THE HIGH PRIEST OF LUXUR. IT WAS HIS GENIUS IDEA TO BRING SUTEKH INTO OUR WORLD.
"THREE MOONS PAST, TATHRA FORCED ME TO AID HIM IN A BLOOD RITUAL...

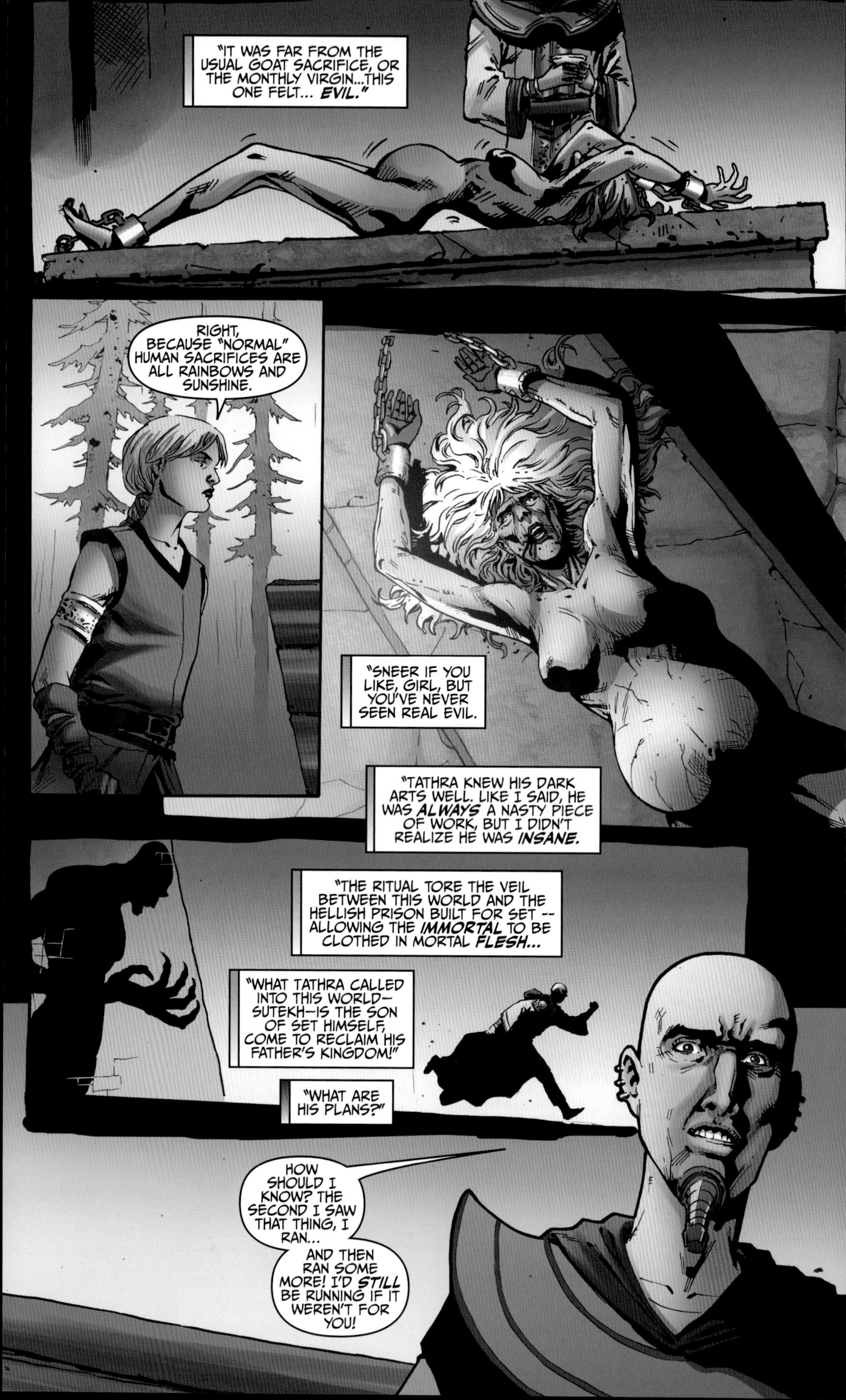
"IT WAS FAR FROM THE USUAL GOAT SACRIFICE, OR THE MONTHLY VIRGIN...THIS ONE FELT... EVIL."
RIGHT, BECAUSE "NORMAL" HUMAN SACRIFICES ARE ALL RAINBOWS AND SUNSHINE.
"SNEER IF YOU LIKE, GIRL, BUT YOU'VE NEVER SEEN REAL EVIL.
"TATHRA KNEW HIS DARK ARTS WELL. LIKE I SAID, HE WAS ALWAYS A NASTY PIECE OF WORK, BUT I DIDN'T REALIZE HE WAS INSANE.
"THE RITUAL TORE THE VEIL BETWEEN THIS WORLD AND THE HELLISH PRISON BUILT FOR SET -- ALLOWING THE IMMORTAL TO BE CLOTHED IN MORTAL FLESH...
"WHAT TATHRA CALLED INTO THIS WORLD—SUTEKH—IS THE SON OF SET HIMSELF, COME TO RECLAIM HIS FATHER'S KINGDOM!"
"WHAT ARE HIS PLANS?"
HOW SHOULD I KNOW? THE SECOND I SAW THAT THING, I RAN...
AND THEN RAN SOME MORE! I'D STILL BE RUNNING IF IT WEREN'T FOR YOU!

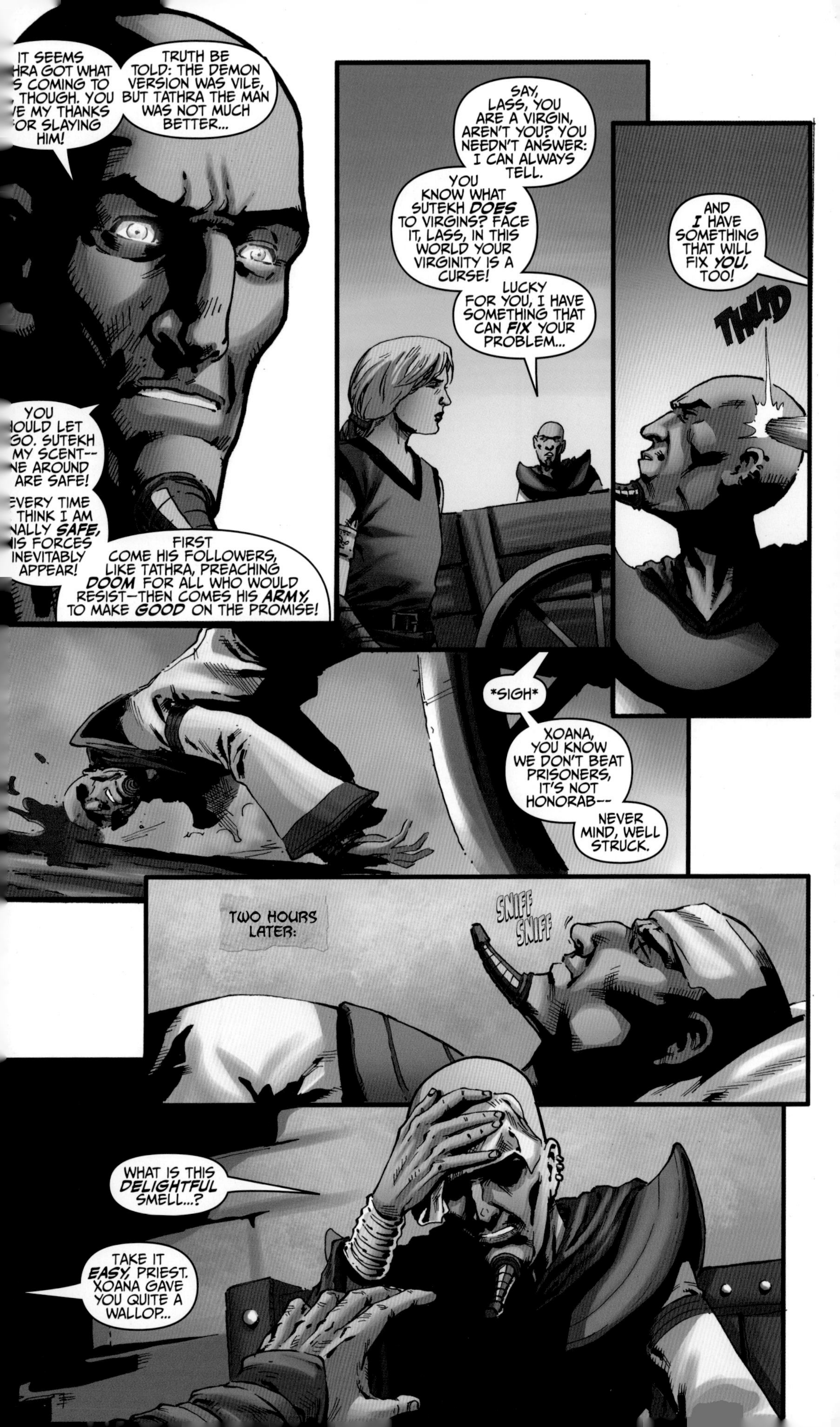
IT SEEMS
HRA GOT WHAT
S COMING TO
, THOUGH. YOU
E MY THANKS
FOR SLAYING
HIM!
TRUTH BE TOLD: THE DEMON VERSION WAS VILE, BUT TATHRA THE MAN WAS NOT MUCH BETTER...
YOU
HOULD LET
GO. SUTEKH
MY SCENT--
NE AROUND
ARE SAFE!
EVERY TIME
THINK I AM
NALLY SAFE,
IS FORCES
INEVITABLY
APPEAR!
FIRST COME HIS FOLLOWERS, LIKE TATHRA, PREACHING DOOM FOR ALL WHO WOULD RESIST--THEN COMES HIS ARMY, TO MAKE GOOD ON THE PROMISE!
SAY, LASS, YOU ARE A VIRGIN, AREN'T YOU? YOU NEEDN'T ANSWER: I CAN ALWAYS TELL.
YOU KNOW WHAT SUTEKH DOES TO VIRGINS? FACE IT, LASS, IN THIS WORLD YOUR VIRGINITY IS A CURSE!
LUCKY FOR YOU, I HAVE SOMETHING THAT CAN FIX YOUR PROBLEM...
AND I HAVE SOMETHING THAT WILL FIX YOU, TOO!
THUD
SIGH
XOANA, YOU KNOW WE DON'T BEAT PRISONERS, IT'S NOT HONORAB--
NEVER MIND, WELL STRUCK.
TWO HOURS LATER:
SNIFF SNIFF
WHAT IS THIS DELIGHTFUL SMELL...?
TAKE IT EASY, PRIEST. XOANA GAVE YOU QUITE A WALLOP...

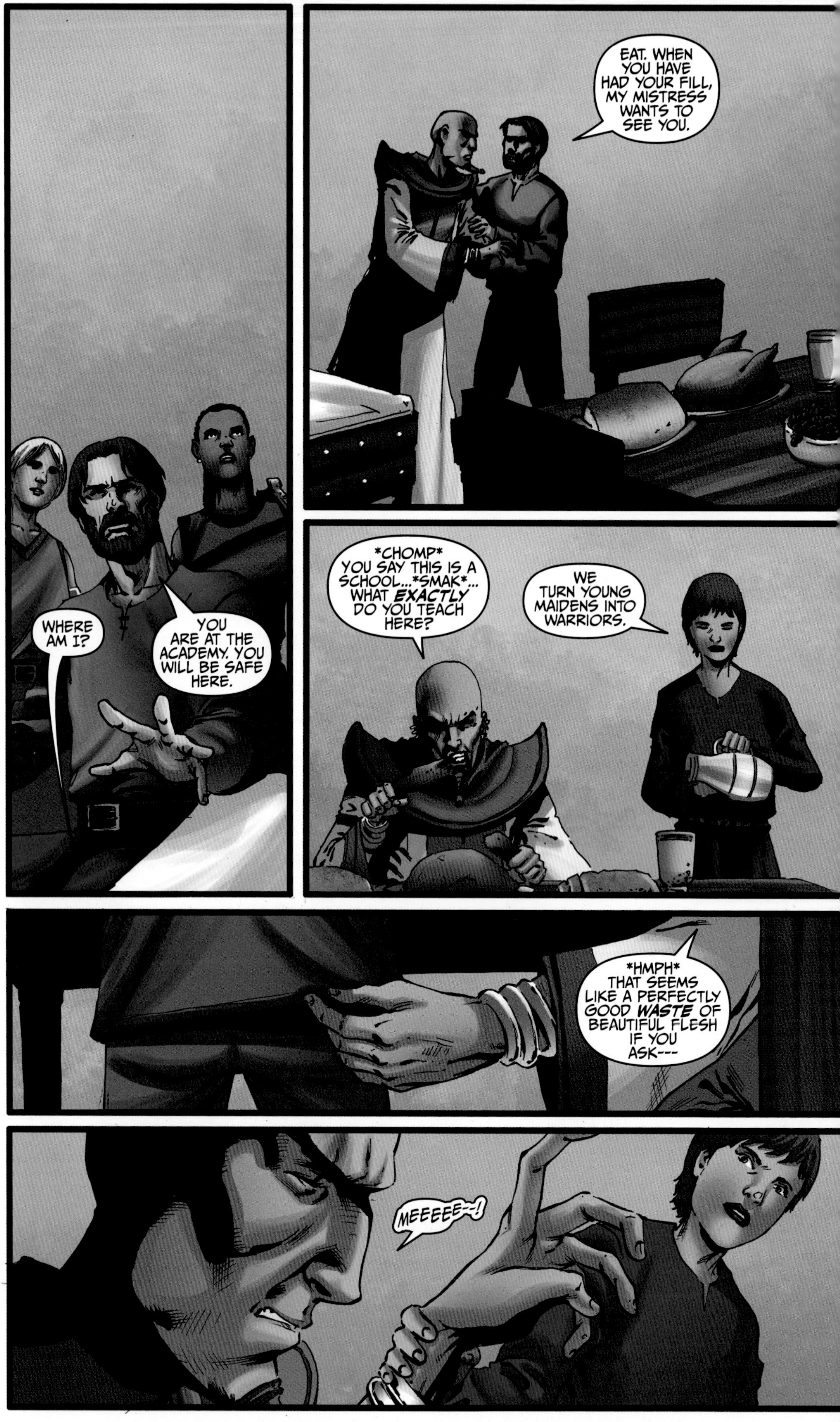
EAT. WHEN YOU HAVE HAD YOUR FILL, MY MISTRESS WANTS TO SEE YOU.
WHERE AM I?
YOU ARE AT THE ACADEMY. YOU WILL BE SAFE HERE.
CHOMP YOU SAY THIS IS A SCHOOL...*SMAK*... WHAT EXACTLY DO YOU TEACH HERE?
WE TURN YOUNG MAIDENS INTO WARRIORS.
HMPH THAT SEEMS LIKE A PERFECTLY GOOD WASTE OF BEAUTIFUL FLESH IF YOU ASK---
MEEEEE--!

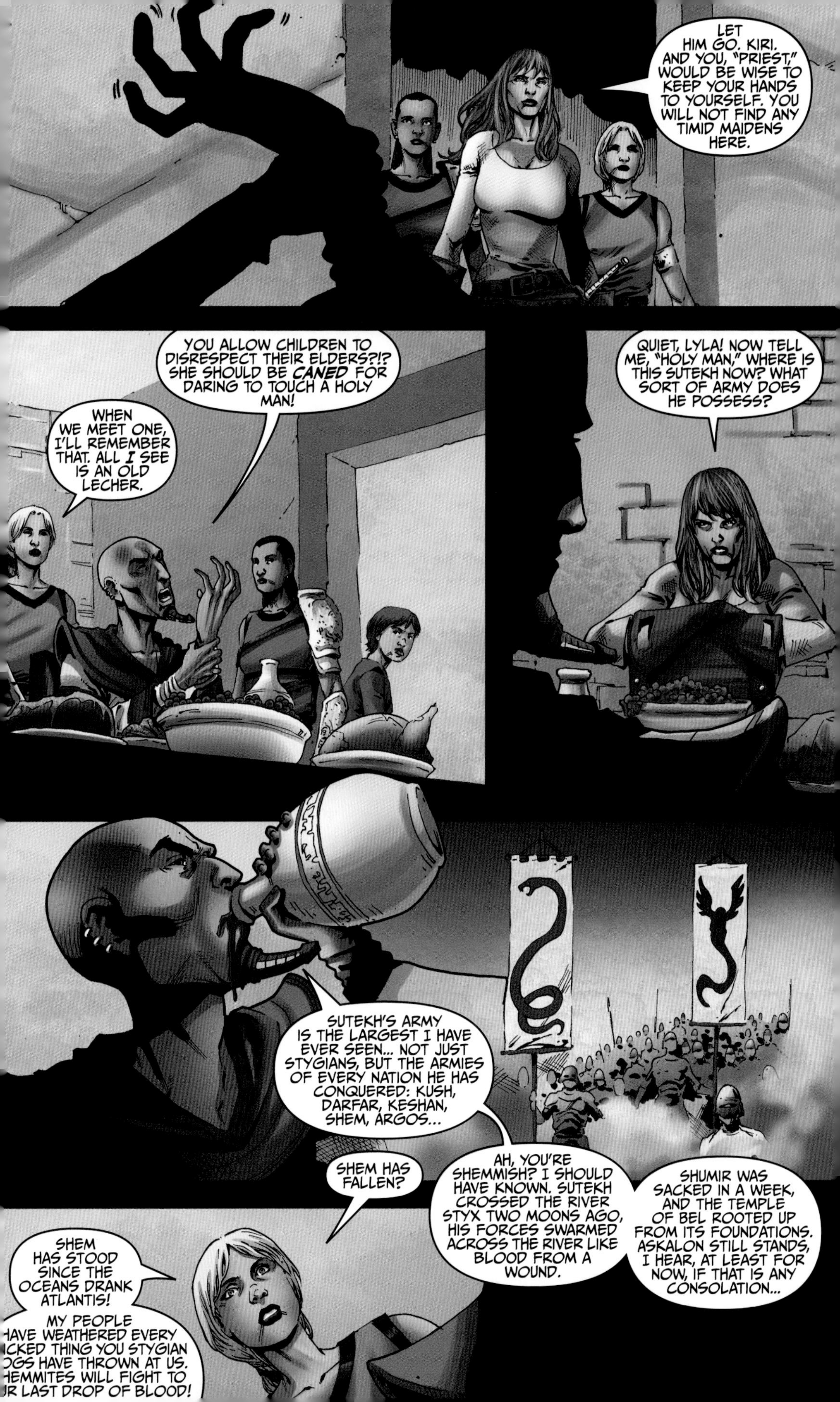
LET HIM GO, KIRI. AND YOU, "PRIEST," WOULD BE WISE TO KEEP YOUR HANDS TO YOURSELF. YOU WILL NOT FIND ANY TIMID MAIDENS HERE.
YOU ALLOW CHILDREN TO DISRESPECT THEIR ELDERS?!? SHE SHOULD BE *CANED* FOR DARING TO TOUCH A HOLY MAN!
WHEN WE MEET ONE, I'LL REMEMBER THAT. ALL *I* SEE IS AN OLD LECHER.
QUIET, LYLA! NOW TELL ME, "HOLY MAN," WHERE IS THIS SUTEKH NOW? WHAT SORT OF ARMY DOES HE POSSESS?
SUTEKH'S ARMY IS THE LARGEST I HAVE EVER SEEN... NOT JUST STYGIANS, BUT THE ARMIES OF EVERY NATION HE HAS CONQUERED: KUSH, DARFAR, KESHAN, SHEM, ARGOS...
SHEM HAS FALLEN?
AH, YOU'RE SHEMMISH? I SHOULD HAVE KNOWN. SUTEKH CROSSED THE RIVER STYX TWO MOONS AGO, HIS FORCES SWARMED ACROSS THE RIVER LIKE BLOOD FROM A WOUND.
SHUMIR WAS SACKED IN A WEEK, AND THE TEMPLE OF BEL ROOTED UP FROM ITS FOUNDATIONS. ASKALON STILL STANDS, I HEAR, AT LEAST FOR NOW, IF THAT IS ANY CONSOLATION...
SHEM HAS STOOD SINCE THE OCEANS DRANK ATLANTIS!
MY PEOPLE HAVE WEATHERED EVERY ICKED THING YOU STYGIAN OGS HAVE THROWN AT US. HEMMITES WILL FIGHT TO R LAST DROP OF BLOOD!

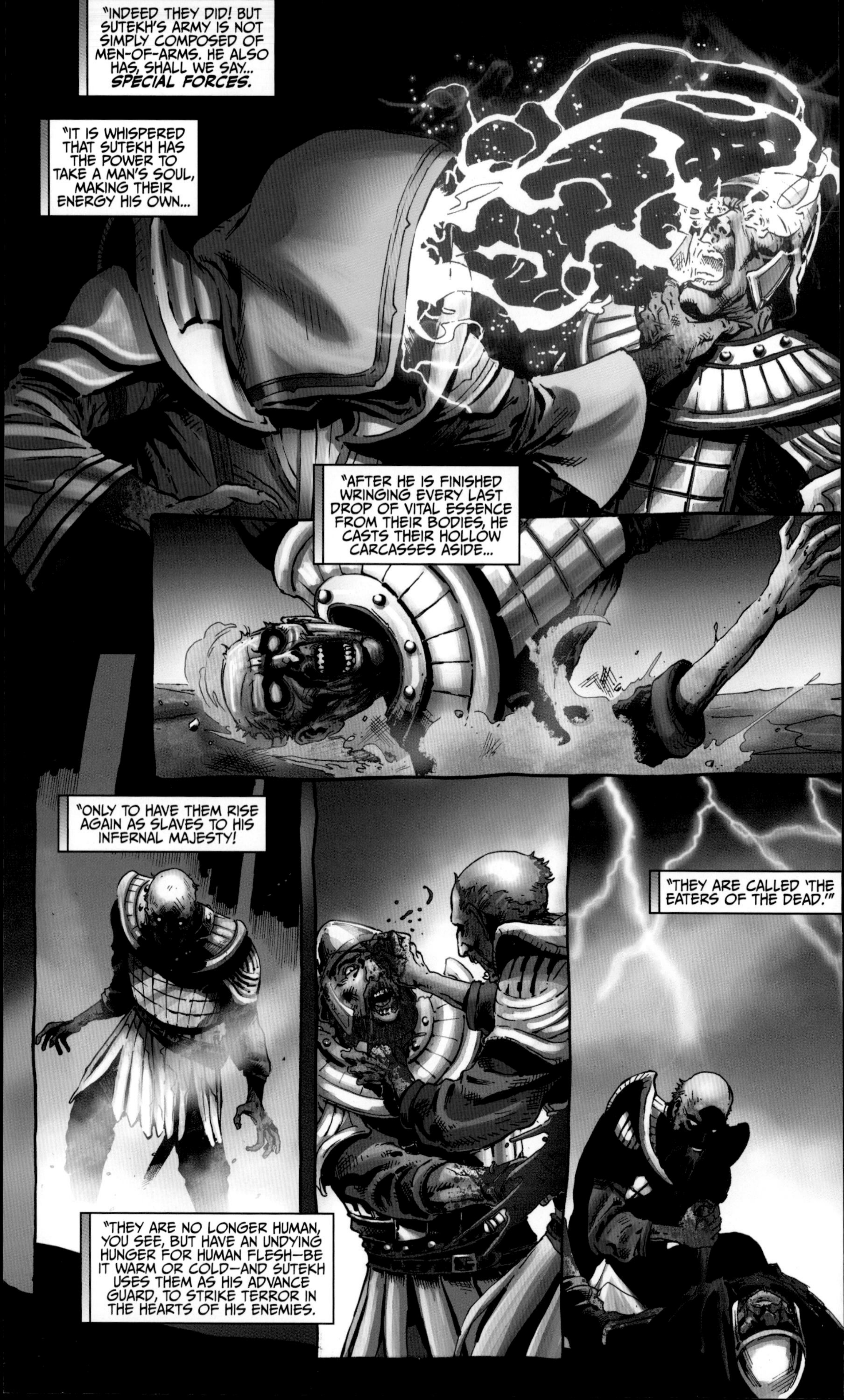
"INDEED THEY DID! BUT SUTEKH'S ARMY IS NOT SIMPLY COMPOSED OF MEN-OF-ARMS. HE ALSO HAS, SHALL WE SAY... SPECIAL FORCES.
"IT IS WHISPERED THAT SUTEKH HAS THE POWER TO TAKE A MAN'S SOUL, MAKING THEIR ENERGY HIS OWN...
"AFTER HE IS FINISHED WRINGING EVERY LAST DROP OF VITAL ESSENCE FROM THEIR BODIES, HE CASTS THEIR HOLLOW CARCASSES ASIDE...
"ONLY TO HAVE THEM RISE AGAIN AS SLAVES TO HIS INFERNAL MAJESTY!
"THEY ARE NO LONGER HUMAN, YOU SEE, BUT HAVE AN UNDYING HUNGER FOR HUMAN FLESH—BE IT WARM OR COLD—AND SUTEKH USES THEM AS HIS ADVANCE GUARD, TO STRIKE TERROR IN THE HEARTS OF HIS ENEMIES.
"THEY ARE CALLED 'THE EATERS OF THE DEAD.'"

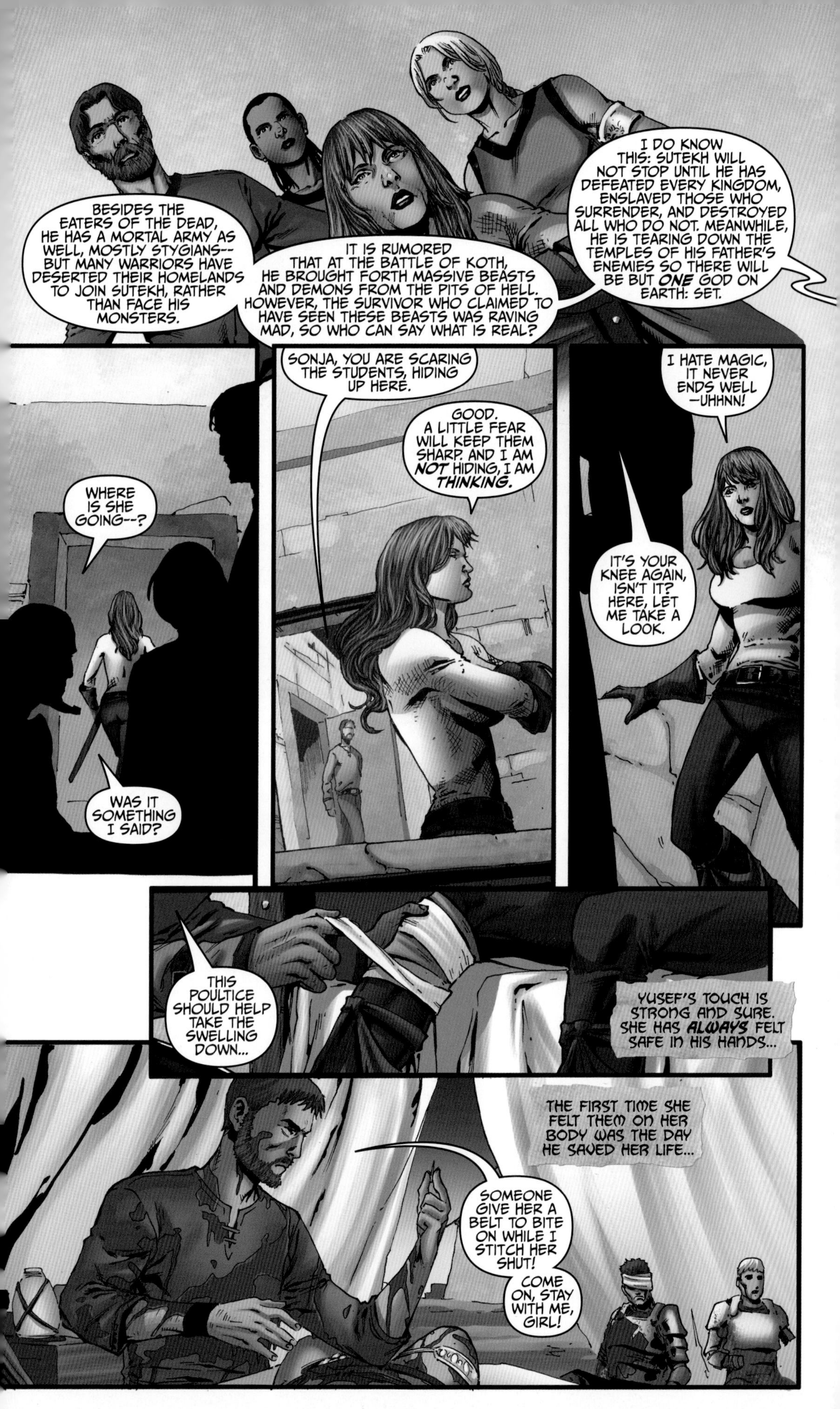
BESIDES THE EATERS OF THE DEAD, HE HAS A MORTAL ARMY AS WELL, MOSTLY STYGIANS--BUT MANY WARRIORS HAVE DESERTED THEIR HOMELANDS TO JOIN SUTEKH, RATHER THAN FACE HIS MONSTERS.
IT IS RUMORED THAT AT THE BATTLE OF KOTH, HE BROUGHT FORTH MASSIVE BEASTS AND DEMONS FROM THE PITS OF HELL. HOWEVER, THE SURVIVOR WHO CLAIMED TO HAVE SEEN THESE BEASTS WAS RAVING MAD, SO WHO CAN SAY WHAT IS REAL?
I DO KNOW THIS: SUTEKH WILL NOT STOP UNTIL HE HAS DEFEATED EVERY KINGDOM, ENSLAVED THOSE WHO SURRENDER, AND DESTROYED ALL WHO DO NOT. MEANWHILE, HE IS TEARING DOWN THE TEMPLES OF HIS FATHER'S ENEMIES SO THERE WILL BE BUT ONE GOD ON EARTH: SET.
WHERE IS SHE GOING--?
WAS IT SOMETHING I SAID?
SONJA, YOU ARE SCARING THE STUDENTS, HIDING UP HERE.
GOOD. A LITTLE FEAR WILL KEEP THEM SHARP. AND I AM NOT HIDING, I AM THINKING.
I HATE MAGIC, IT NEVER ENDS WELL —UHHNN!
IT'S YOUR KNEE AGAIN, ISN'T IT? HERE, LET ME TAKE A LOOK.
THIS POULTICE SHOULD HELP TAKE THE SWELLING DOWN...
YUSEF'S TOUCH IS STRONG AND SURE. SHE HAS ALWAYS FELT SAFE IN HIS HANDS...
THE FIRST TIME SHE FELT THEM ON HER BODY WAS THE DAY HE SAVED HER LIFE...
SOMEONE GIVE HER A BELT TO BITE ON WHILE I STITCH HER SHUT!
COME ON, STAY WITH ME, GIRL!

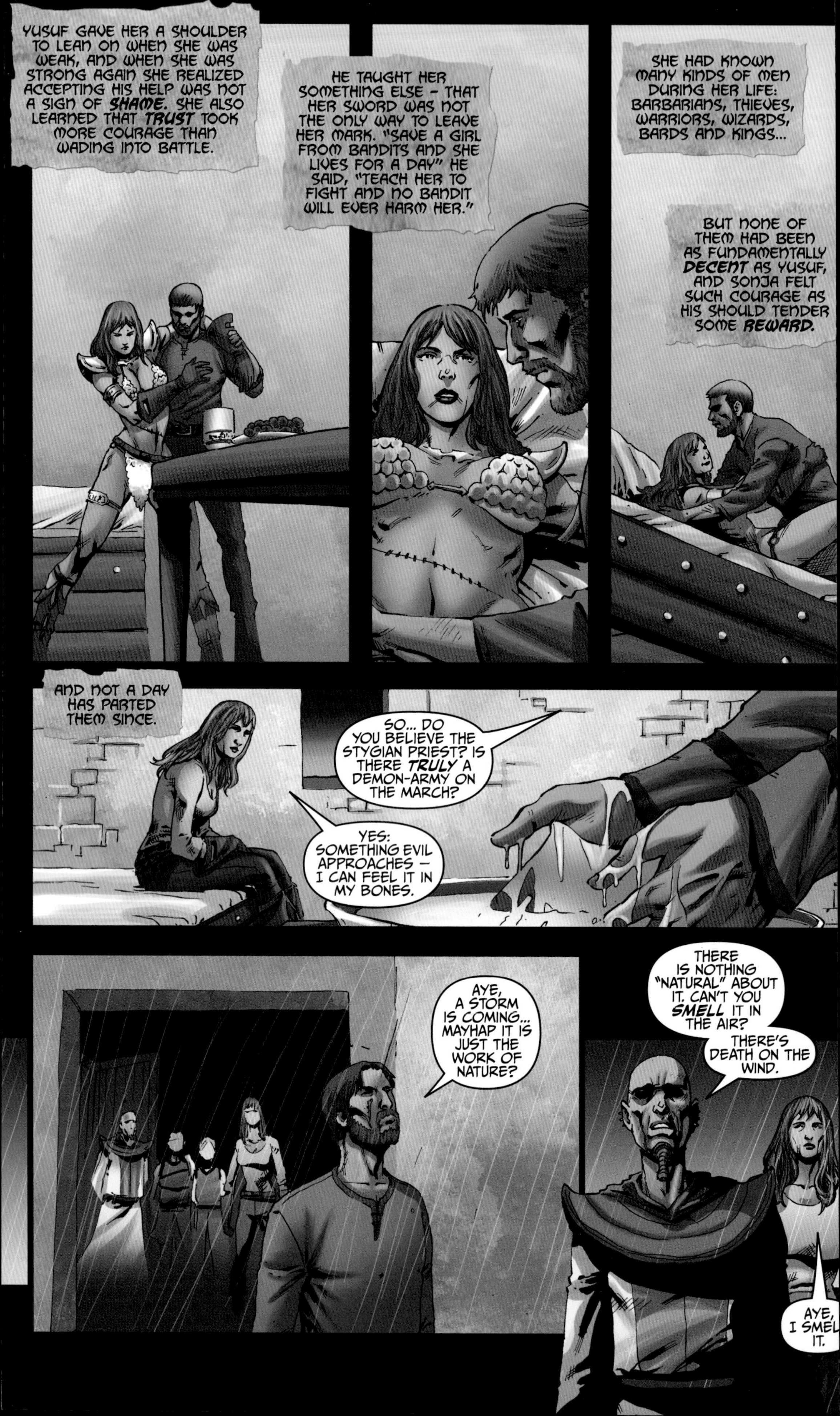
YUSUF GAVE HER A SHOULDER TO LEAN ON WHEN SHE WAS WEAK, AND WHEN SHE WAS STRONG AGAIN SHE REALIZED ACCEPTING HIS HELP WAS NOT A SIGN OF SHAME. SHE ALSO LEARNED THAT TRUST TOOK MORE COURAGE THAN WADING INTO BATTLE.
HE TAUGHT HER SOMETHING ELSE – THAT HER SWORD WAS NOT THE ONLY WAY TO LEAVE HER MARK. "SAVE A GIRL FROM BANDITS AND SHE LIVES FOR A DAY" HE SAID, "TEACH HER TO FIGHT AND NO BANDIT WILL EVER HARM HER."
SHE HAD KNOWN MANY KINDS OF MEN DURING HER LIFE: BARBARIANS, THIEVES, WARRIORS, WIZARDS, BARDS AND KINGS...
BUT NONE OF THEM HAD BEEN AS FUNDAMENTALLY DECENT AS YUSUF, AND SONJA FELT SUCH COURAGE AS HIS SHOULD TENDER SOME REWARD.
AND NOT A DAY HAS PARTED THEM SINCE.
SO... DO YOU BELIEVE THE STYGIAN PRIEST? IS THERE TRULY A DEMON-ARMY ON THE MARCH?
YES: SOMETHING EVIL APPROACHES — I CAN FEEL IT IN MY BONES.
AYE, A STORM IS COMING... MAYHAP IT IS JUST THE WORK OF NATURE?
THERE IS NOTHING "NATURAL" ABOUT IT. CAN'T YOU SMELL IT IN THE AIR?
THERE'S DEATH ON THE WIND.
AYE, I SMEL IT.

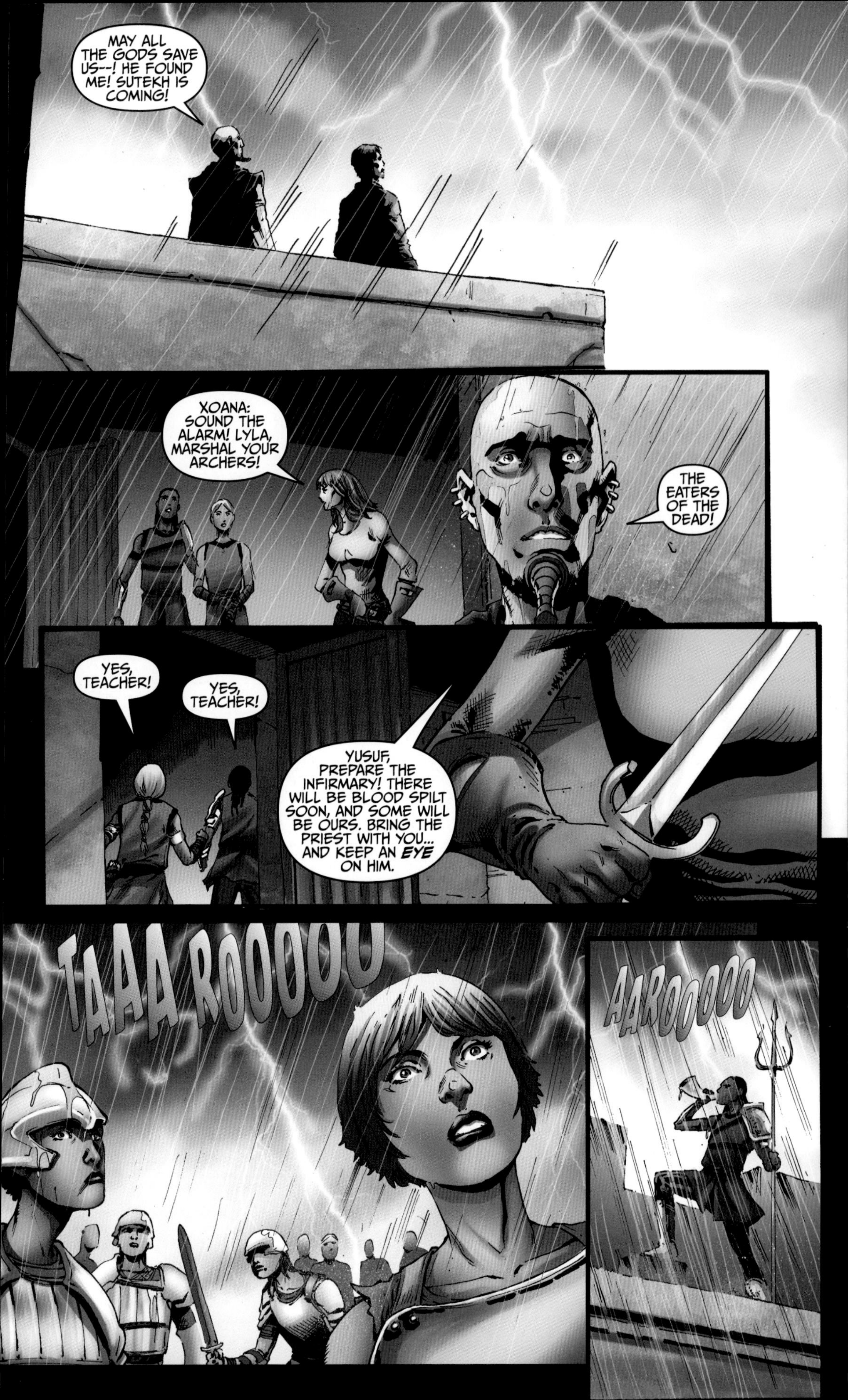
MAY ALL THE GODS SAVE US--! HE FOUND ME! SUTEKH IS COMING!
XOANA: SOUND THE ALARM! LYLA, MARSHAL YOUR ARCHERS!
THE EATERS OF THE DEAD!
YES, TEACHER!
YES, TEACHER!
YUSUF, PREPARE THE INFIRMARY! THERE WILL BE BLOOD SPILT SOON, AND SOME WILL BE OURS. BRING THE PRIEST WITH YOU... AND KEEP AN *EYE* ON HIM.
TAAA ROOOOO
AAROOOOO

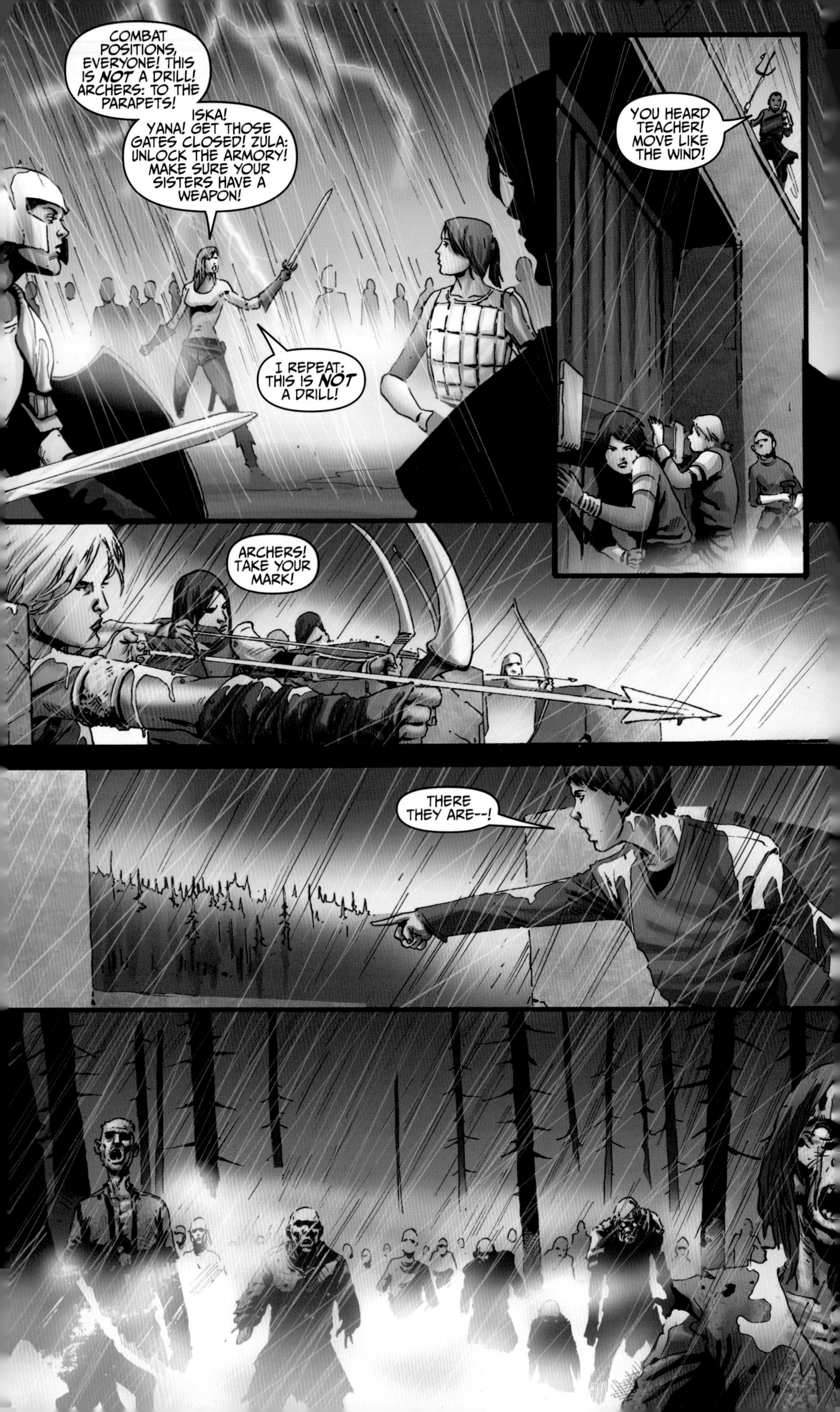
COMBAT POSITIONS, EVERYONE! THIS IS NOT A DRILL! ARCHERS: TO THE PARAPETS!
ISKA! YANA! GET THOSE GATES CLOSED! ZULA: UNLOCK THE ARMORY! MAKE SURE YOUR SISTERS HAVE A WEAPON!
I REPEAT: THIS IS NOT A DRILL!
YOU HEARD TEACHER! MOVE LIKE THE WIND!
ARCHERS! TAKE YOUR MARK!
THERE THEY ARE--!

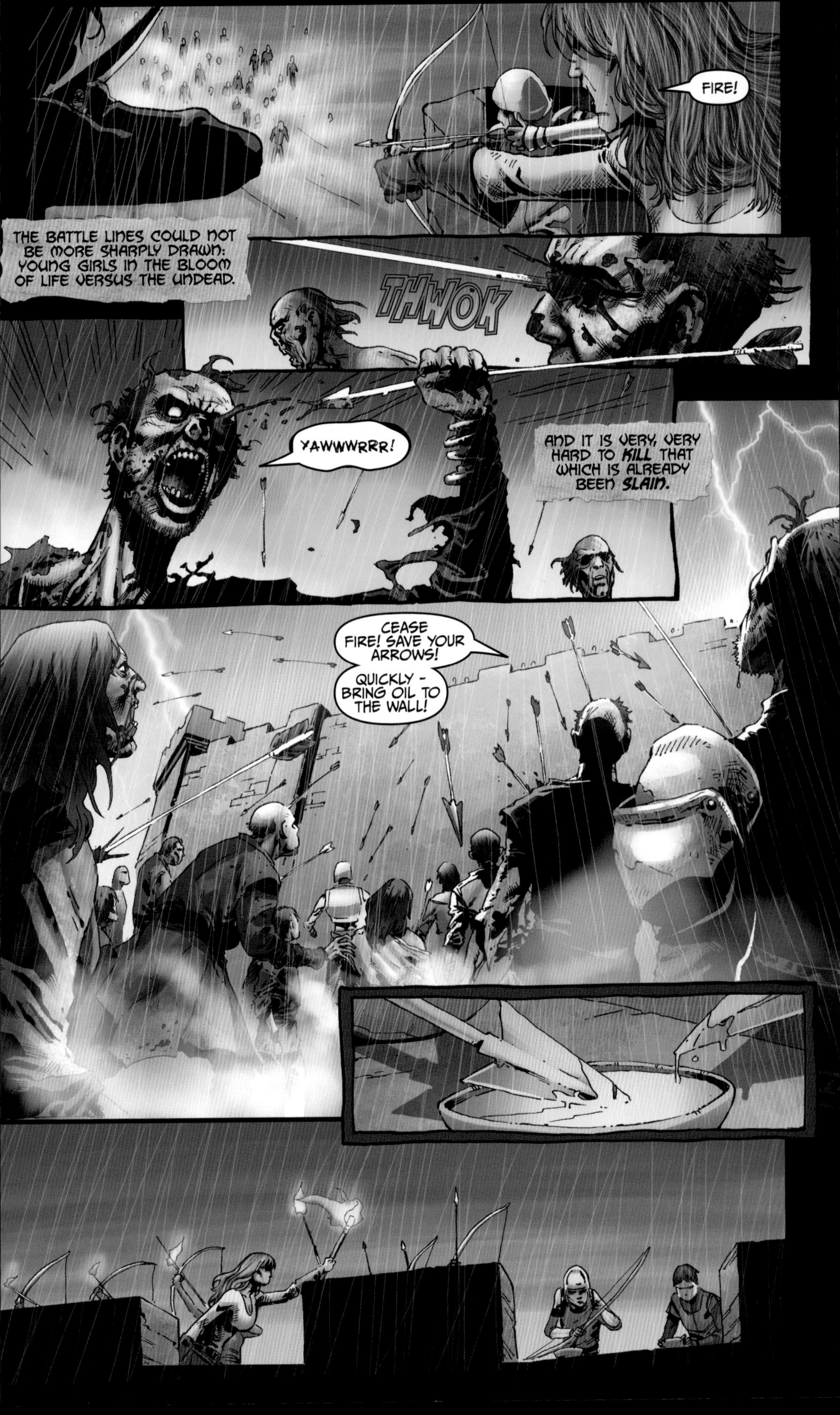
FIRE!
THE BATTLE LINES COULD NOT BE MORE SHARPLY DRAWN: YOUNG GIRLS IN THE BLOOM OF LIFE VERSUS THE UNDEAD.
THWOK
YAWWWRRR!
AND IT IS VERY, VERY HARD TO KILL THAT WHICH IS ALREADY BEEN SLAIN.
CEASE FIRE! SAVE YOUR ARROWS!
QUICKLY - BRING OIL TO THE WALL!

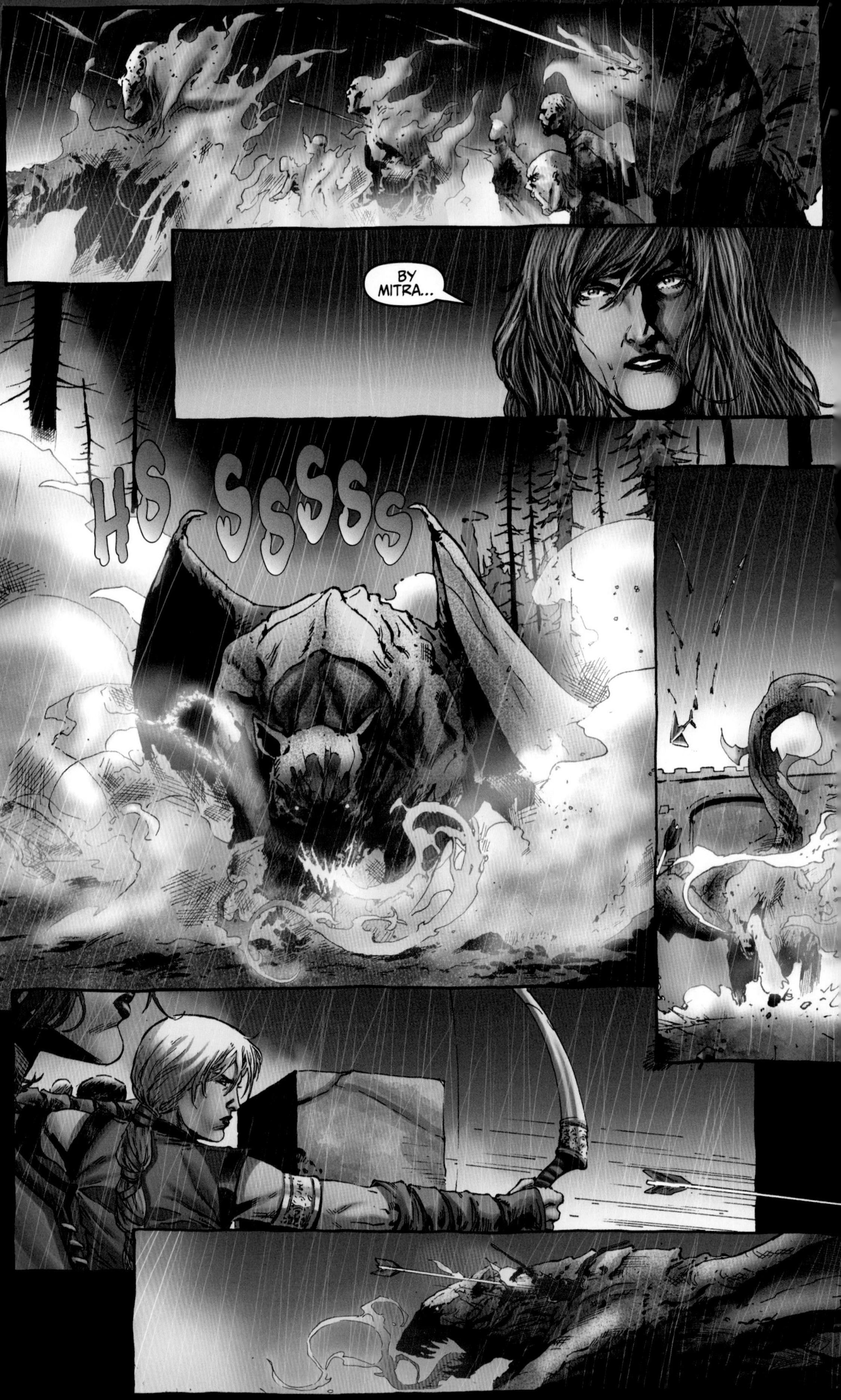
BY MITRA...
HS SSSSS

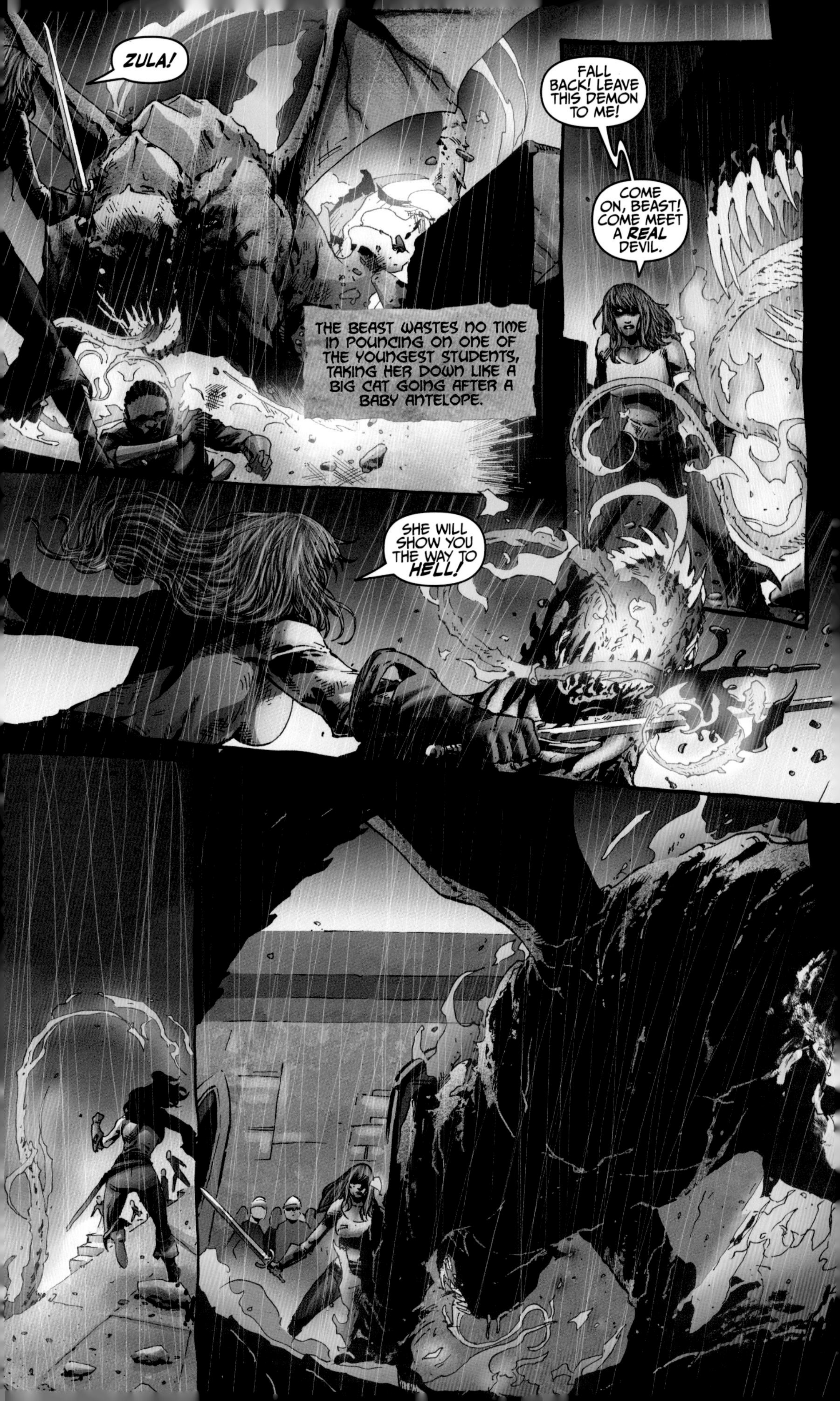
ZULA!
FALL BACK! LEAVE THIS DEMON TO ME!
COME ON, BEAST! COME MEET A REAL DEVIL.
THE BEAST WASTES NO TIME IN POUNCING ON ONE OF THE YOUNGEST STUDENTS, TAKING HER DOWN LIKE A BIG CAT GOING AFTER A BABY ANTELOPE.
SHE WILL SHOW YOU THE WAY TO HELL!

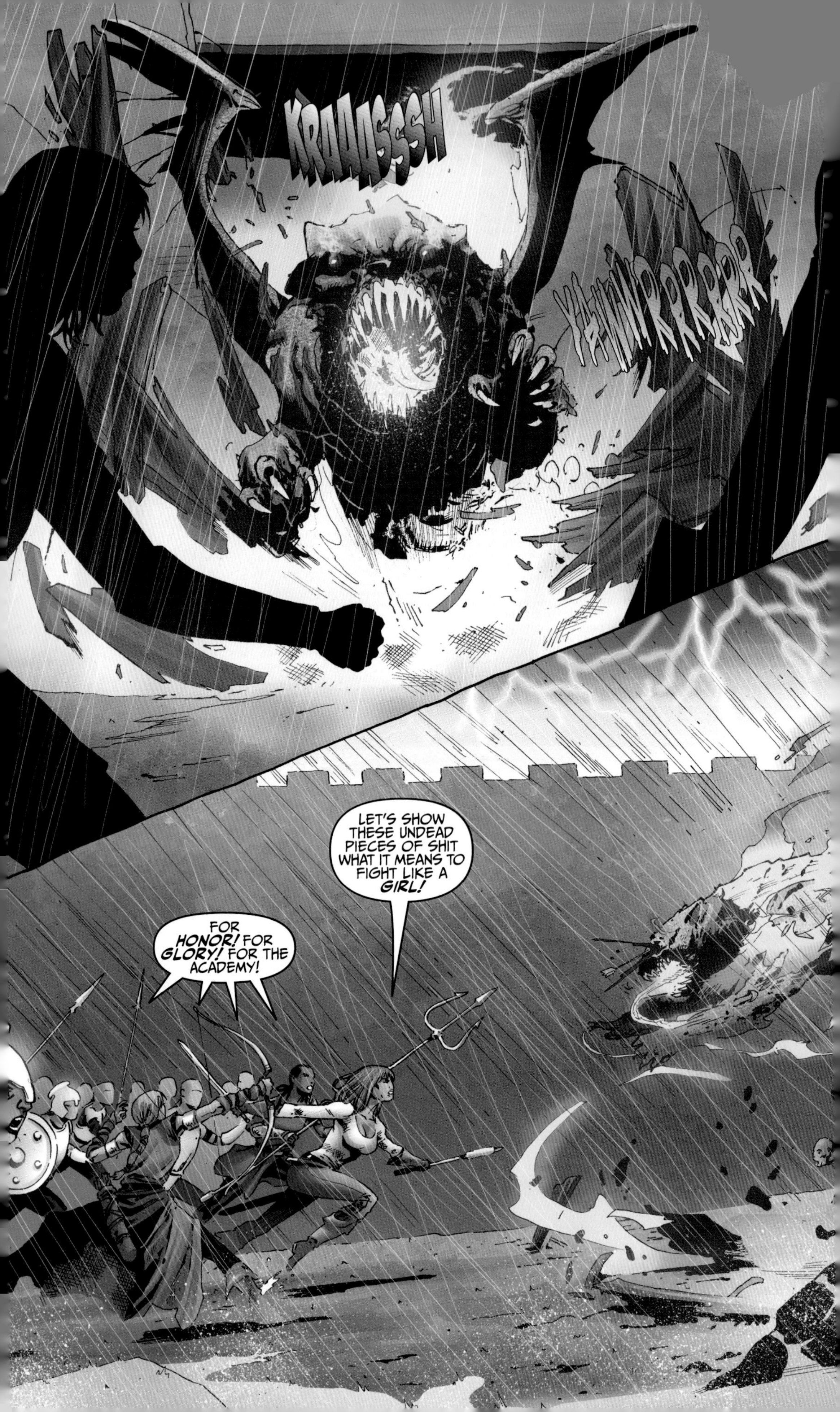
KRAAASSSH
YAWWRRRRRR
LET'S SHOW THESE UNDEAD PIECES OF SHIT WHAT IT MEANS TO FIGHT LIKE A *GIRL!*
FOR *HONOR!* FOR *GLORY!* FOR THE ACADEMY!

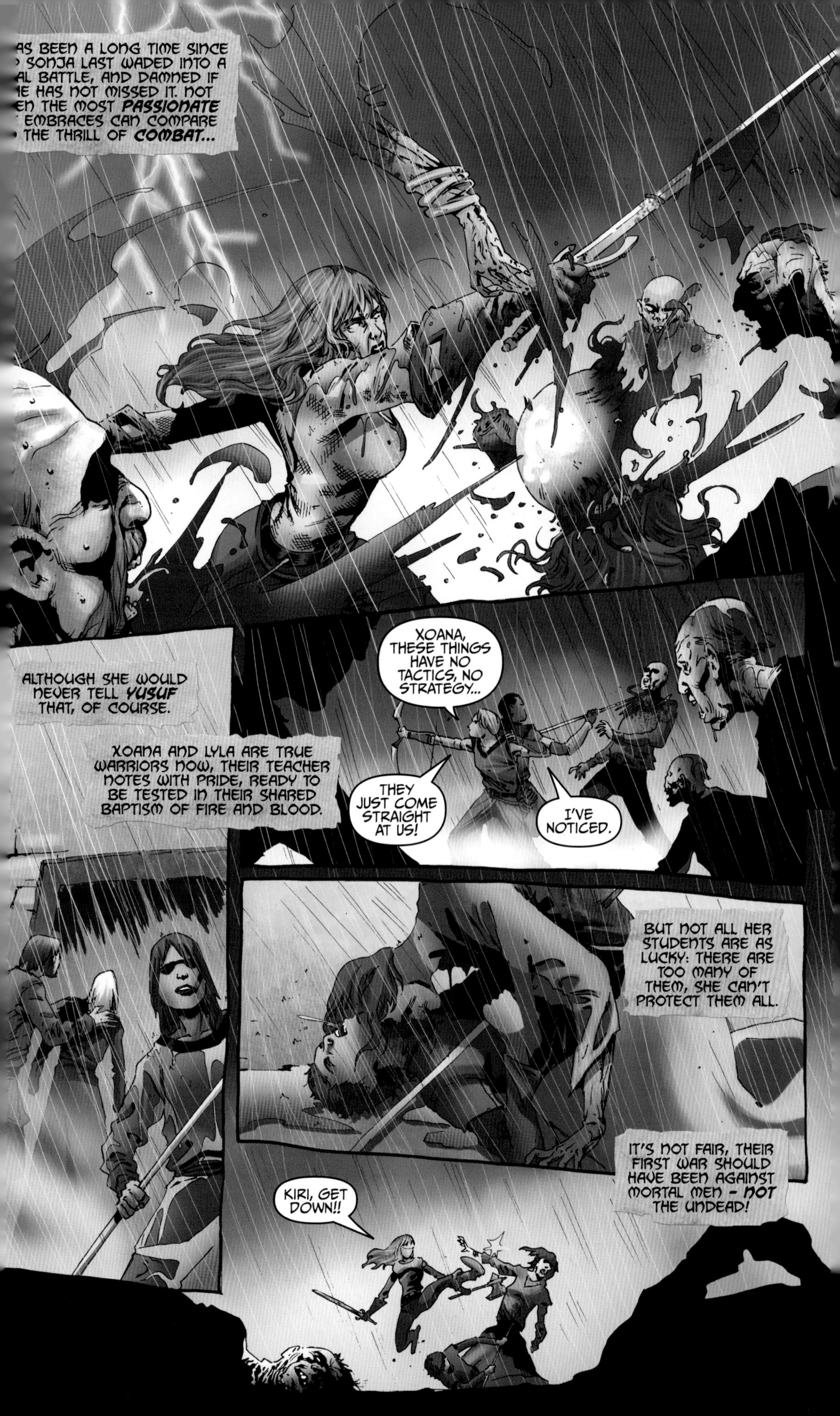

AS BEEN A LONG TIME SINCE
SONJA LAST WADED INTO A
AL BATTLE, AND DAMNED IF
HE HAS NOT MISSED IT. NOT
EN THE MOST PASSIONATE
EMBRACES CAN COMPARE
THE THRILL OF COMBAT...
ALTHOUGH SHE WOULD NEVER TELL YUSUF THAT, OF COURSE.
XOANA AND LYLA ARE TRUE WARRIORS NOW, THEIR TEACHER NOTES WITH PRIDE, READY TO BE TESTED IN THEIR SHARED BAPTISM OF FIRE AND BLOOD.
XOANA, THESE THINGS HAVE NO TACTICS, NO STRATEGY...
THEY JUST COME STRAIGHT AT US!
I'VE NOTICED.
BUT NOT ALL HER STUDENTS ARE AS LUCKY: THERE ARE TOO MANY OF THEM, SHE CAN'T PROTECT THEM ALL.
IT'S NOT FAIR, THEIR FIRST WAR SHOULD HAVE BEEN AGAINST MORTAL MEN - NOT THE UNDEAD!
KIRI, GET DOWN!!

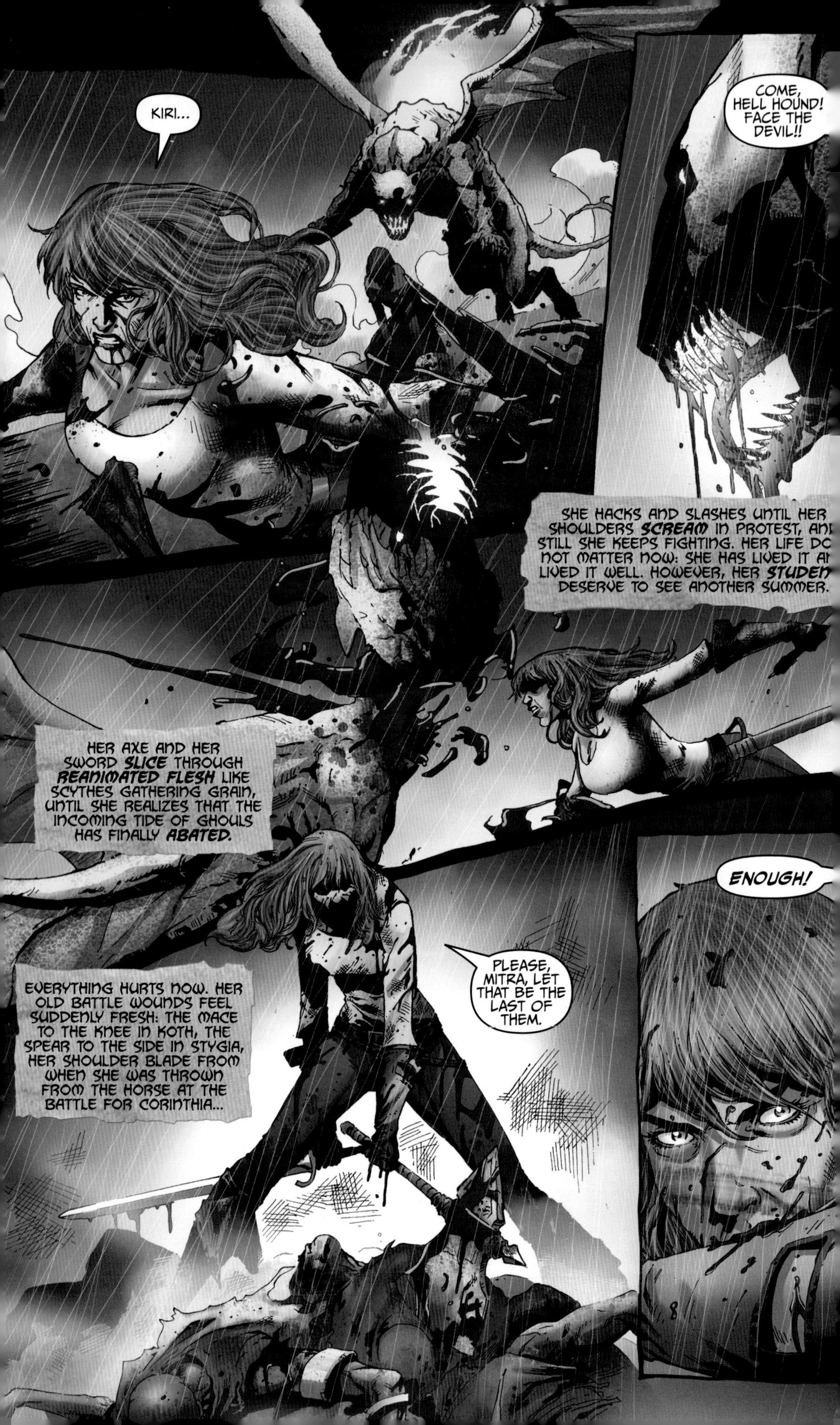
KIRI...
COME, HELL HOUND! FACE THE DEVIL!!
SHE HACKS AND SLASHES UNTIL HER SHOULDERS SCREAM IN PROTEST, AN STILL SHE KEEPS FIGHTING. HER LIFE DO NOT MATTER NOW: SHE HAS LIVED IT A LIVED IT WELL. HOWEVER, HER STUDEN DESERVE TO SEE ANOTHER SUMMER.
HER AXE AND HER SWORD SLICE THROUGH REANIMATED FLESH LIKE SCYTHES GATHERING GRAIN, UNTIL SHE REALIZES THAT THE INCOMING TIDE OF GHOULS HAS FINALLY ABATED.
ENOUGH!
EVERYTHING HURTS NOW. HER OLD BATTLE WOUNDS FEEL SUDDENLY FRESH: THE MACE TO THE KNEE IN KOTH, THE SPEAR TO THE SIDE IN STYGIA, HER SHOULDER BLADE FROM WHEN SHE WAS THROWN FROM THE HORSE AT THE BATTLE FOR CORINTHIA...
PLEASE, MITRA, LET THAT BE THE LAST OF THEM.

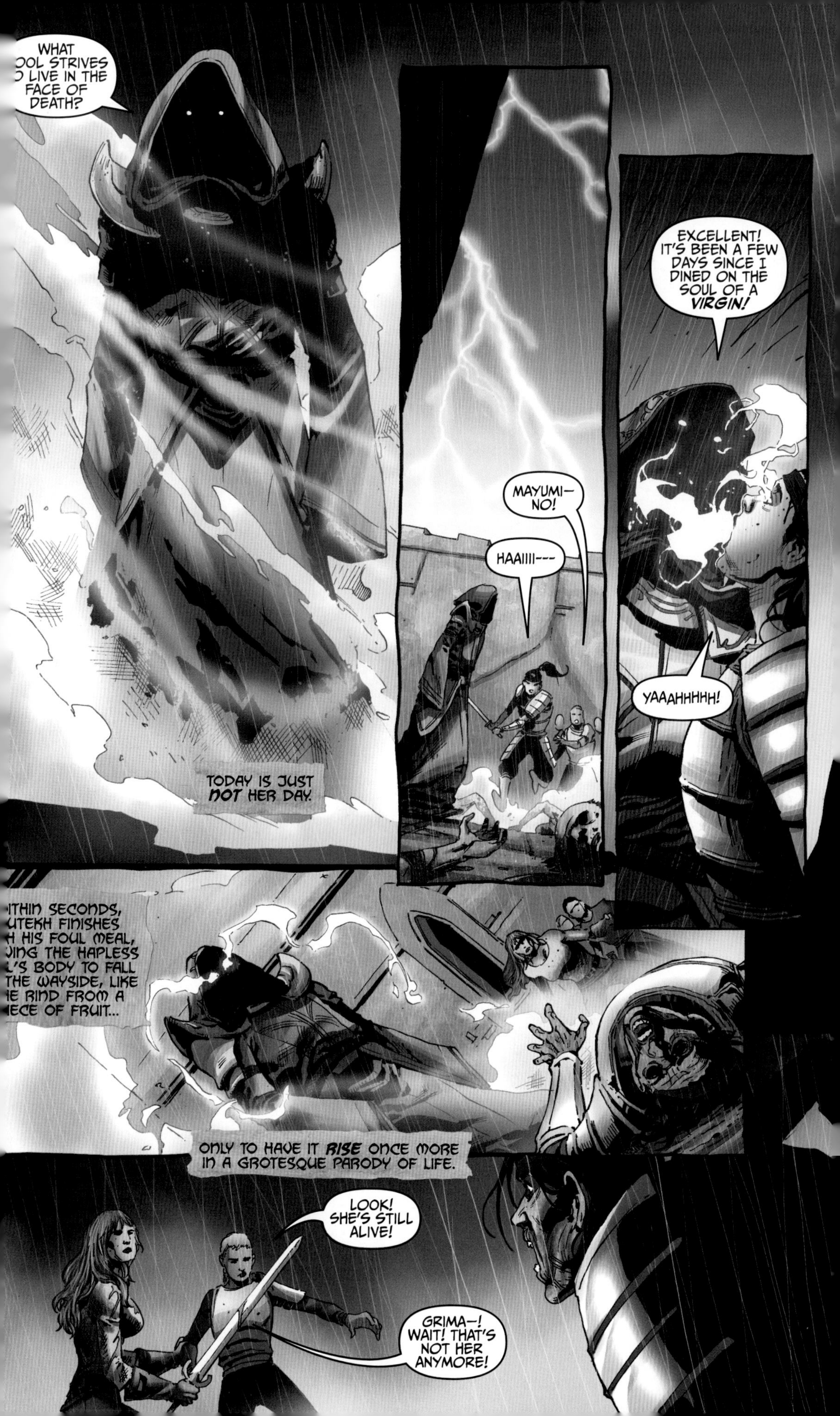
WHAT
OOL STRIVES
O LIVE IN THE
FACE OF
DEATH?
TODAY IS JUST NOT HER DAY.
MAYUMI—NO!
HAAIIII---
EXCELLENT! IT'S BEEN A FEW DAYS SINCE I DINED ON THE SOUL OF A VIRGIN!
YAAAHHHHH!
ITHIN SECONDS,
UTEKH FINISHES
H HIS FOUL MEAL,
VING THE HAPLESS
L'S BODY TO FALL
THE WAYSIDE, LIKE
E RIND FROM A
ECE OF FRUIT...
ONLY TO HAVE IT RISE ONCE MORE IN A GROTESQUE PARODY OF LIFE.
LOOK! SHE'S STILL ALIVE!
GRIMA—! WAIT! THAT'S NOT HER ANYMORE!

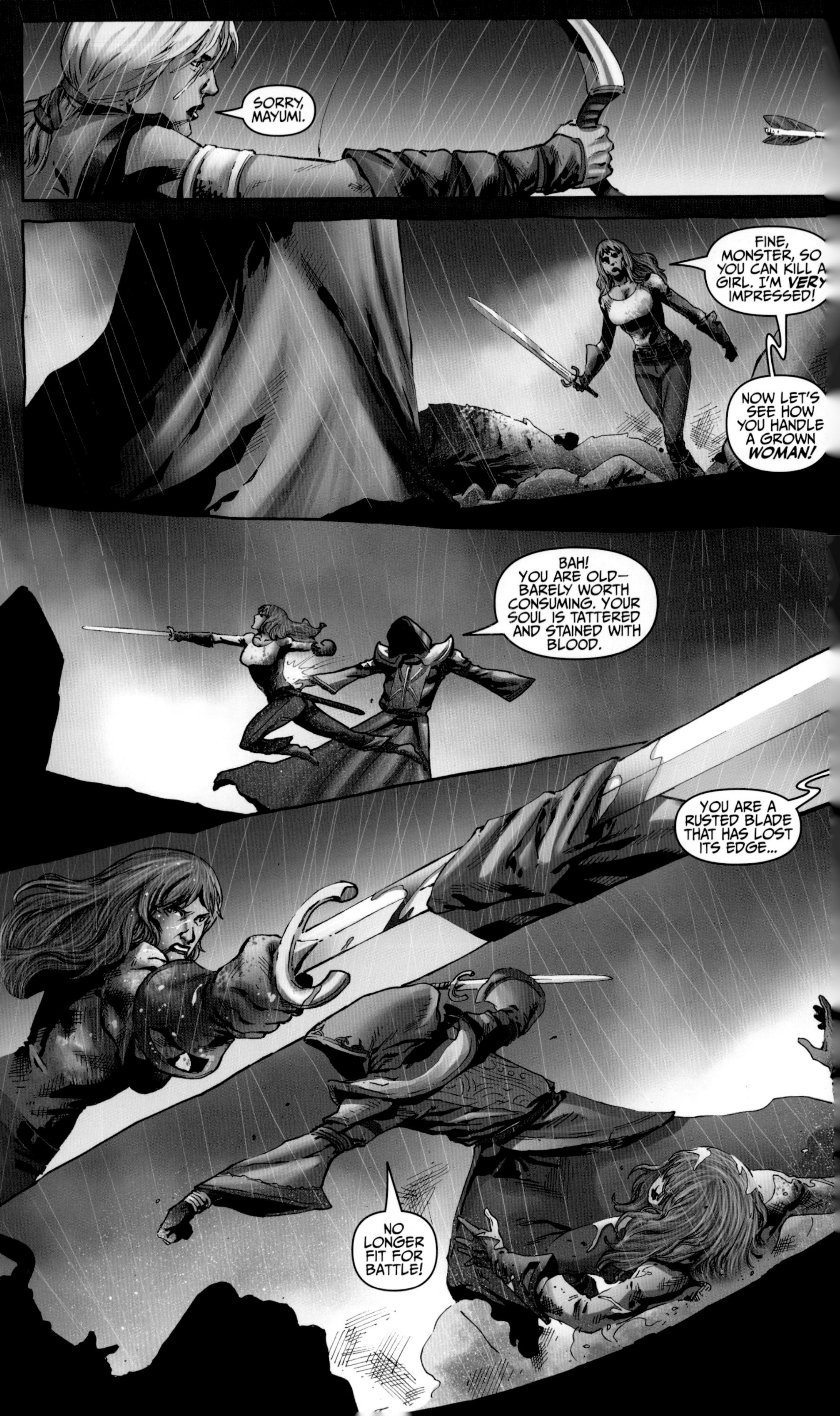
SORRY, MAYUMI.
FINE, MONSTER, SO YOU CAN KILL A GIRL. I'M *VERY* IMPRESSED!
NOW LET'S SEE HOW YOU HANDLE A GROWN *WOMAN!*
BAH! YOU ARE OLD— BARELY WORTH CONSUMING. YOUR SOUL IS TATTERED AND STAINED WITH BLOOD.
YOU ARE A RUSTED BLADE THAT HAS LOST ITS EDGE...
NO LONGER FIT FOR BATTLE!

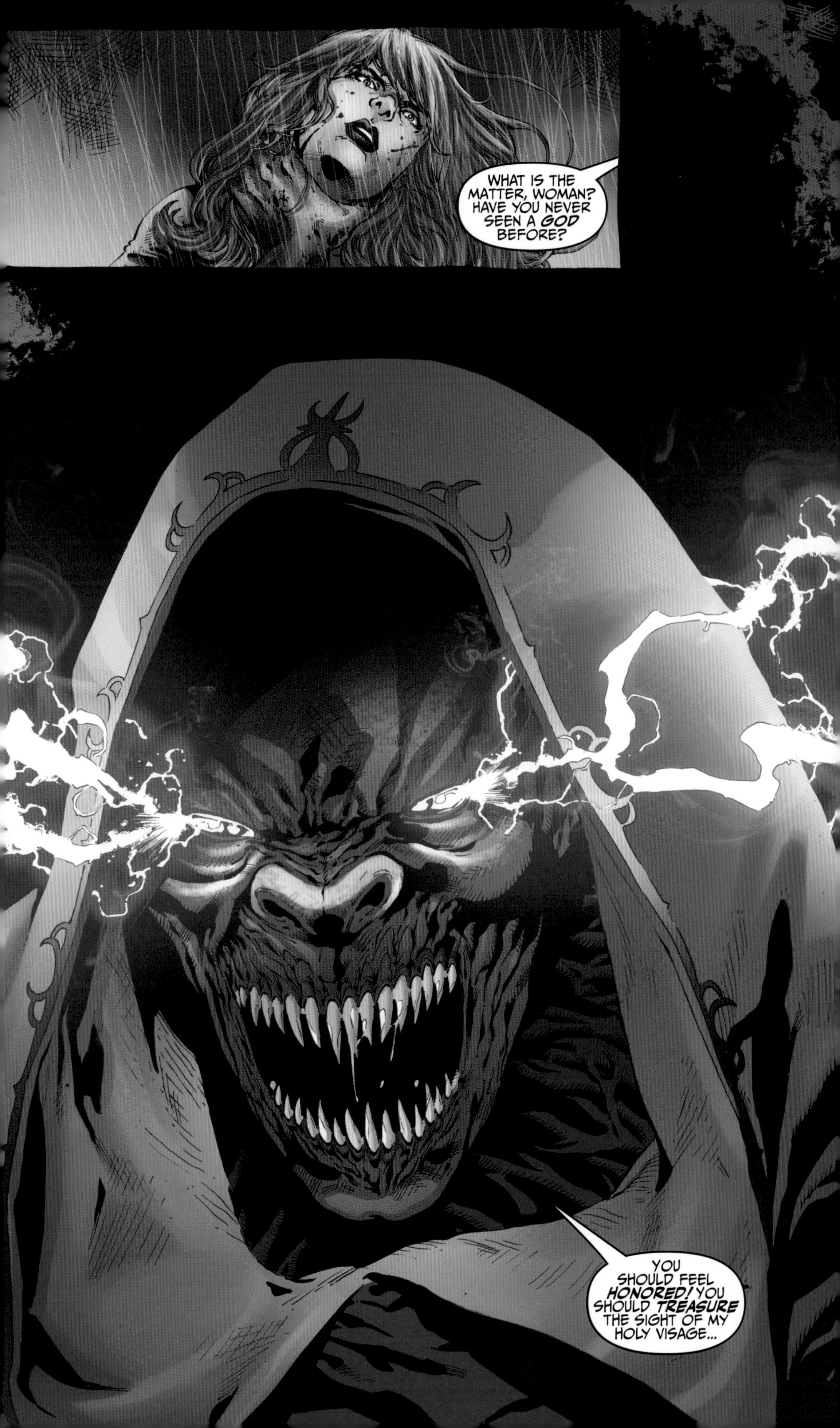
WHAT IS THE MATTER, WOMAN? HAVE YOU NEVER SEEN A GOD BEFORE?
YOU SHOULD FEEL HONORED! YOU SHOULD TREASURE THE SIGHT OF MY HOLY VISAGE...

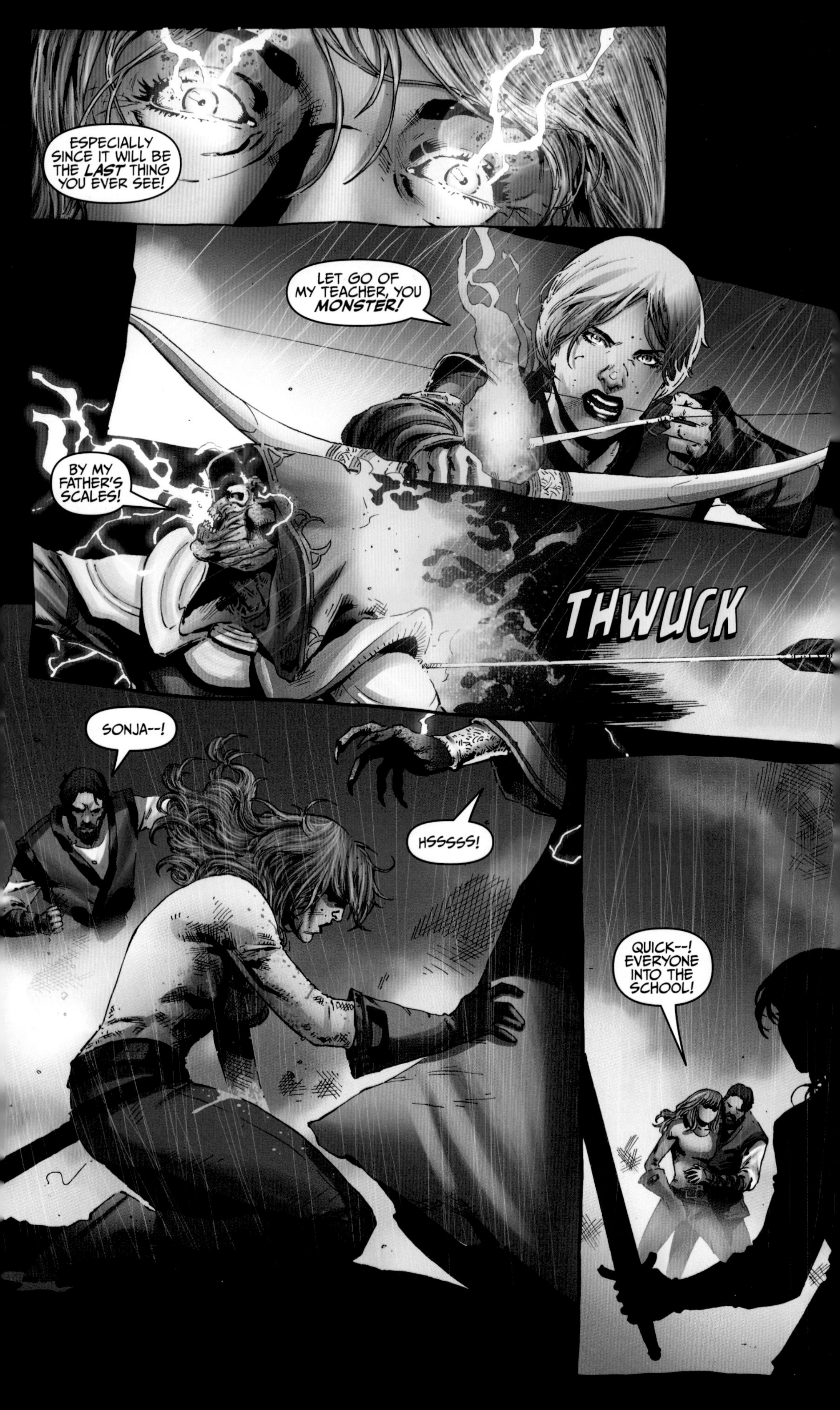
ESPECIALLY SINCE IT WILL BE THE *LAST* THING YOU EVER SEE!
LET GO OF MY TEACHER, YOU *MONSTER!*
BY MY FATHER'S SCALES!
THWUCK
SONJA--!
HSSSSS!
QUICK--! EVERYONE INTO THE SCHOOL!

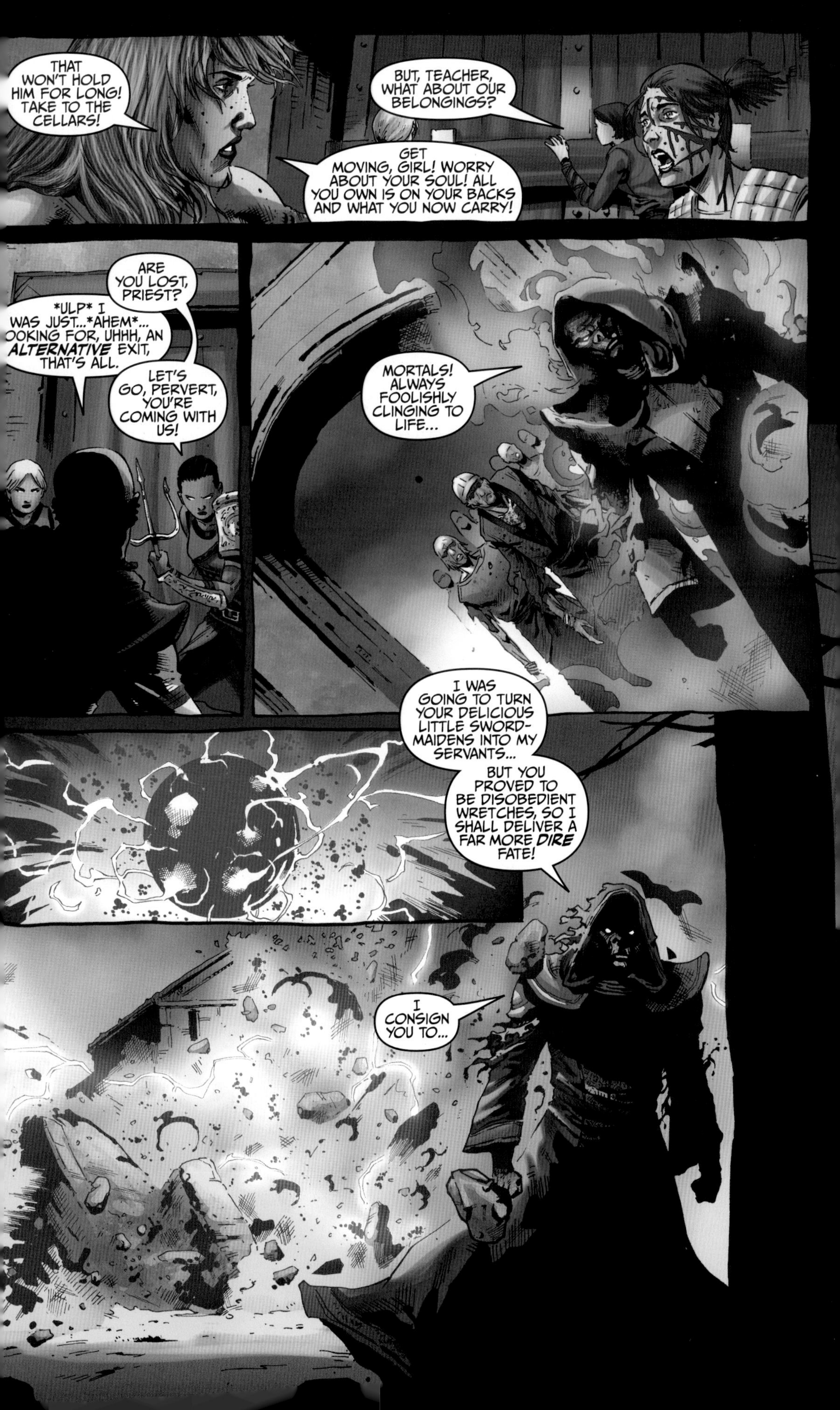
THAT WON'T HOLD HIM FOR LONG! TAKE TO THE CELLARS!
BUT, TEACHER, WHAT ABOUT OUR BELONGINGS?
GET MOVING, GIRL! WORRY ABOUT YOUR SOUL! ALL YOU OWN IS ON YOUR BACKS AND WHAT YOU NOW CARRY!
ARE YOU LOST, PRIEST?
ULP I WAS JUST...*AHEM*...OOKING FOR, UHHH, AN ALTERNATIVE EXIT, THAT'S ALL.
LET'S GO, PERVERT, YOU'RE COMING WITH US!
MORTALS! ALWAYS FOOLISHLY CLINGING TO LIFE...
I WAS GOING TO TURN YOUR DELICIOUS LITTLE SWORD-MAIDENS INTO MY SERVANTS...
BUT YOU PROVED TO BE DISOBEDIENT WRETCHES, SO I SHALL DELIVER A FAR MORE DIRE FATE!
I CONSIGN YOU TO...

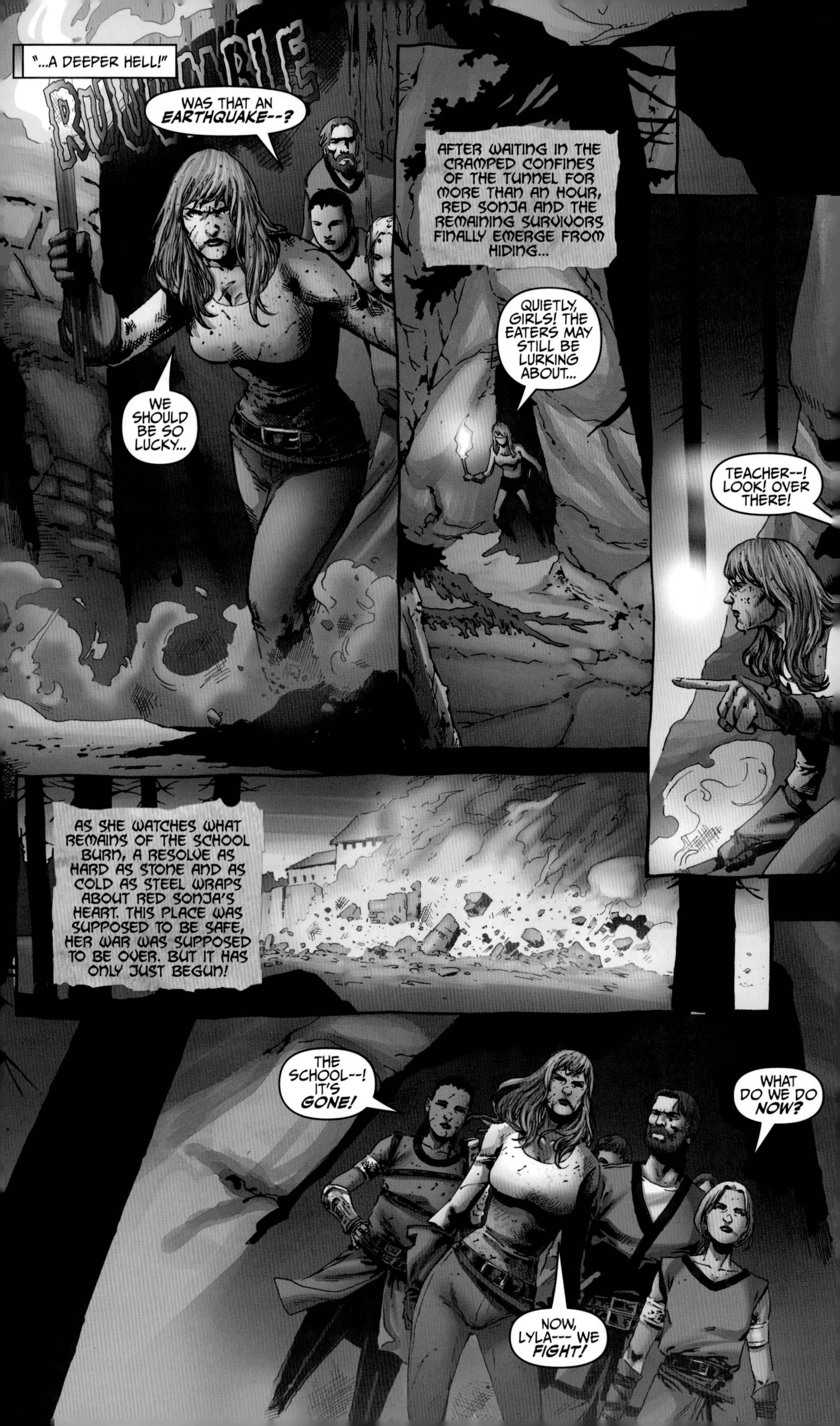
"...A DEEPER HELL!"
ROUUMBLE
WAS THAT AN *EARTHQUAKE*--?
WE SHOULD BE SO LUCKY...
AFTER WAITING IN THE CRAMPED CONFINES OF THE TUNNEL FOR MORE THAN AN HOUR, RED SONJA AND THE REMAINING SURVIVORS FINALLY EMERGE FROM HIDING...
QUIETLY, GIRLS! THE EATERS MAY STILL BE LURKING ABOUT...
TEACHER--! LOOK! OVER THERE!
AS SHE WATCHES WHAT REMAINS OF THE SCHOOL BURN, A RESOLVE AS HARD AS STONE AND AS COLD AS STEEL WRAPS ABOUT RED SONJA'S HEART. THIS PLACE WAS SUPPOSED TO BE SAFE, HER WAR WAS SUPPOSED TO BE OVER. BUT IT HAS ONLY JUST BEGUN!
THE SCHOOL--! IT'S *GONE!*
WHAT DO WE DO *NOW?*
NOW, LYLA--- WE *FIGHT!*

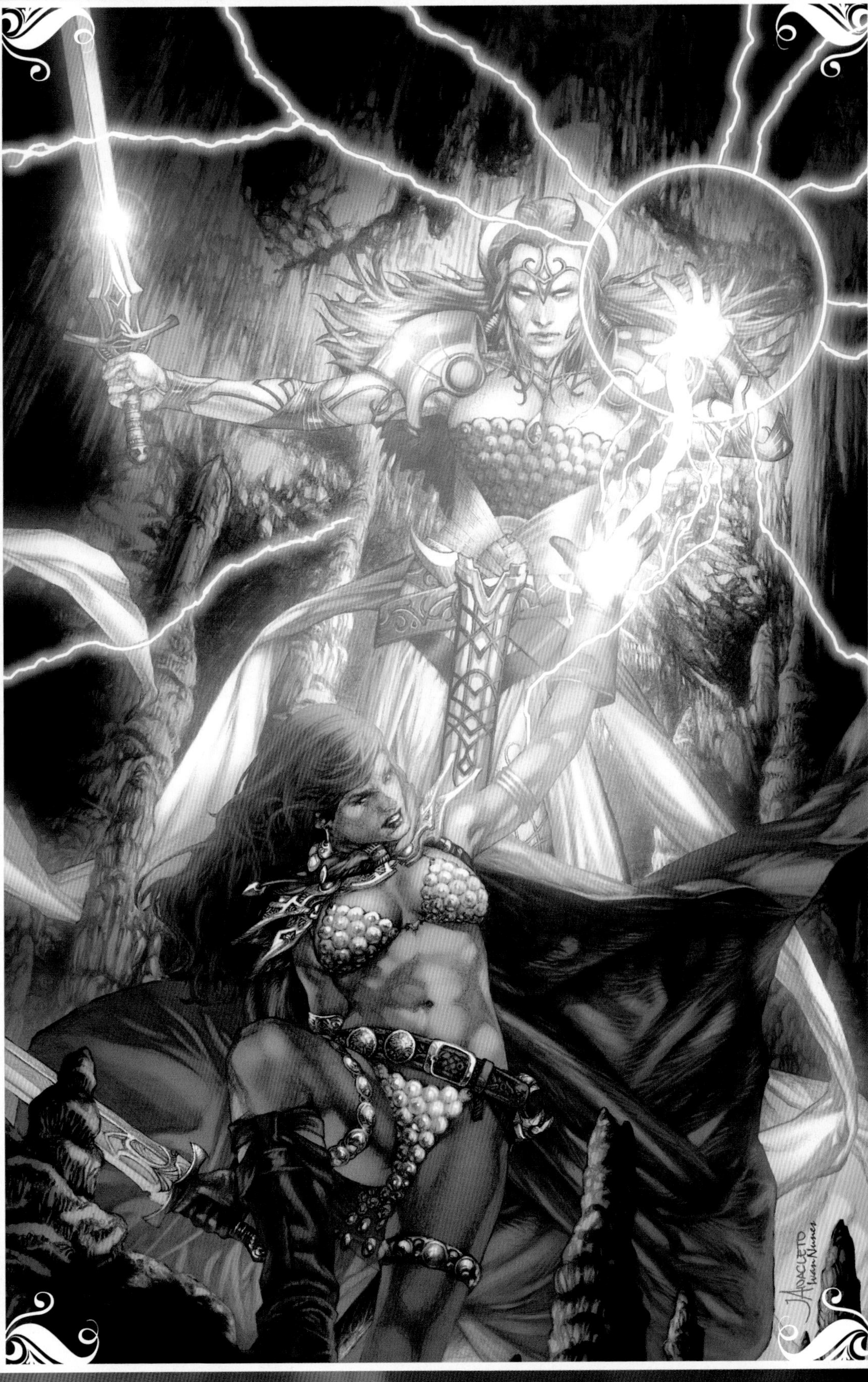
J. Anacleto
Ivan Nunes

ISSUE THREE

cover art by Jay Anacleto and Ivan Nunes

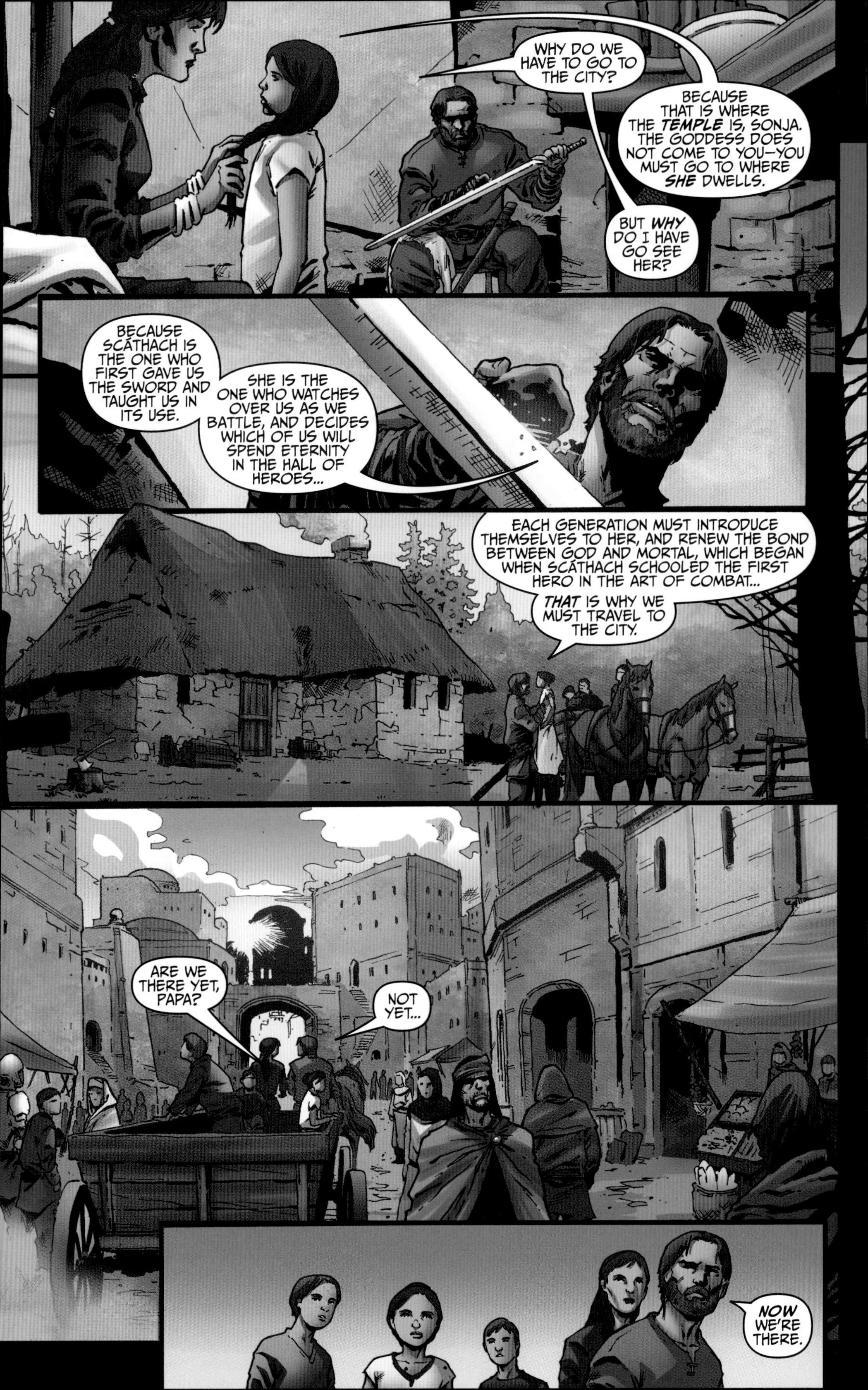
WHY DO WE HAVE TO GO TO THE CITY?
BECAUSE THAT IS WHERE THE ***TEMPLE*** IS, SONJA. THE GODDESS DOES NOT COME TO YOU—YOU MUST GO TO WHERE ***SHE*** DWELLS.
BUT ***WHY*** DO I HAVE GO SEE HER?
BECAUSE SCÁTHACH IS THE ONE WHO FIRST GAVE US THE SWORD AND TAUGHT US IN ITS USE.
SHE IS THE ONE WHO WATCHES OVER US AS WE BATTLE, AND DECIDES WHICH OF US WILL SPEND ETERNITY IN THE HALL OF HEROES...
EACH GENERATION MUST INTRODUCE THEMSELVES TO HER, AND RENEW THE BOND BETWEEN GOD AND MORTAL, WHICH BEGAN WHEN SCÁTHACH SCHOOLED THE FIRST HERO IN THE ART OF COMBAT...
THAT IS WHY WE MUST TRAVEL TO THE CITY.
ARE WE THERE YET, PAPA?
NOT YET...
NOW WE'RE THERE.

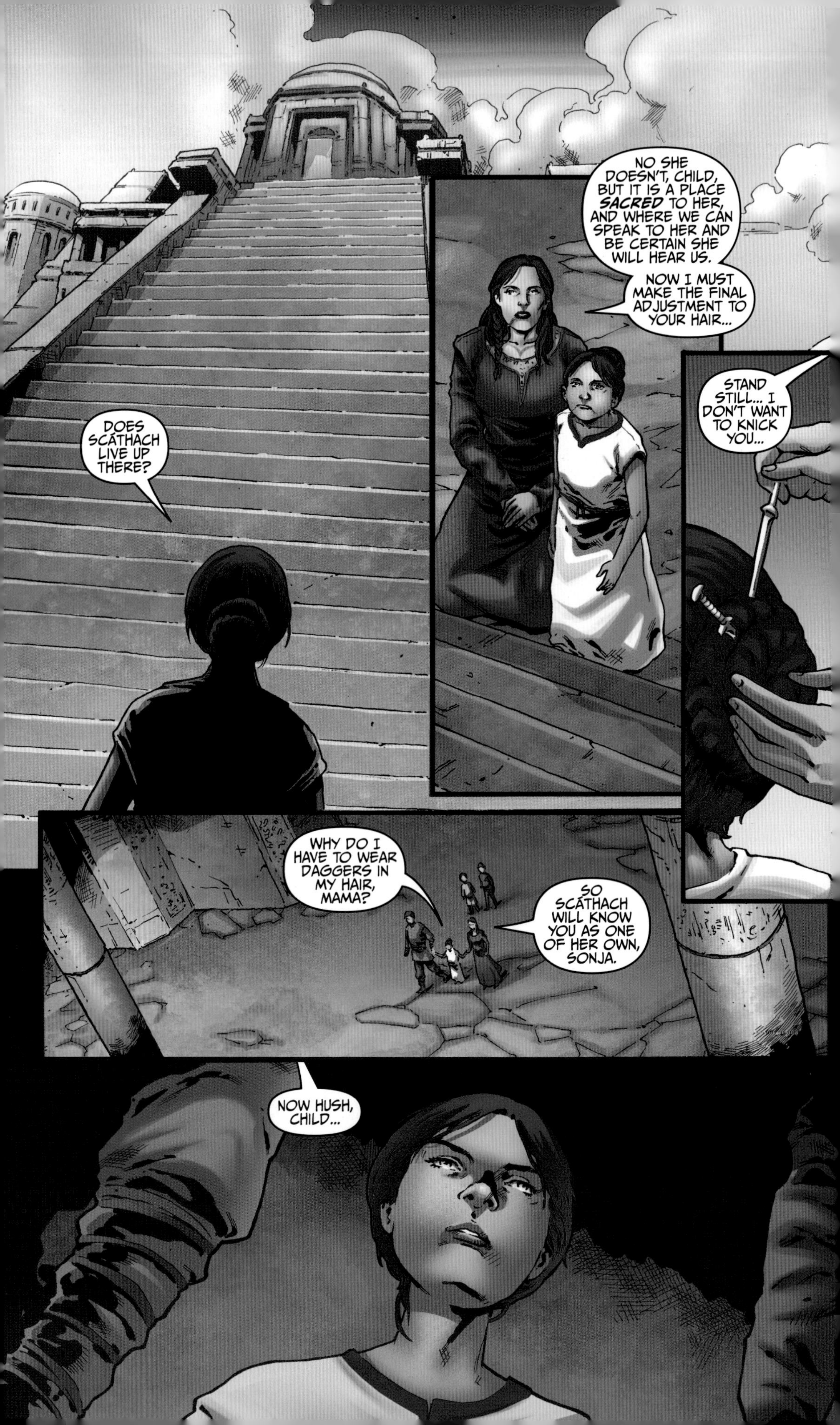
DOES SCÁTHACH LIVE UP THERE?
NO SHE DOESN'T, CHILD, BUT IT IS A PLACE SACRED TO HER, AND WHERE WE CAN SPEAK TO HER AND BE CERTAIN SHE WILL HEAR US.
NOW I MUST MAKE THE FINAL ADJUSTMENT TO YOUR HAIR...
STAND STILL... I DON'T WANT TO KNICK YOU...
WHY DO I HAVE TO WEAR DAGGERS IN MY HAIR, MAMA?
SO SCÁTHACH WILL KNOW YOU AS ONE OF HER OWN, SONJA.
NOW HUSH, CHILD...

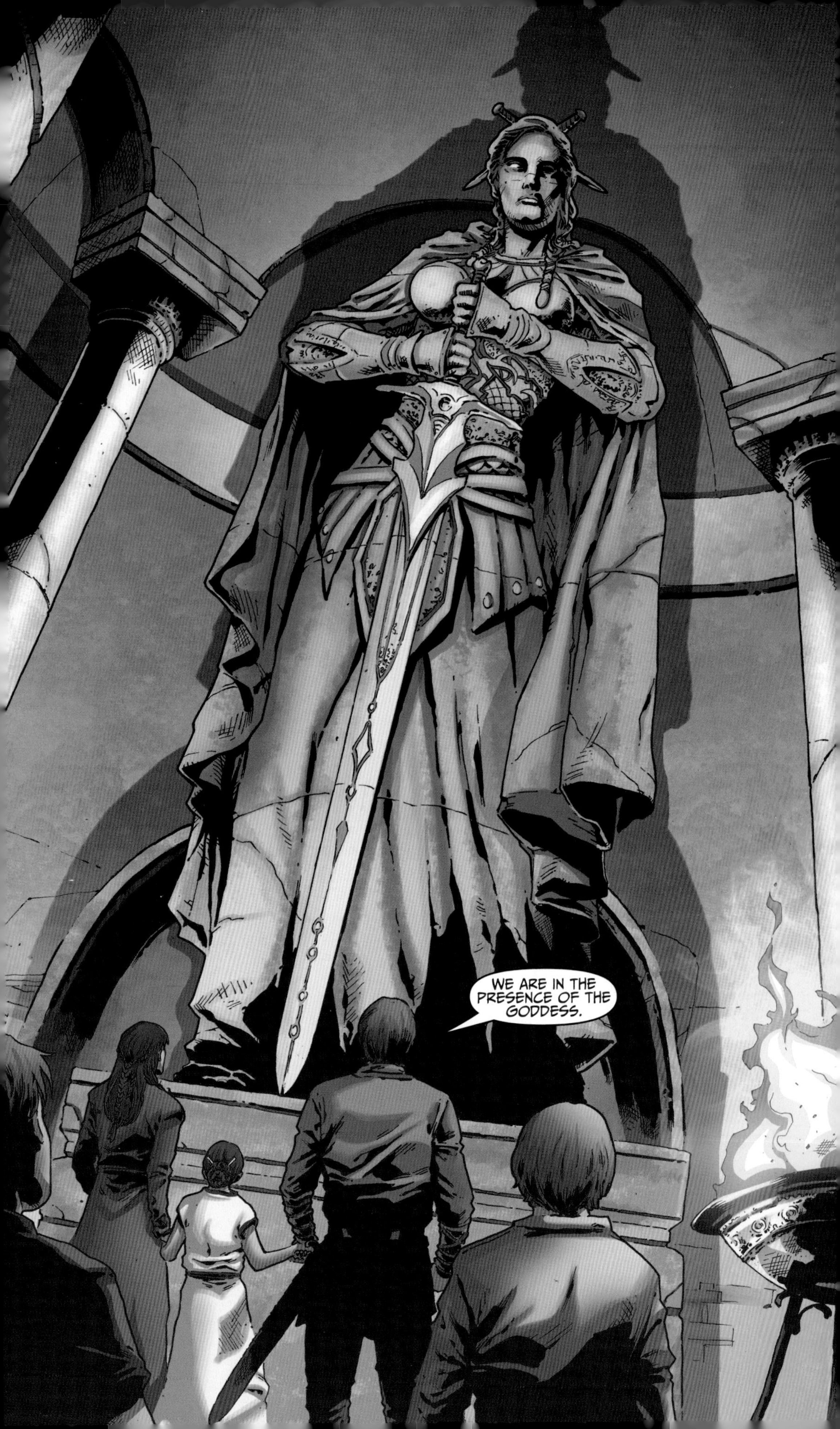
WE ARE IN THE PRESENCE OF THE GODDESS.

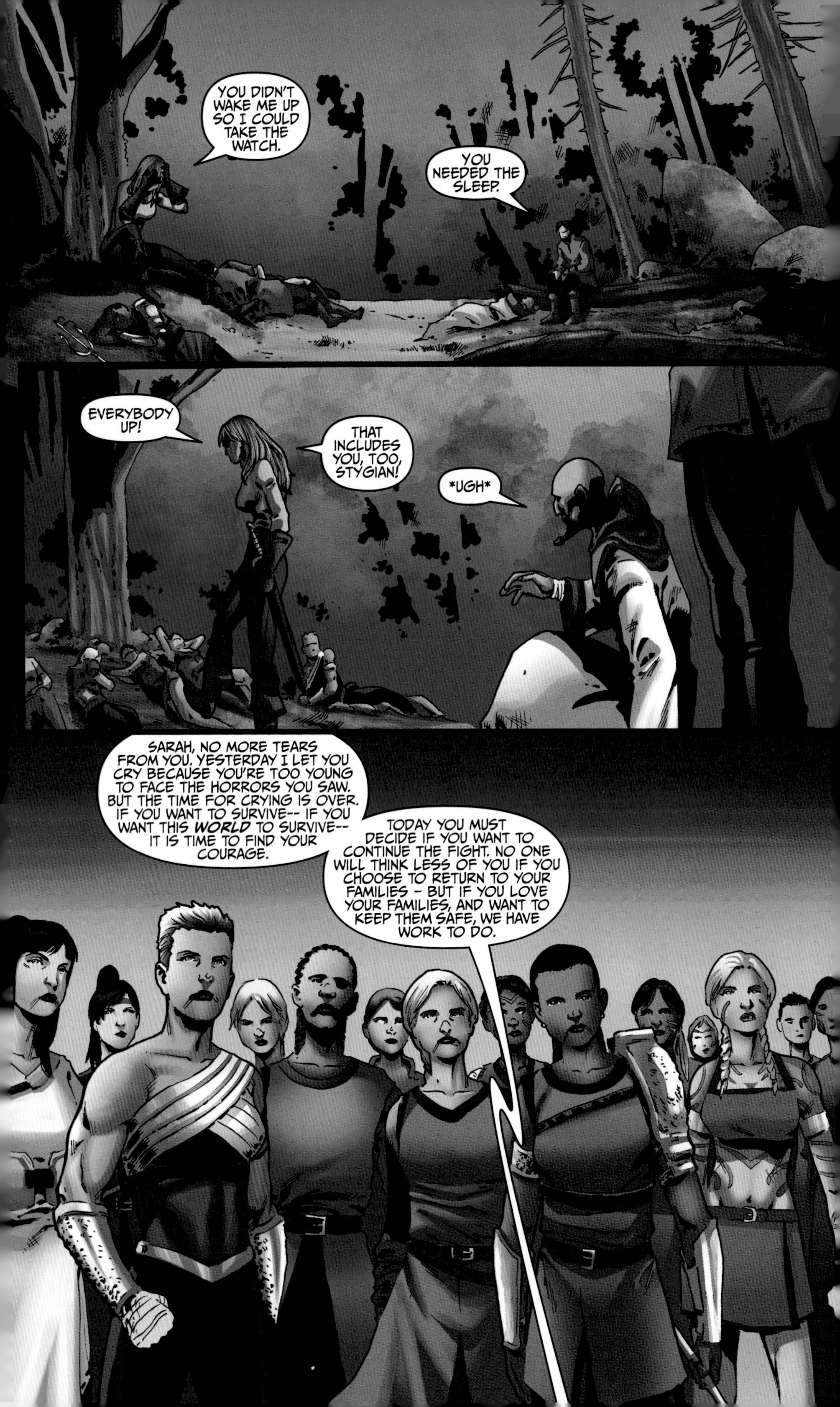
YOU DIDN'T WAKE ME UP SO I COULD TAKE THE WATCH.
YOU NEEDED THE SLEEP.
EVERYBODY UP!
THAT INCLUDES YOU, TOO, STYGIAN!
UGH
SARAH, NO MORE TEARS FROM YOU. YESTERDAY I LET YOU CRY BECAUSE YOU'RE TOO YOUNG TO FACE THE HORRORS YOU SAW. BUT THE TIME FOR CRYING IS OVER. IF YOU WANT TO SURVIVE-- IF YOU WANT THIS **WORLD** TO SURVIVE-- IT IS TIME TO FIND YOUR COURAGE.
TODAY YOU MUST DECIDE IF YOU WANT TO CONTINUE THE FIGHT. NO ONE WILL THINK LESS OF YOU IF YOU CHOOSE TO RETURN TO YOUR FAMILIES - BUT IF YOU LOVE YOUR FAMILIES, AND WANT TO KEEP THEM SAFE, WE HAVE WORK TO DO.

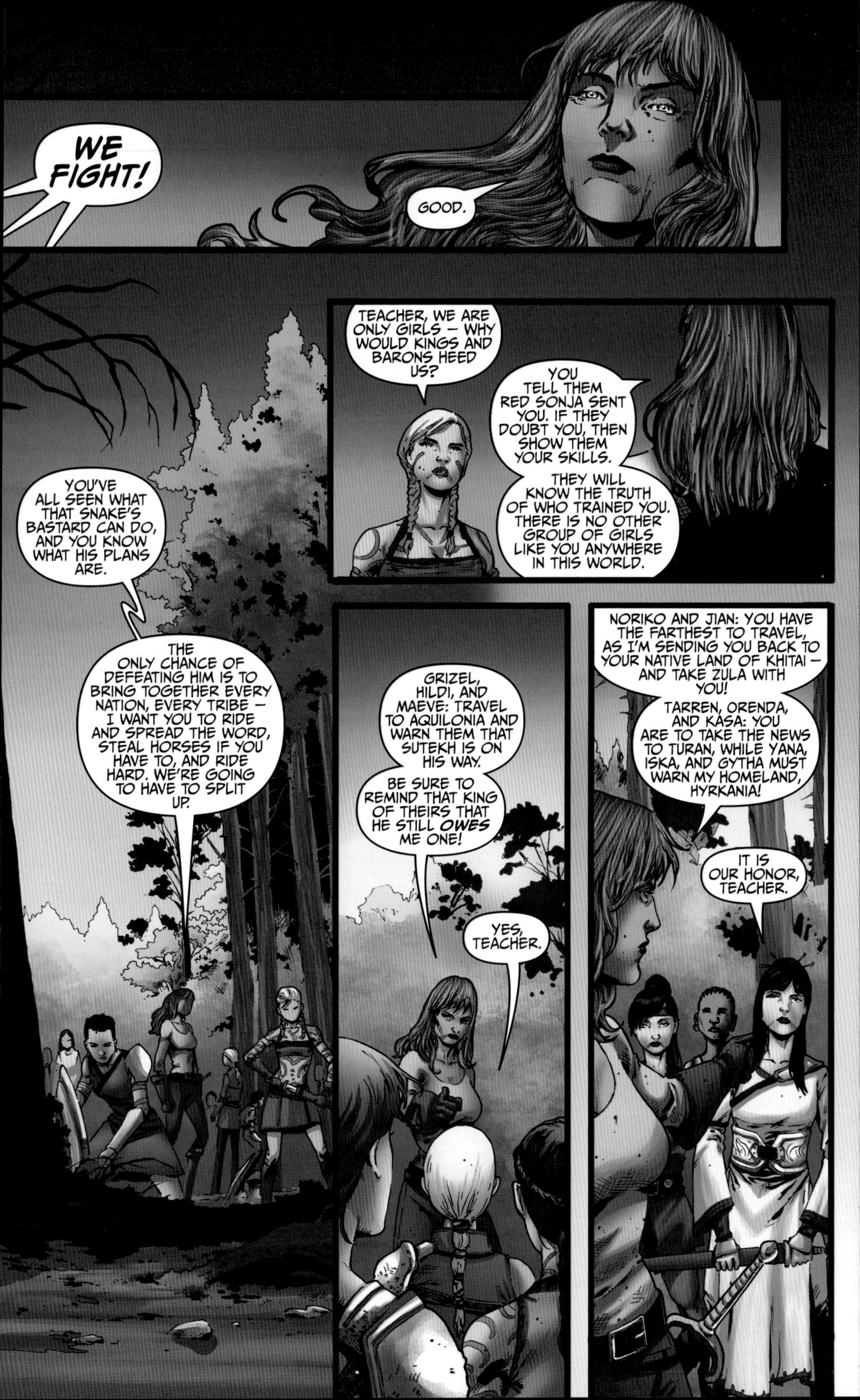
WE FIGHT!
GOOD.
YOU'VE ALL SEEN WHAT THAT SNAKE'S BASTARD CAN DO, AND YOU KNOW WHAT HIS PLANS ARE.
THE ONLY CHANCE OF DEFEATING HIM IS TO BRING TOGETHER EVERY NATION, EVERY TRIBE — I WANT YOU TO RIDE AND SPREAD THE WORD, STEAL HORSES IF YOU HAVE TO, AND RIDE HARD. WE'RE GOING TO HAVE TO SPLIT UP.
TEACHER, WE ARE ONLY GIRLS — WHY WOULD KINGS AND BARONS HEED US?
YOU TELL THEM RED SONJA SENT YOU. IF THEY DOUBT YOU, THEN SHOW THEM YOUR SKILLS.
THEY WILL KNOW THE TRUTH OF WHO TRAINED YOU. THERE IS NO OTHER GROUP OF GIRLS LIKE YOU ANYWHERE IN THIS WORLD.
GRIZEL, HILDI, AND MAEVE: TRAVEL TO AQUILONIA AND WARN THEM THAT SUTEKH IS ON HIS WAY.
BE SURE TO REMIND THAT KING OF THEIRS THAT HE STILL OWES ME ONE!
YES, TEACHER.
NORIKO AND JIAN: YOU HAVE THE FARTHEST TO TRAVEL, AS I'M SENDING YOU BACK TO YOUR NATIVE LAND OF KHITAI — AND TAKE ZULA WITH YOU!
TARREN, ORENDA, AND KASA: YOU ARE TO TAKE THE NEWS TO TURAN, WHILE YANA, ISKA, AND GYTHA MUST WARN MY HOMELAND, HYRKANIA!
IT IS OUR HONOR, TEACHER.

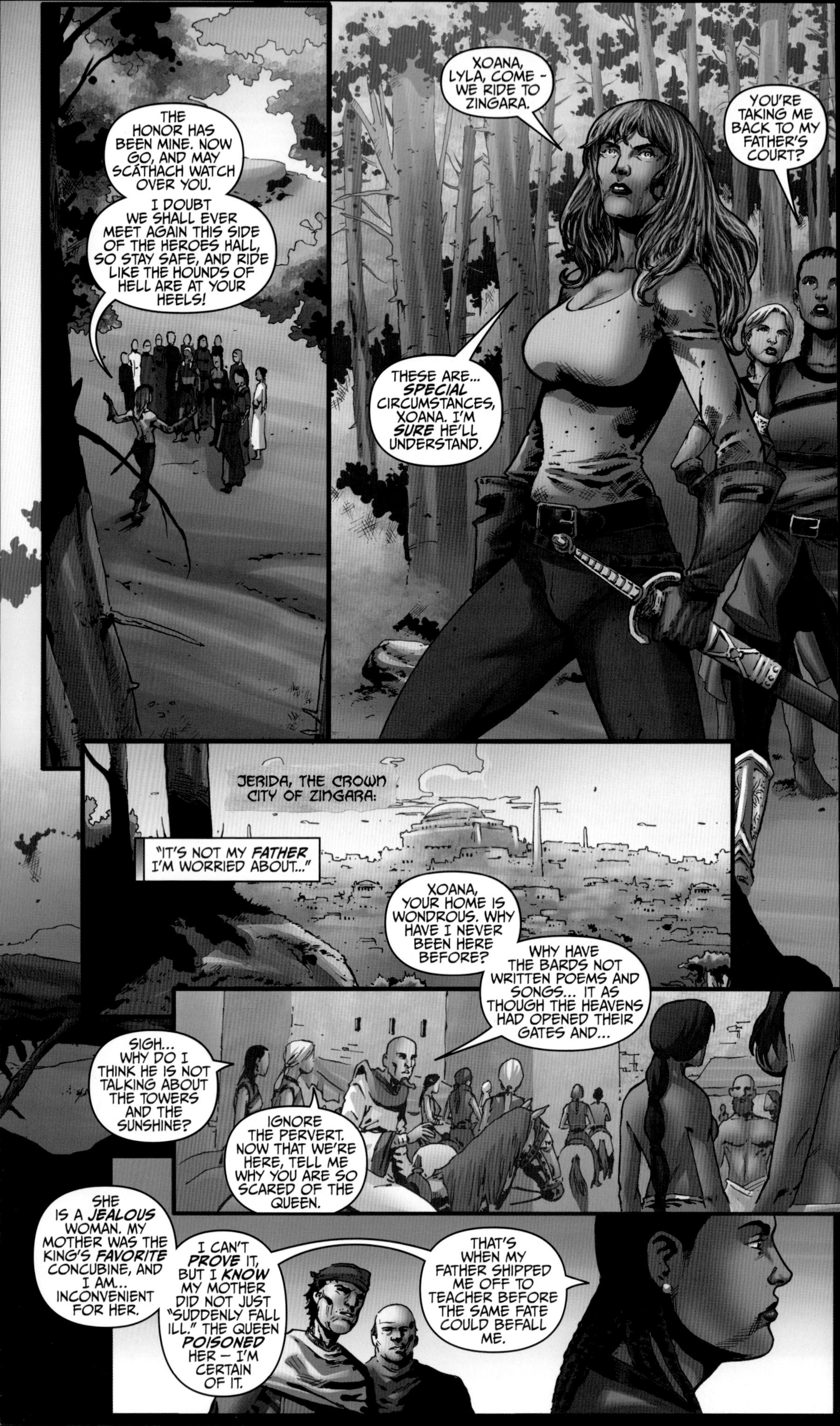
THE HONOR HAS BEEN MINE. NOW GO, AND MAY SCÁTHACH WATCH OVER YOU.
I DOUBT WE SHALL EVER MEET AGAIN THIS SIDE OF THE HEROES HALL, SO STAY SAFE, AND RIDE LIKE THE HOUNDS OF HELL ARE AT YOUR HEELS!
XOANA, LYLA, COME - WE RIDE TO ZINGARA.
YOU'RE TAKING ME BACK TO MY FATHER'S COURT?
THESE ARE... SPECIAL CIRCUMSTANCES, XOANA. I'M SURE HE'LL UNDERSTAND.
JERIDA, THE CROWN CITY OF ZINGARA:
"IT'S NOT MY FATHER I'M WORRIED ABOUT..."
XOANA, YOUR HOME IS WONDROUS. WHY HAVE I NEVER BEEN HERE BEFORE?
WHY HAVE THE BARDS NOT WRITTEN POEMS AND SONGS... IT AS THOUGH THE HEAVENS HAD OPENED THEIR GATES AND...
SIGH... WHY DO I THINK HE IS NOT TALKING ABOUT THE TOWERS AND THE SUNSHINE?
IGNORE THE PERVERT. NOW THAT WE'RE HERE, TELL ME WHY YOU ARE SO SCARED OF THE QUEEN.
SHE IS A JEALOUS WOMAN. MY MOTHER WAS THE KING'S FAVORITE CONCUBINE, AND I AM... INCONVENIENT FOR HER.
I CAN'T PROVE IT, BUT I KNOW MY MOTHER DID NOT JUST "SUDDENLY FALL ILL." THE QUEEN POISONED HER — I'M CERTAIN OF IT.
THAT'S WHEN MY FATHER SHIPPED ME OFF TO TEACHER BEFORE THE SAME FATE COULD BEFALL ME.

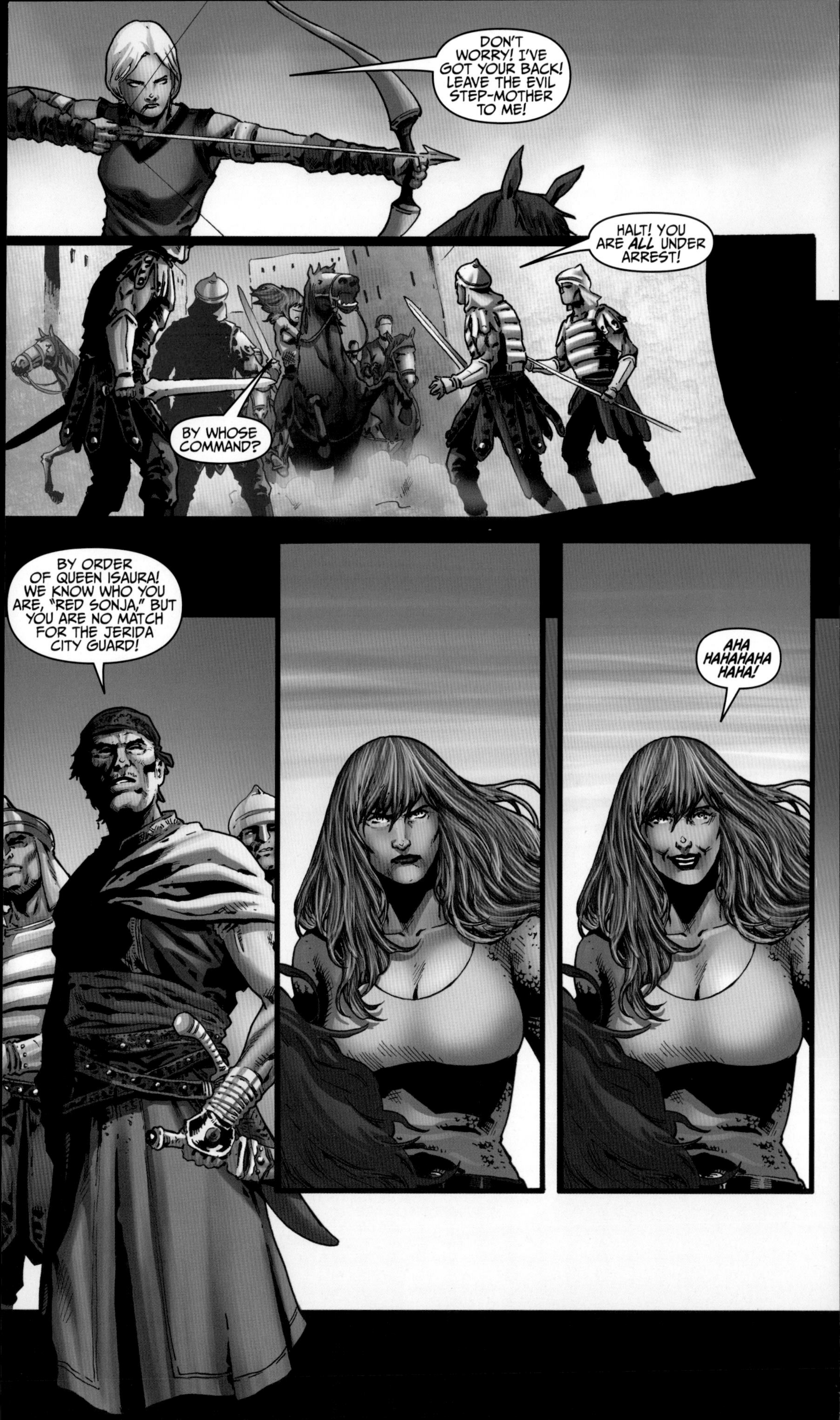
DON'T WORRY! I'VE GOT YOUR BACK! LEAVE THE EVIL STEP-MOTHER TO ME!
HALT! YOU ARE ALL UNDER ARREST!
BY WHOSE COMMAND?
BY ORDER OF QUEEN ISAURA! WE KNOW WHO YOU ARE, "RED SONJA," BUT YOU ARE NO MATCH FOR THE JERIDA CITY GUARD!
AHA HAHAHAHA HAHA!

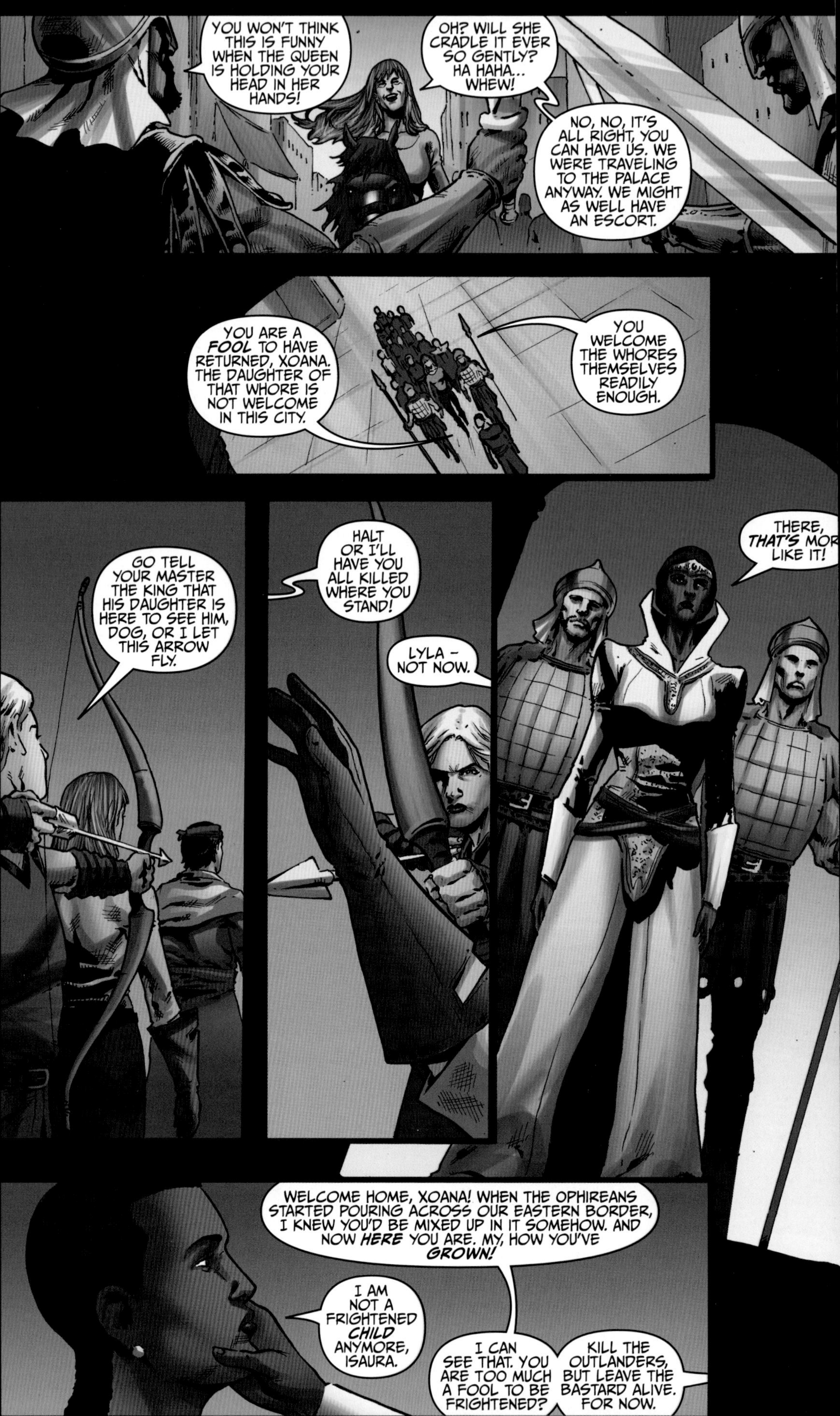
YOU WON'T THINK THIS IS FUNNY WHEN THE QUEEN IS HOLDING YOUR HEAD IN HER HANDS!
OH? WILL SHE CRADLE IT EVER SO GENTLY? HA HAHA... WHEW!
NO, NO, IT'S ALL RIGHT, YOU CAN HAVE US. WE WERE TRAVELING TO THE PALACE ANYWAY. WE MIGHT AS WELL HAVE AN ESCORT.
YOU ARE A FOOL TO HAVE RETURNED, XOANA. THE DAUGHTER OF THAT WHORE IS NOT WELCOME IN THIS CITY.
YOU WELCOME THE WHORES THEMSELVES READILY ENOUGH.
GO TELL YOUR MASTER THE KING THAT HIS DAUGHTER IS HERE TO SEE HIM, DOG, OR I LET THIS ARROW FLY.
HALT OR I'LL HAVE YOU ALL KILLED WHERE YOU STAND!
LYLA - NOT NOW.
THERE, THAT'S MOR LIKE IT!
WELCOME HOME, XOANA! WHEN THE OPHIREANS STARTED POURING ACROSS OUR EASTERN BORDER, I KNEW YOU'D BE MIXED UP IN IT SOMEHOW. AND NOW HERE YOU ARE. MY, HOW YOU'VE GROWN!
I AM NOT A FRIGHTENED CHILD ANYMORE, ISAURA.
I CAN SEE THAT. YOU ARE TOO MUCH A FOOL TO BE FRIGHTENED?
KILL THE OUTLANDERS, BUT LEAVE THE BASTARD ALIVE. FOR NOW.

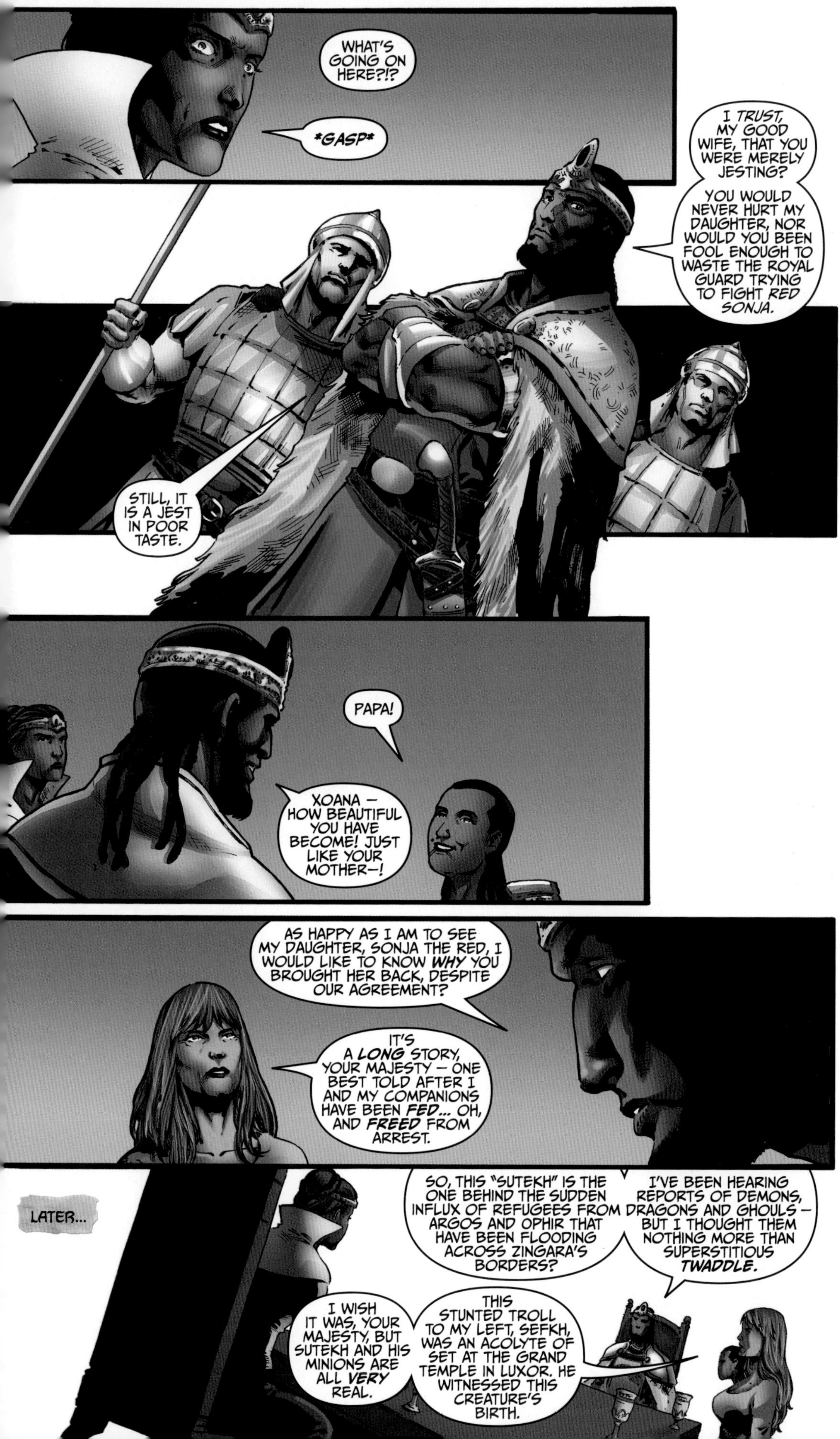
WHAT'S GOING ON HERE?!?
GASP
I TRUST, MY GOOD WIFE, THAT YOU WERE MERELY JESTING?
YOU WOULD NEVER HURT MY DAUGHTER, NOR WOULD YOU BEEN FOOL ENOUGH TO WASTE THE ROYAL GUARD TRYING TO FIGHT RED SONJA.
STILL, IT IS A JEST IN POOR TASTE.
PAPA!
XOANA — HOW BEAUTIFUL YOU HAVE BECOME! JUST LIKE YOUR MOTHER—!
AS HAPPY AS I AM TO SEE MY DAUGHTER, SONJA THE RED, I WOULD LIKE TO KNOW WHY YOU BROUGHT HER BACK, DESPITE OUR AGREEMENT?
IT'S A LONG STORY, YOUR MAJESTY — ONE BEST TOLD AFTER I AND MY COMPANIONS HAVE BEEN FED... OH, AND FREED FROM ARREST.
LATER...
SO, THIS "SUTEKH" IS THE ONE BEHIND THE SUDDEN INFLUX OF REFUGEES FROM ARGOS AND OPHIR THAT HAVE BEEN FLOODING ACROSS ZINGARA'S BORDERS?
I'VE BEEN HEARING REPORTS OF DEMONS, DRAGONS AND GHOULS — BUT I THOUGHT THEM NOTHING MORE THAN SUPERSTITIOUS TWADDLE.
I WISH IT WAS, YOUR MAJESTY, BUT SUTEKH AND HIS MINIONS ARE ALL VERY REAL.
THIS STUNTED TROLL TO MY LEFT, SEFKH, WAS AN ACOLYTE OF SET AT THE GRAND TEMPLE IN LUXOR. HE WITNESSED THIS CREATURE'S BIRTH.

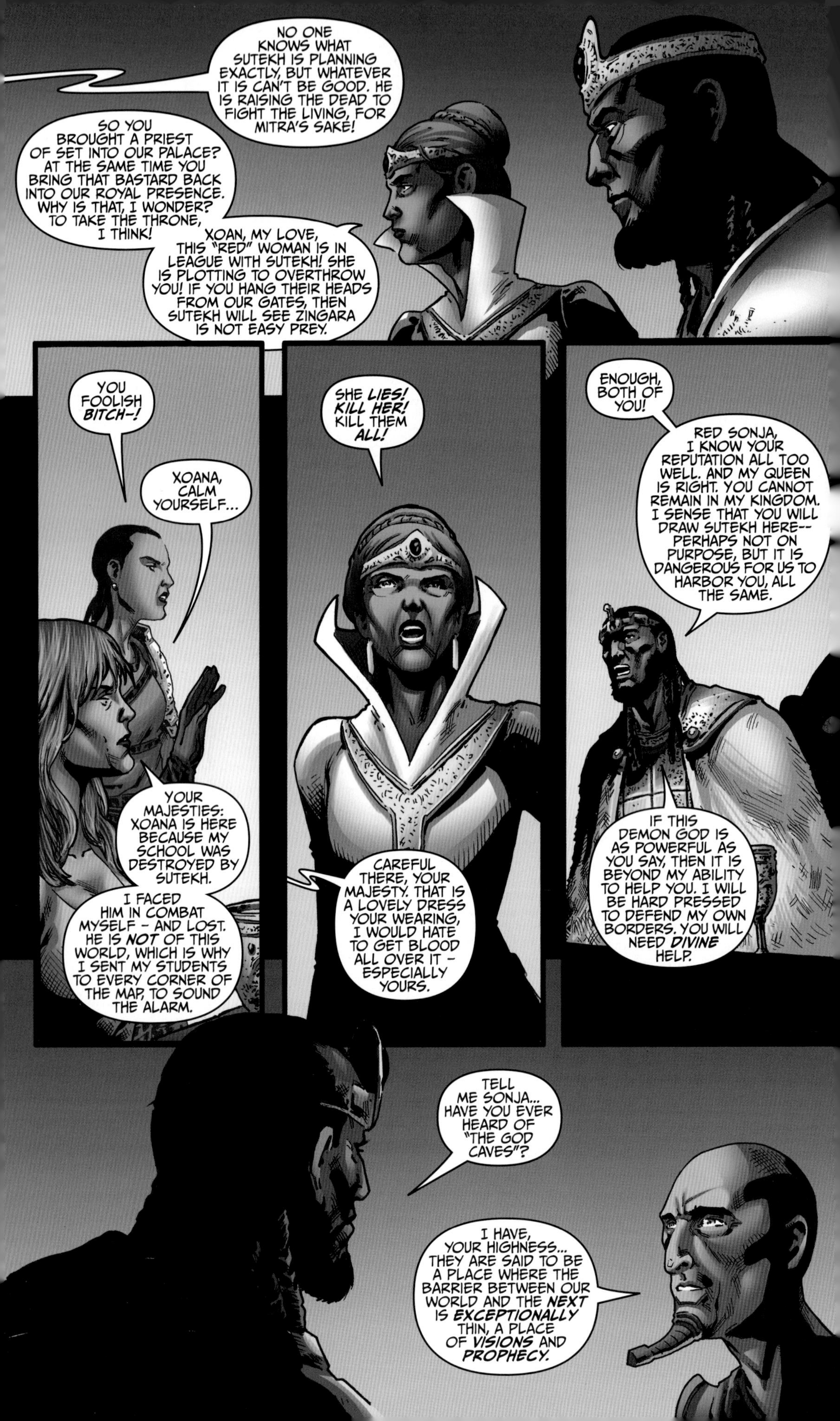
NO ONE KNOWS WHAT SUTEKH IS PLANNING EXACTLY, BUT WHATEVER IT IS CAN'T BE GOOD. HE IS RAISING THE DEAD TO FIGHT THE LIVING, FOR MITRA'S SAKE!
SO YOU BROUGHT A PRIEST OF SET INTO OUR PALACE? AT THE SAME TIME YOU BRING THAT BASTARD BACK INTO OUR ROYAL PRESENCE. WHY IS THAT, I WONDER? TO TAKE THE THRONE, I THINK!
XOAN, MY LOVE, THIS "RED" WOMAN IS IN LEAGUE WITH SUTEKH! SHE IS PLOTTING TO OVERTHROW YOU! IF YOU HANG THEIR HEADS FROM OUR GATES, THEN SUTEKH WILL SEE ZINGARA IS NOT EASY PREY.
YOU FOOLISH *BITCH-!*
XOANA, CALM YOURSELF...
YOUR MAJESTIES: XOANA IS HERE BECAUSE MY SCHOOL WAS DESTROYED BY SUTEKH.
I FACED HIM IN COMBAT MYSELF - AND LOST. HE IS *NOT* OF THIS WORLD, WHICH IS WHY I SENT MY STUDENTS TO EVERY CORNER OF THE MAP, TO SOUND THE ALARM.
SHE *LIES! KILL HER!* KILL THEM *ALL!*
CAREFUL THERE, YOUR MAJESTY. THAT IS A LOVELY DRESS YOUR WEARING, I WOULD HATE TO GET BLOOD ALL OVER IT - ESPECIALLY YOURS.
ENOUGH, BOTH OF YOU!
RED SONJA, I KNOW YOUR REPUTATION ALL TOO WELL. AND MY QUEEN IS RIGHT. YOU CANNOT REMAIN IN MY KINGDOM. I SENSE THAT YOU WILL DRAW SUTEKH HERE-- PERHAPS NOT ON PURPOSE, BUT IT IS DANGEROUS FOR US TO HARBOR YOU, ALL THE SAME.
IF THIS DEMON GOD IS AS POWERFUL AS YOU SAY, THEN IT IS BEYOND MY ABILITY TO HELP YOU. I WILL BE HARD PRESSED TO DEFEND MY OWN BORDERS. YOU WILL NEED *DIVINE* HELP.
TELL ME SONJA... HAVE YOU EVER HEARD OF "THE GOD CAVES"?
I HAVE, YOUR HIGHNESS... THEY ARE SAID TO BE A PLACE WHERE THE BARRIER BETWEEN OUR WORLD AND THE *NEXT* IS *EXCEPTIONALLY* THIN, A PLACE OF *VISIONS* AND *PROPHECY.*

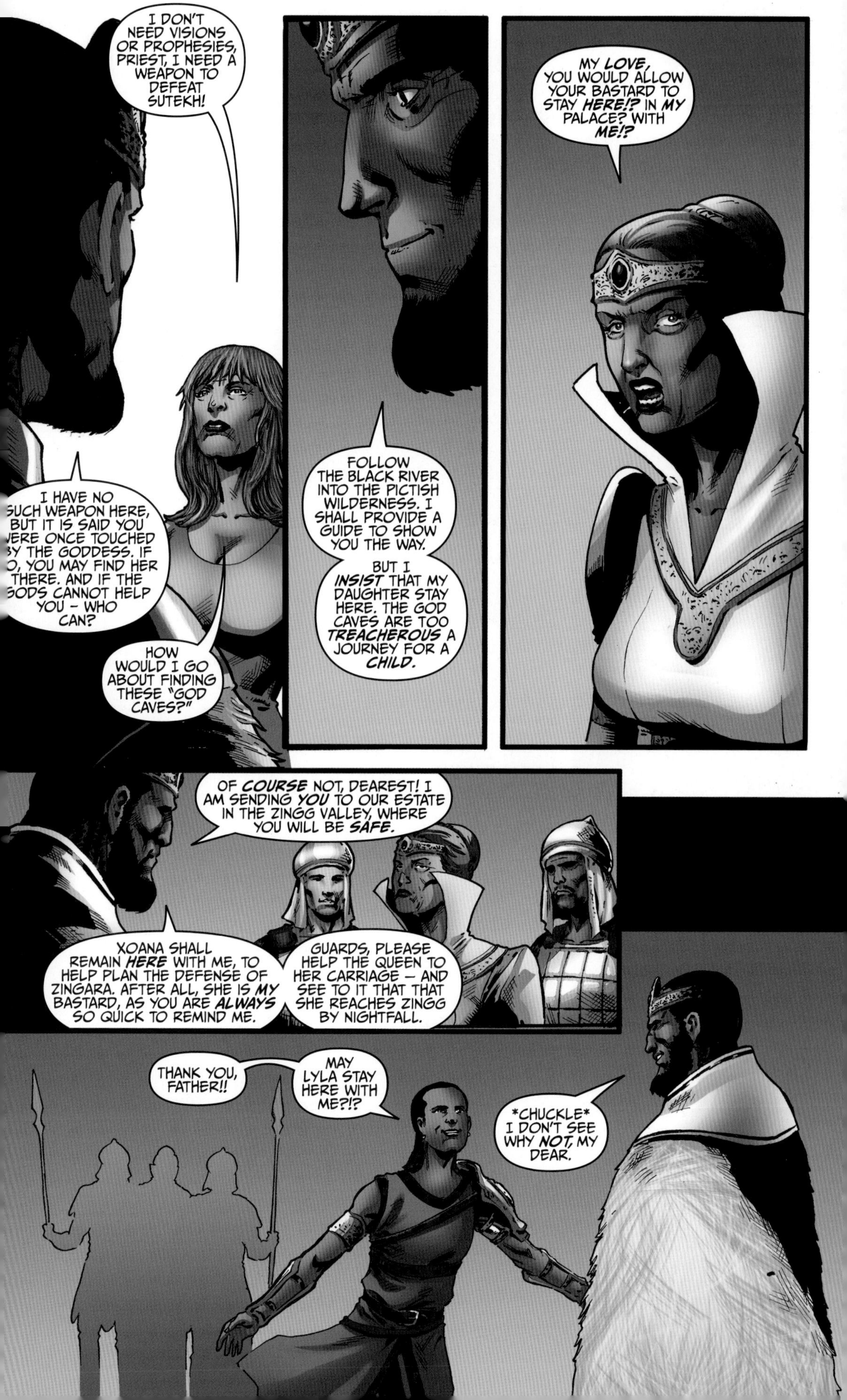
I DON'T NEED VISIONS OR PROPHESIES, PRIEST, I NEED A WEAPON TO DEFEAT SUTEKH!
I HAVE NO SUCH WEAPON HERE, BUT IT IS SAID YOU WERE ONCE TOUCHED BY THE GODDESS. IF SO, YOU MAY FIND HER THERE. AND IF THE GODS CANNOT HELP YOU – WHO CAN?
HOW WOULD I GO ABOUT FINDING THESE "GOD CAVES?"
FOLLOW THE BLACK RIVER INTO THE PICTISH WILDERNESS. I SHALL PROVIDE A GUIDE TO SHOW YOU THE WAY.
BUT I INSIST THAT MY DAUGHTER STAY HERE. THE GOD CAVES ARE TOO TREACHEROUS A JOURNEY FOR A CHILD.
MY LOVE, YOU WOULD ALLOW YOUR BASTARD TO STAY HERE!? IN MY PALACE? WITH ME!?
OF COURSE NOT, DEAREST! I AM SENDING YOU TO OUR ESTATE IN THE ZINGG VALLEY, WHERE YOU WILL BE SAFE.
XOANA SHALL REMAIN HERE WITH ME, TO HELP PLAN THE DEFENSE OF ZINGARA. AFTER ALL, SHE IS MY BASTARD, AS YOU ARE ALWAYS SO QUICK TO REMIND ME.
GUARDS, PLEASE HELP THE QUEEN TO HER CARRIAGE – AND SEE TO IT THAT THAT SHE REACHES ZINGG BY NIGHTFALL.
THANK YOU, FATHER!!
MAY LYLA STAY HERE WITH ME?!?
CHUCKLE I DON'T SEE WHY NOT, MY DEAR.

THE NEXT DAY:

YES, BUT THEY ARE NEEDED HERE. THEY CAN HELP THE ZINGARAN ARMY TO PREPARE AGAINST SUTEKH'S HORDES. BESIDES, WILL BE EASIER FOR A SMALL PARTY SUCH AS OURS TO INFILTRATE THE PICTISH WILDERNESS...

THERE IS THE GUIDE THE KING PROMISED US.

IT FEELS STRANGE, LEAVING THE GIRLS BEHIND...

PICTS! UGH! SUCH DISGUSTING SAVAGES! AND THE WOMEN LOOK JUST LIKE THE MEN!

DEEP IN THE WILDERNESS:

IT'S BEEN TWO DAYS, AND WE'VE YET TO SEE A SINGLE PICT!

BELIEVE ME, THEY'RE OUT THERE, YUSUF!

YOU *NEVER* SEE A PICT UNTIL HE'S ALMOST ON TOP OF YOU.

LOOK—! UP THERE!

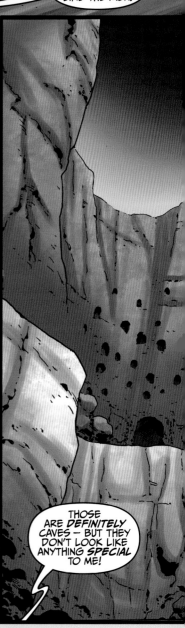

THOSE ARE *DEFINITELY* CAVES — BUT THEY DON'T LOOK LIKE ANYTHING *SPECIAL* TO ME!

IT'S THE PICTS! QUICKLY — TO THE CAVES!!

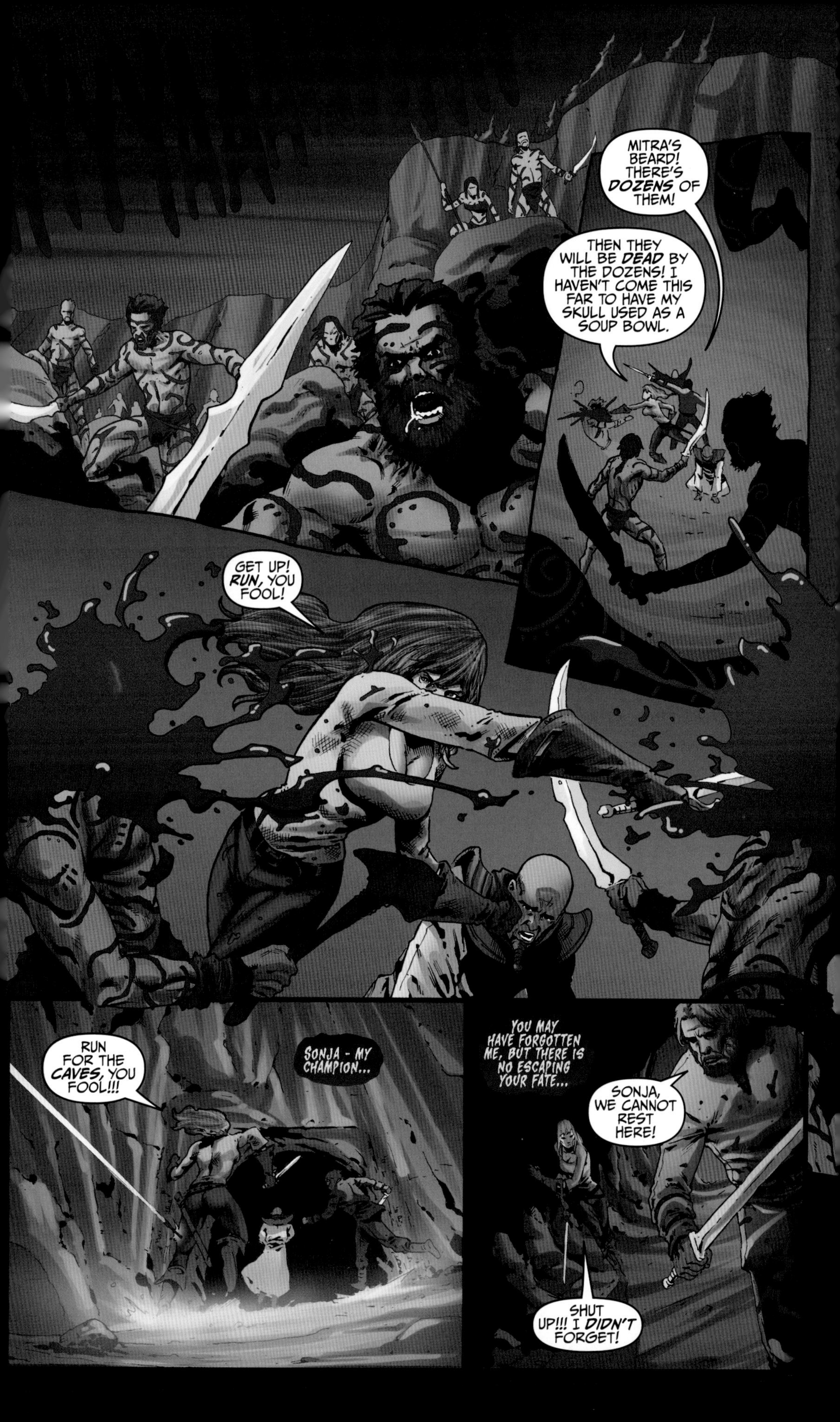
MITRA'S BEARD! THERE'S DOZENS OF THEM!
THEN THEY WILL BE DEAD BY THE DOZENS! I HAVEN'T COME THIS FAR TO HAVE MY SKULL USED AS A SOUP BOWL.
GET UP! RUN, YOU FOOL!
RUN FOR THE CAVES, YOU FOOL!!!
SONJA - MY CHAMPION...
YOU MAY HAVE FORGOTTEN ME, BUT THERE IS NO ESCAPING YOUR FATE...
SONJA, WE CANNOT REST HERE!
SHUT UP!!! I DIDN'T FORGET!

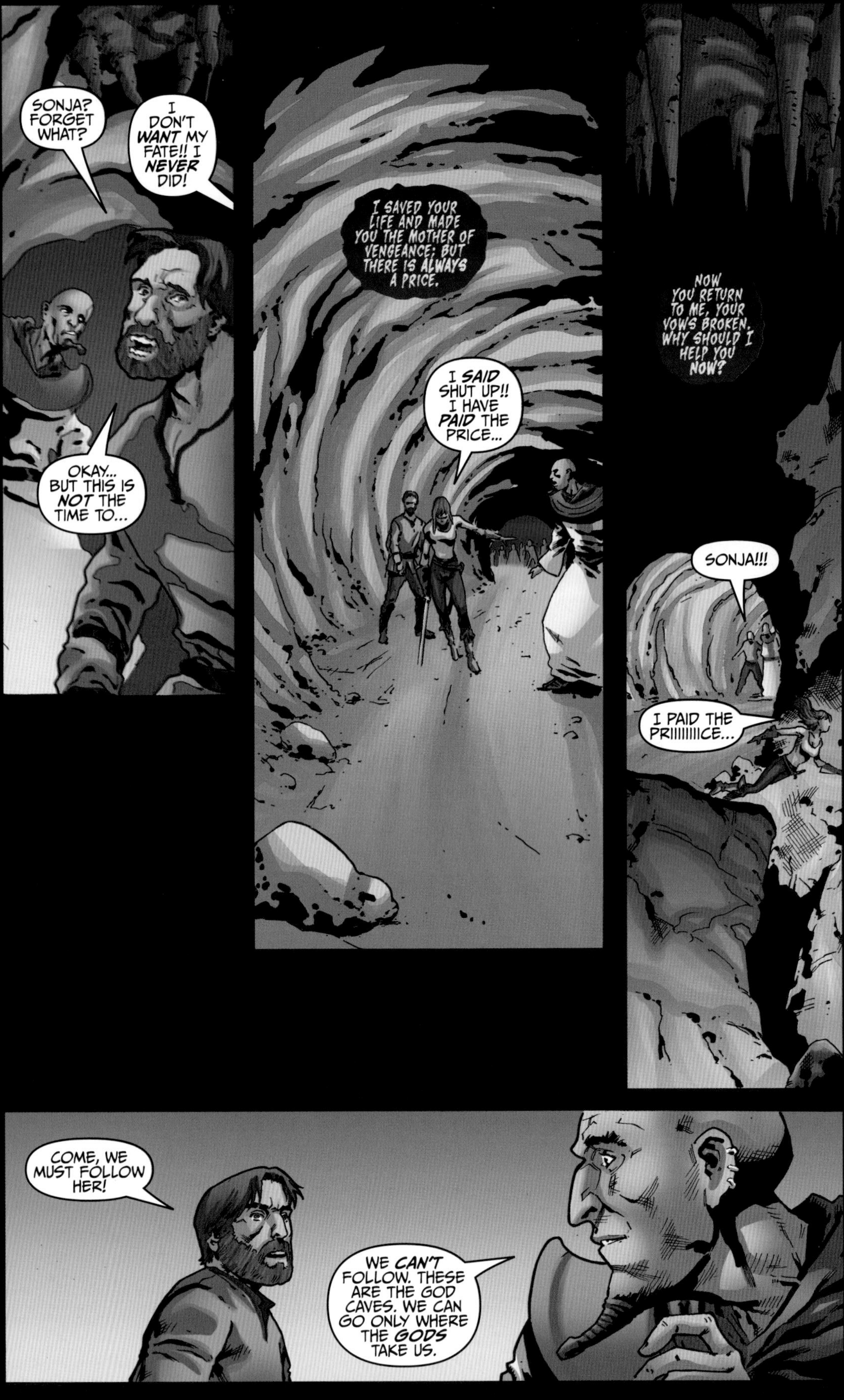
SONJA? FORGET WHAT?
I DON'T WANT MY FATE!! I NEVER DID!
OKAY... BUT THIS IS NOT THE TIME TO...
I SAVED YOUR LIFE AND MADE YOU THE MOTHER OF VENGEANCE; BUT THERE IS ALWAYS A PRICE.
I SAID SHUT UP!! I HAVE PAID THE PRICE...
NOW YOU RETURN TO ME, YOUR VOWS BROKEN. WHY SHOULD I HELP YOU NOW?
SONJA!!!
I PAID THE PRIIIIIIICE...
COME, WE MUST FOLLOW HER!
WE CAN'T FOLLOW. THESE ARE THE GOD CAVES. WE CAN GO ONLY WHERE THE GODS TAKE US.

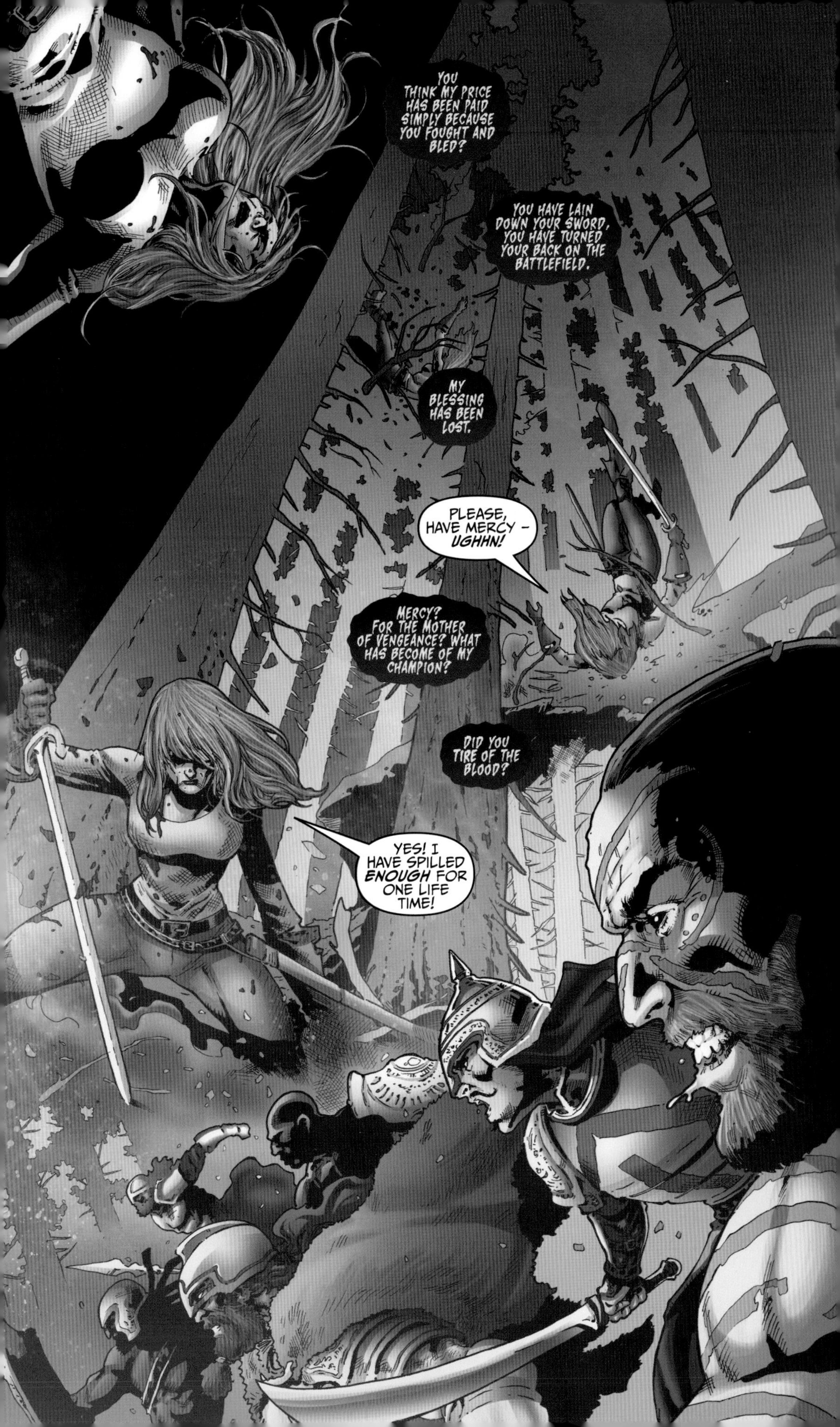
YOU THINK MY PRICE HAS BEEN PAID SIMPLY BECAUSE YOU FOUGHT AND BLED?
YOU HAVE LAIN DOWN YOUR SWORD, YOU HAVE TURNED YOUR BACK ON THE BATTLEFIELD.
MY BLESSING HAS BEEN LOST.
PLEASE, HAVE MERCY - *UGHHN!*
MERCY? FOR THE MOTHER OF VENGEANCE? WHAT HAS BECOME OF MY CHAMPION?
DID YOU TIRE OF THE BLOOD?
YES! I HAVE SPILLED **ENOUGH** FOR ONE LIFE TIME!

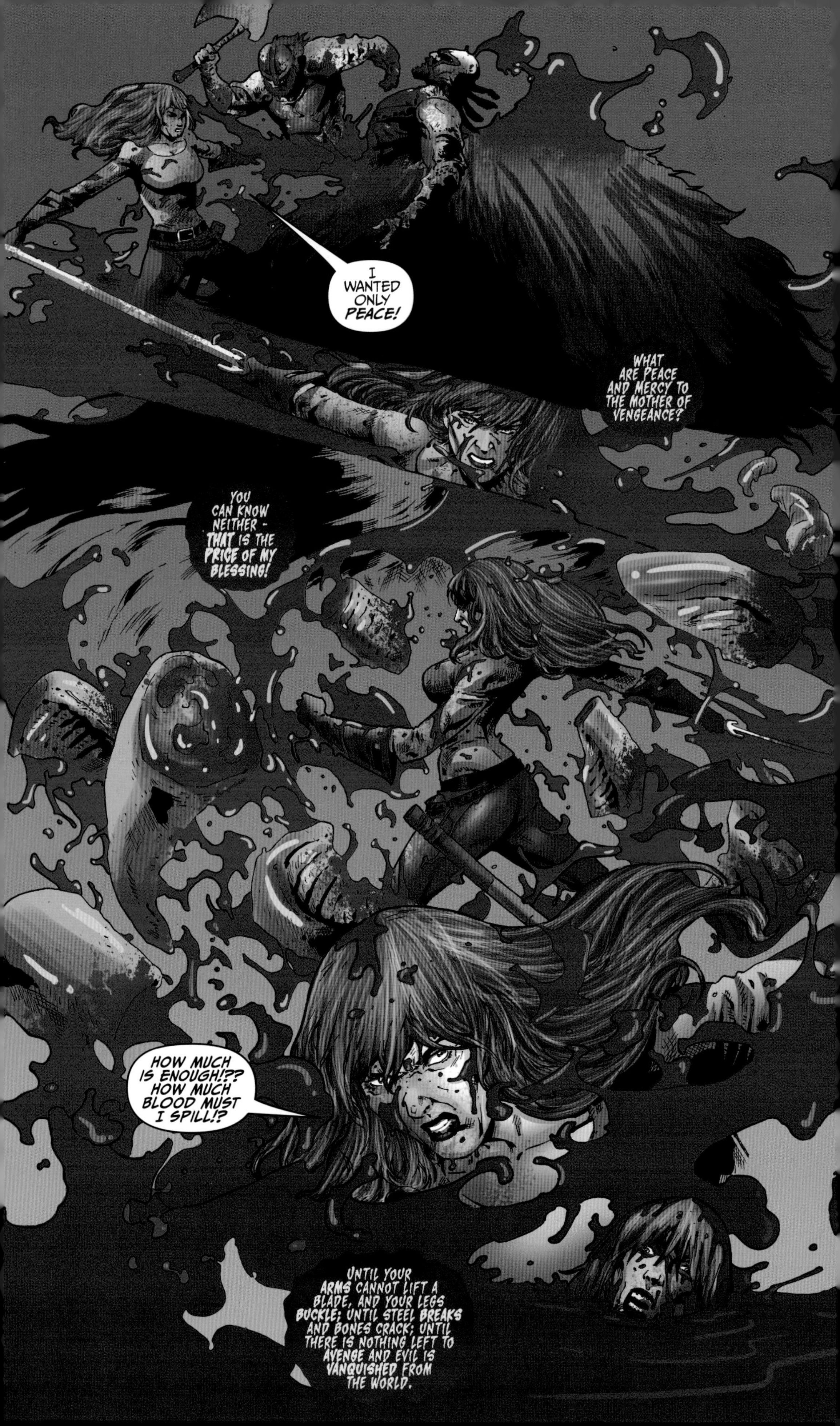
I WANTED ONLY PEACE!
WHAT ARE PEACE AND MERCY TO THE MOTHER OF VENGEANCE?
YOU CAN KNOW NEITHER - THAT IS THE PRICE OF MY BLESSING!
HOW MUCH IS ENOUGH!?? HOW MUCH BLOOD MUST I SPILL!?
UNTIL YOUR ARMS CANNOT LIFT A BLADE, AND YOUR LEGS BUCKLE; UNTIL STEEL BREAKS AND BONES CRACK; UNTIL THERE IS NOTHING LEFT TO AVENGE AND EVIL IS VANQUISHED FROM THE WORLD.

YOU HAVE LOST YOUR EDGE, MY DAUGHTER. A DULL BLADE IS A WORTHLESS WEAPON.
YOU ARE UNWORTHY!
SCÁTHATCH! LISTEN TO ME! THE SON OF SET WALKS THE LAND! HIS ARMIES BUTCHER THE INNOCENT, AND RAPE THE WEAK!
HE WILL SWALLOW THE WHOLE WORLD! ALL WILL BE LOST!
I KNOW THE DARKNESS COMES, BUT YOU CANNOT DEFEAT HIM IF YOUR HEART IS WEIGHTED BY GUILT AND YOUR SOUL IS WEARY.
I HAVE LOST SO MANY...
AND YOU WILL LOSE SO MANY MORE!

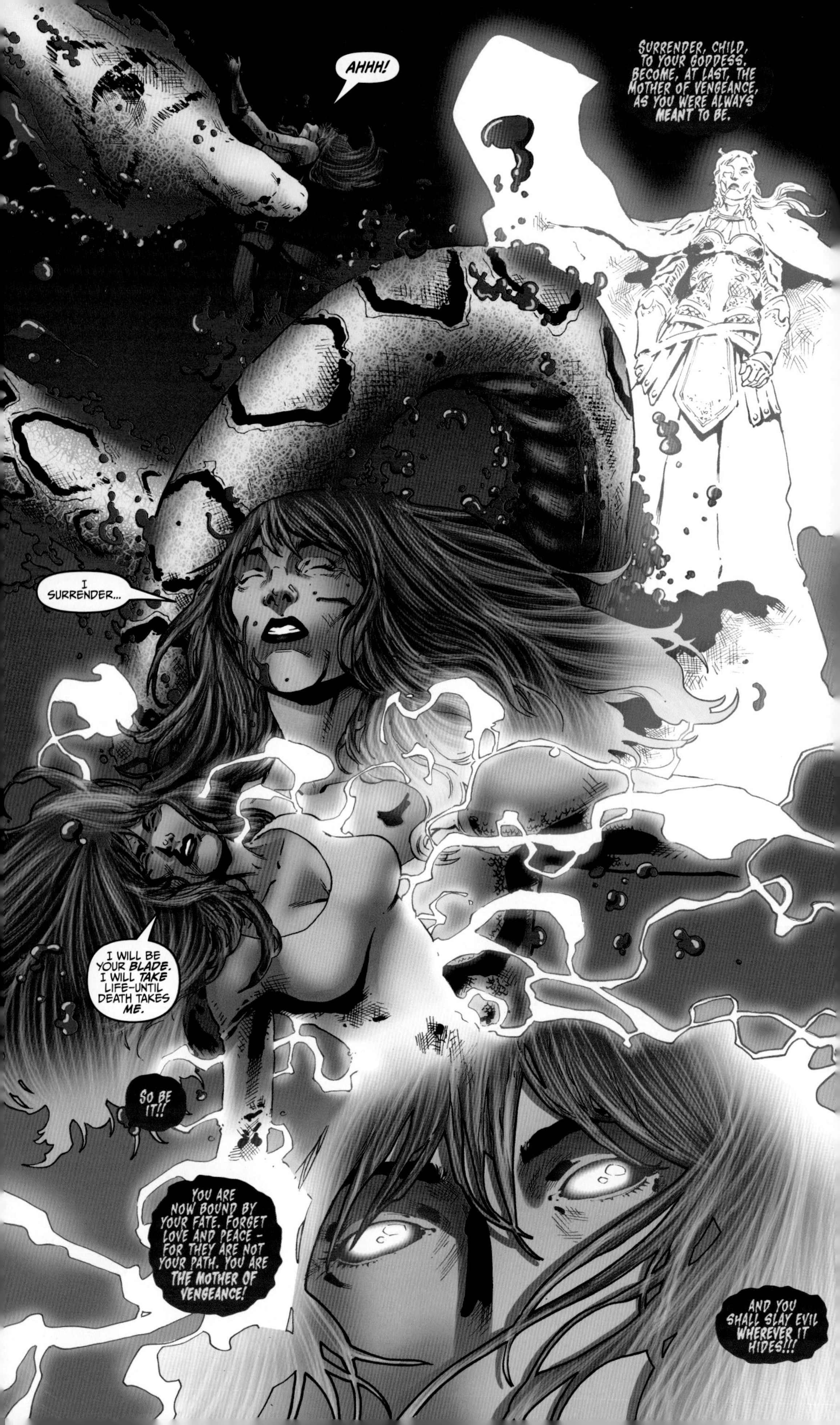
AHHH!
SURRENDER, CHILD, TO YOUR GODDESS. BECOME, AT LAST, THE MOTHER OF VENGEANCE, AS YOU WERE ALWAYS MEANT TO BE.
I SURRENDER...
I WILL BE YOUR *BLADE*. I WILL *TAKE* LIFE–UNTIL DEATH TAKES *ME*.
SO BE IT!!
YOU ARE NOW BOUND BY YOUR FATE. FORGET LOVE AND PEACE – FOR THEY ARE NOT YOUR PATH. YOU ARE **THE MOTHER OF VENGEANCE!**
AND YOU SHALL SLAY EVIL WHEREVER IT HIDES!!!

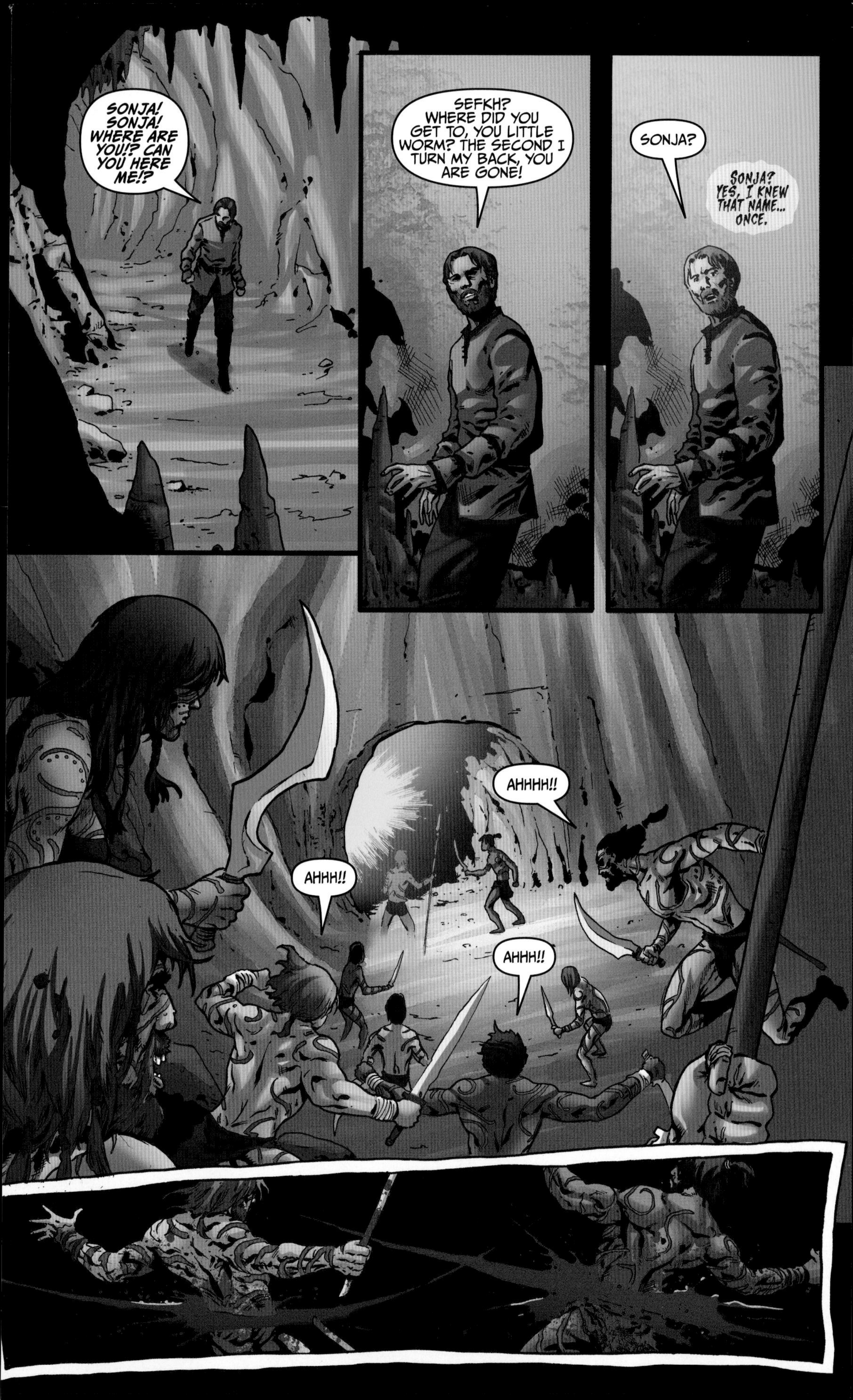
SONJA! SONJA! WHERE ARE YOU!? CAN YOU HERE ME!?
SEFKH? WHERE DID YOU GET TO, YOU LITTLE WORM? THE SECOND I TURN MY BACK, YOU ARE GONE!
SONJA?
SONJA? YES, I KNEW THAT NAME... ONCE.
AHHHH!!
AHHH!!
AHHH!!

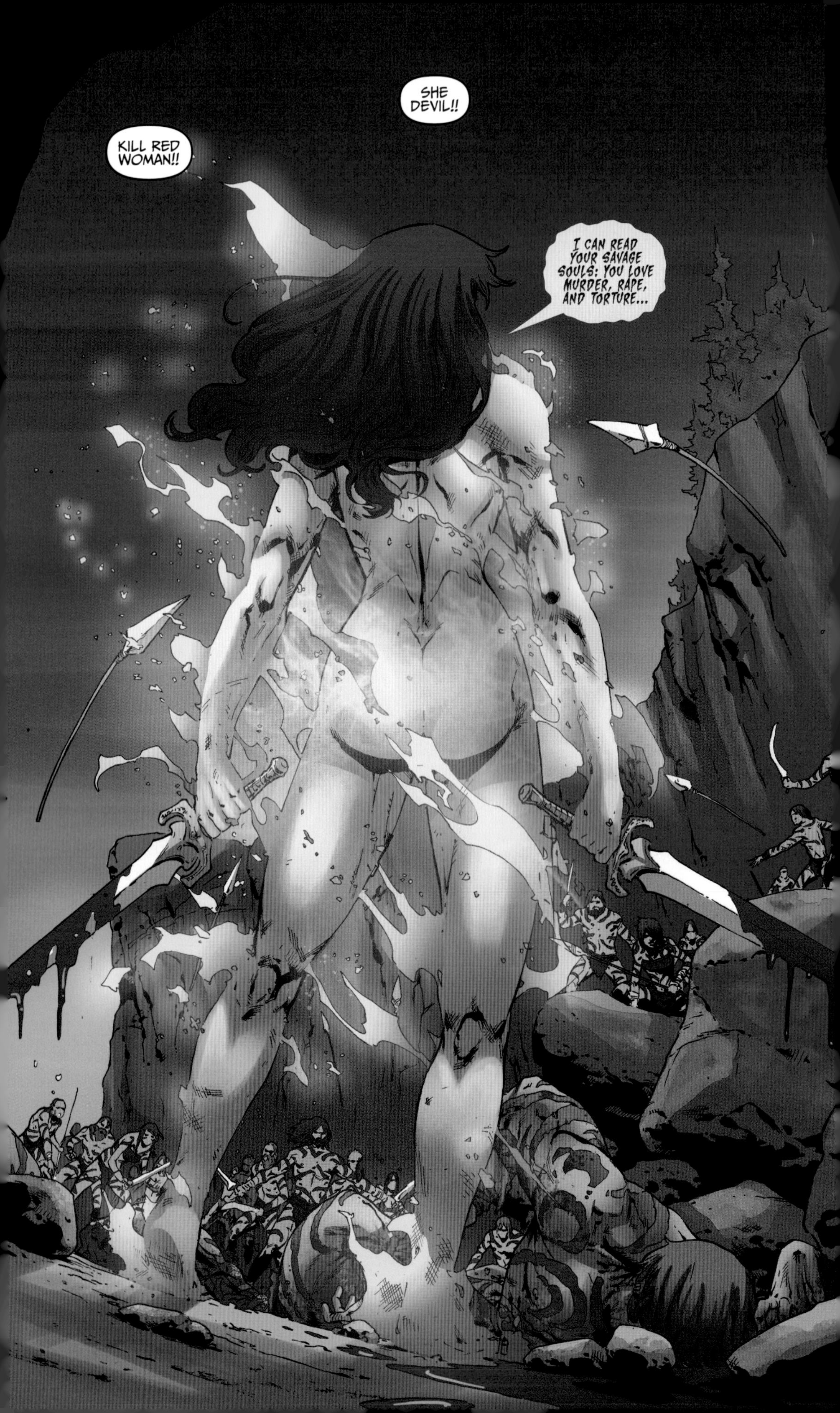
KILL RED WOMAN!!
SHE DEVIL!!
I CAN READ YOUR SAVAGE SOULS: YOU LOVE MURDER, RAPE, AND TORTURE...

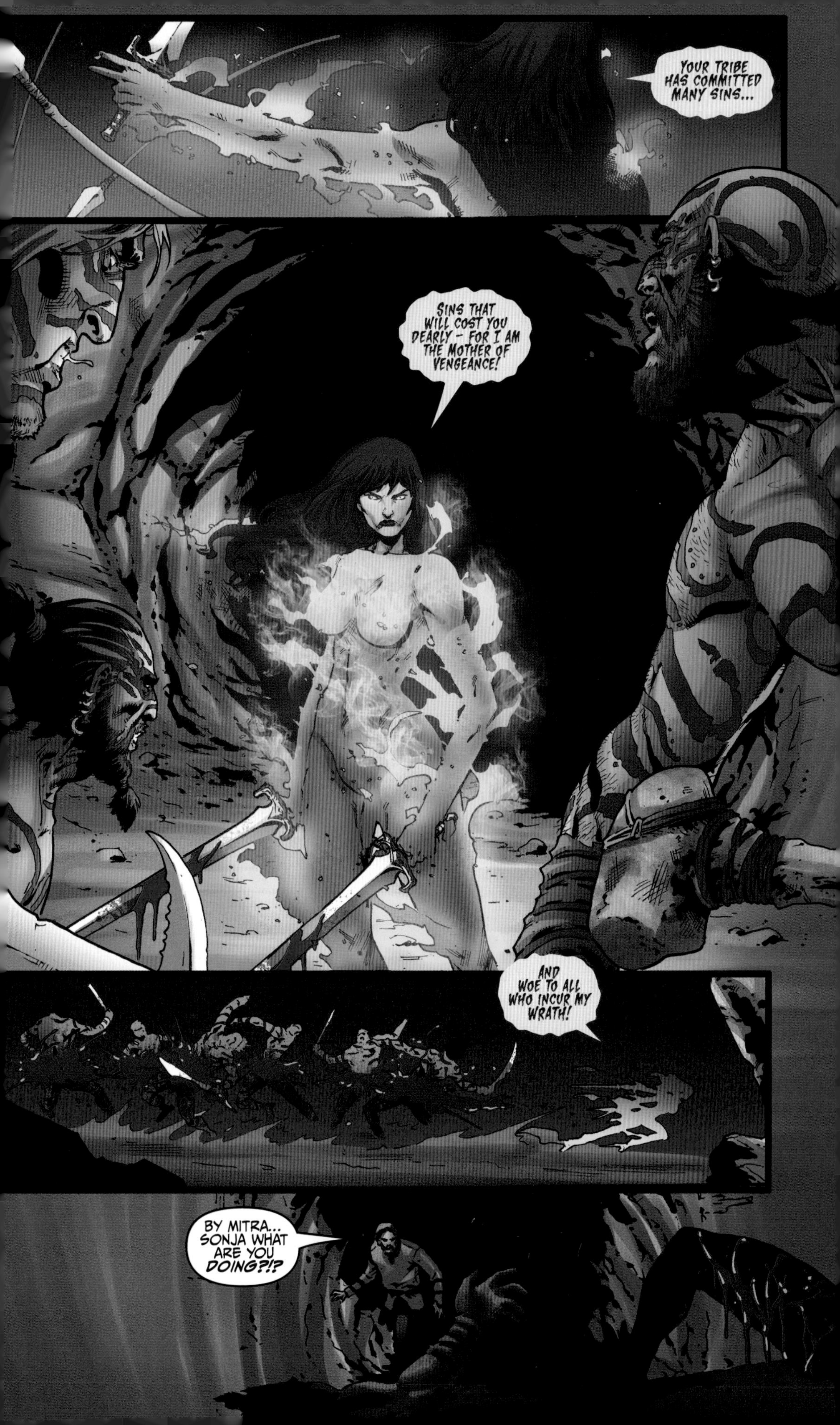
YOUR TRIBE HAS COMMITTED MANY SINS...
SINS THAT WILL COST YOU DEARLY - FOR I AM THE MOTHER OF VENGEANCE!
AND WOE TO ALL WHO INCUR MY WRATH!
BY MITRA... SONJA WHAT ARE YOU DOING?!?

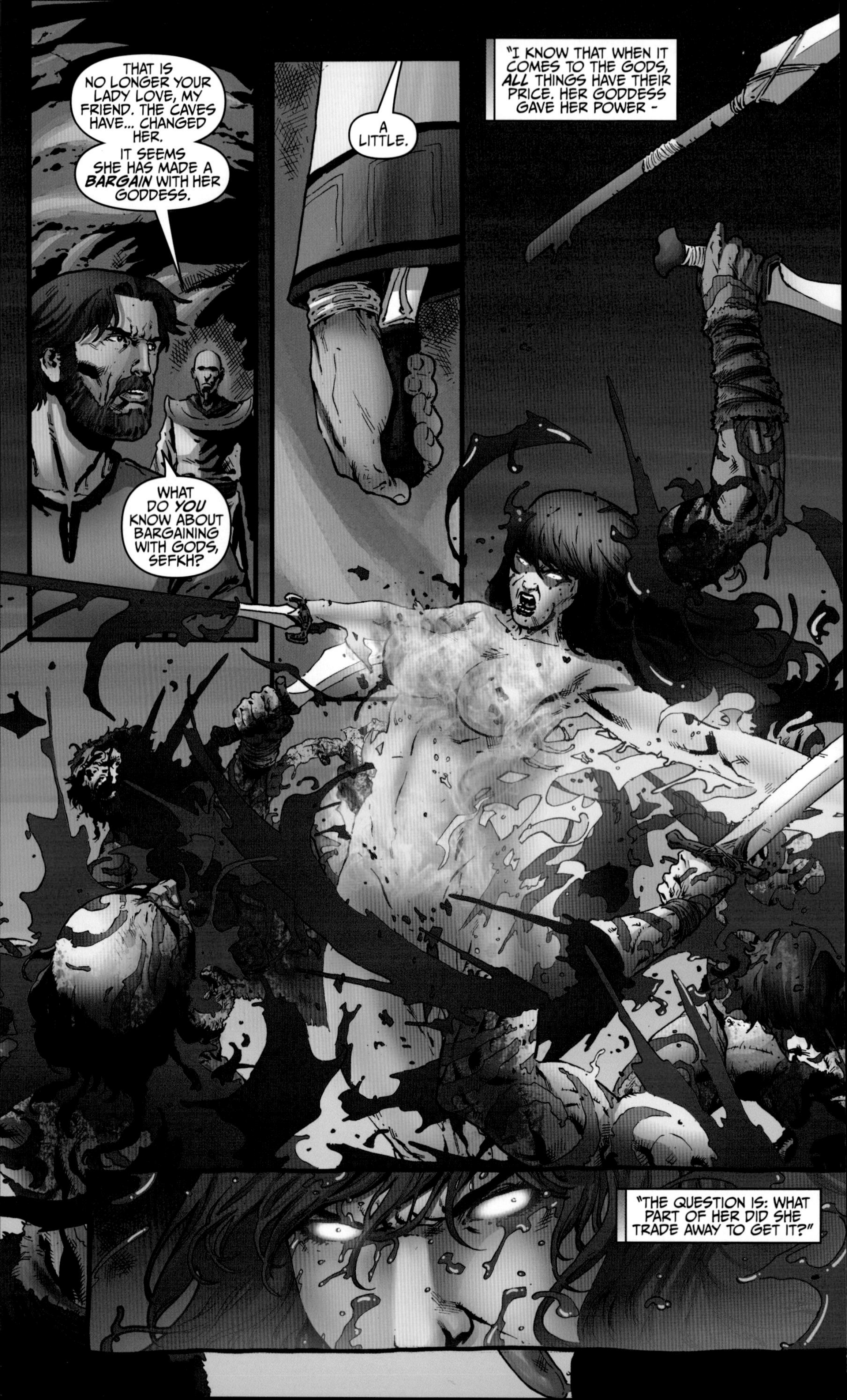
THAT IS NO LONGER YOUR LADY LOVE, MY FRIEND. THE CAVES HAVE... CHANGED HER.
IT SEEMS SHE HAS MADE A *BARGAIN* WITH HER GODDESS.
WHAT DO *YOU* KNOW ABOUT BARGAINING WITH GODS, SEFKH?
A LITTLE.
"I KNOW THAT WHEN IT COMES TO THE GODS, *ALL* THINGS HAVE THEIR PRICE. HER GODDESS GAVE HER POWER -
"THE QUESTION IS: WHAT PART OF HER DID SHE TRADE AWAY TO GET IT?"

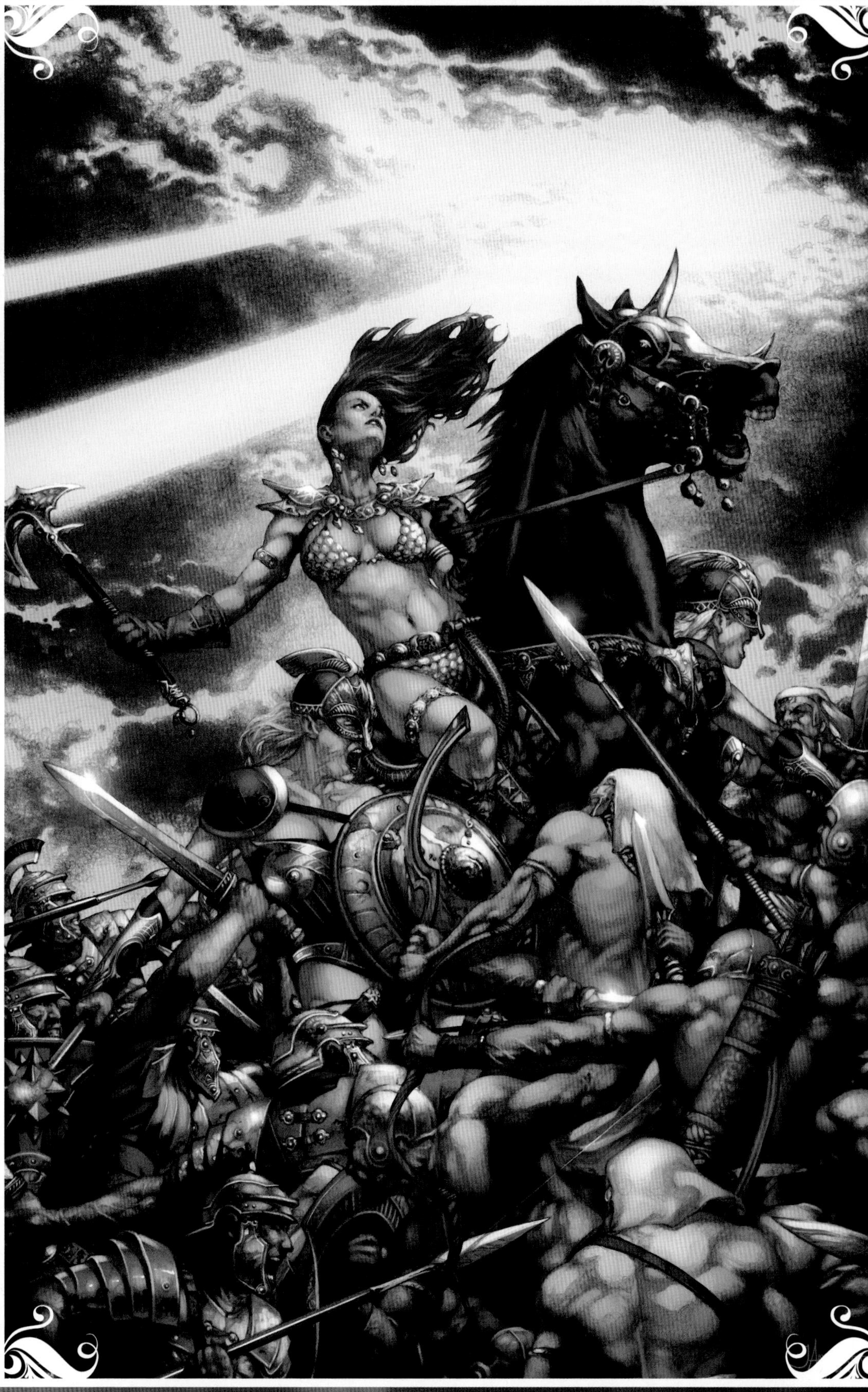

ISSUE FOUR

cover art by Jay Anacleto and Ivan Nunes

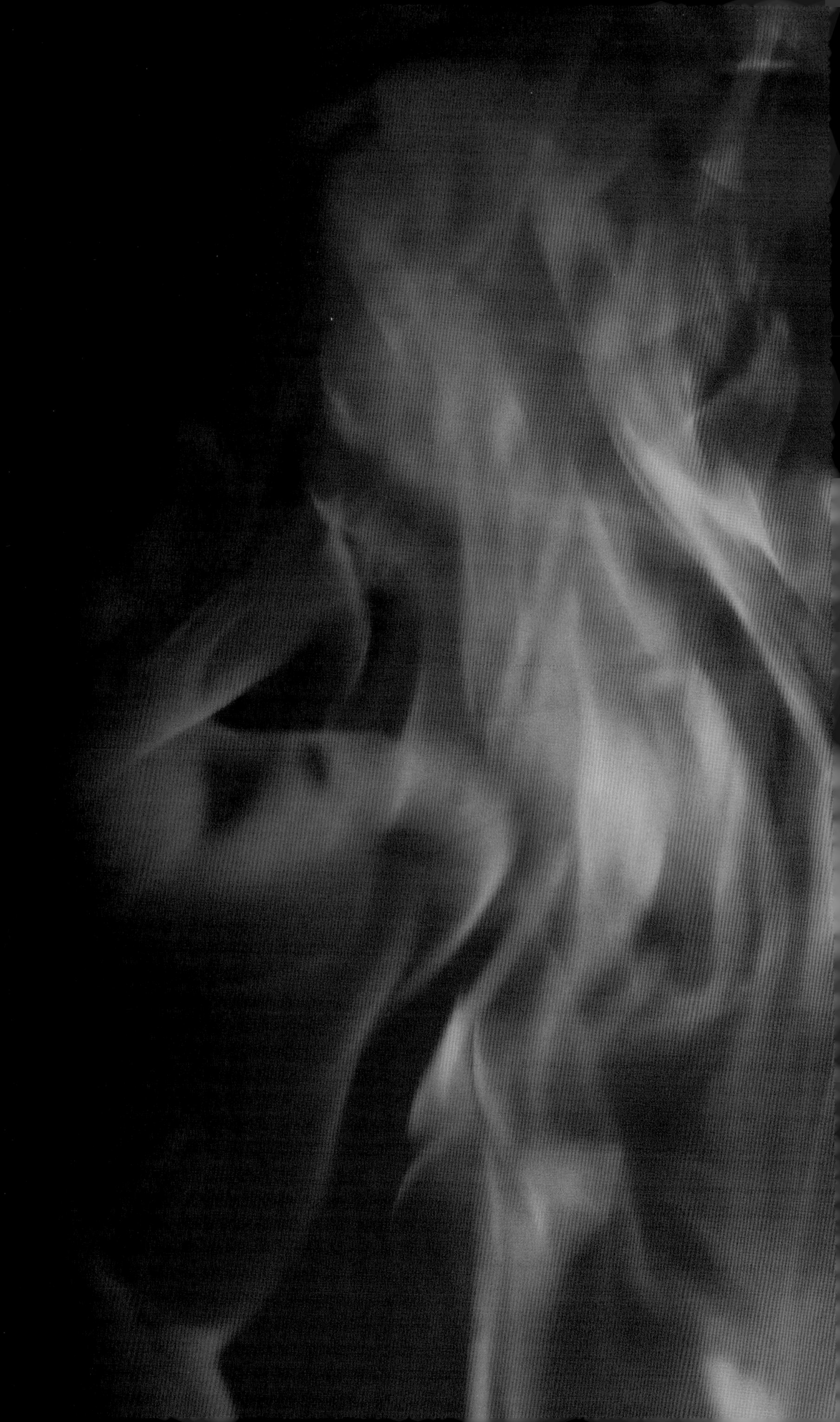

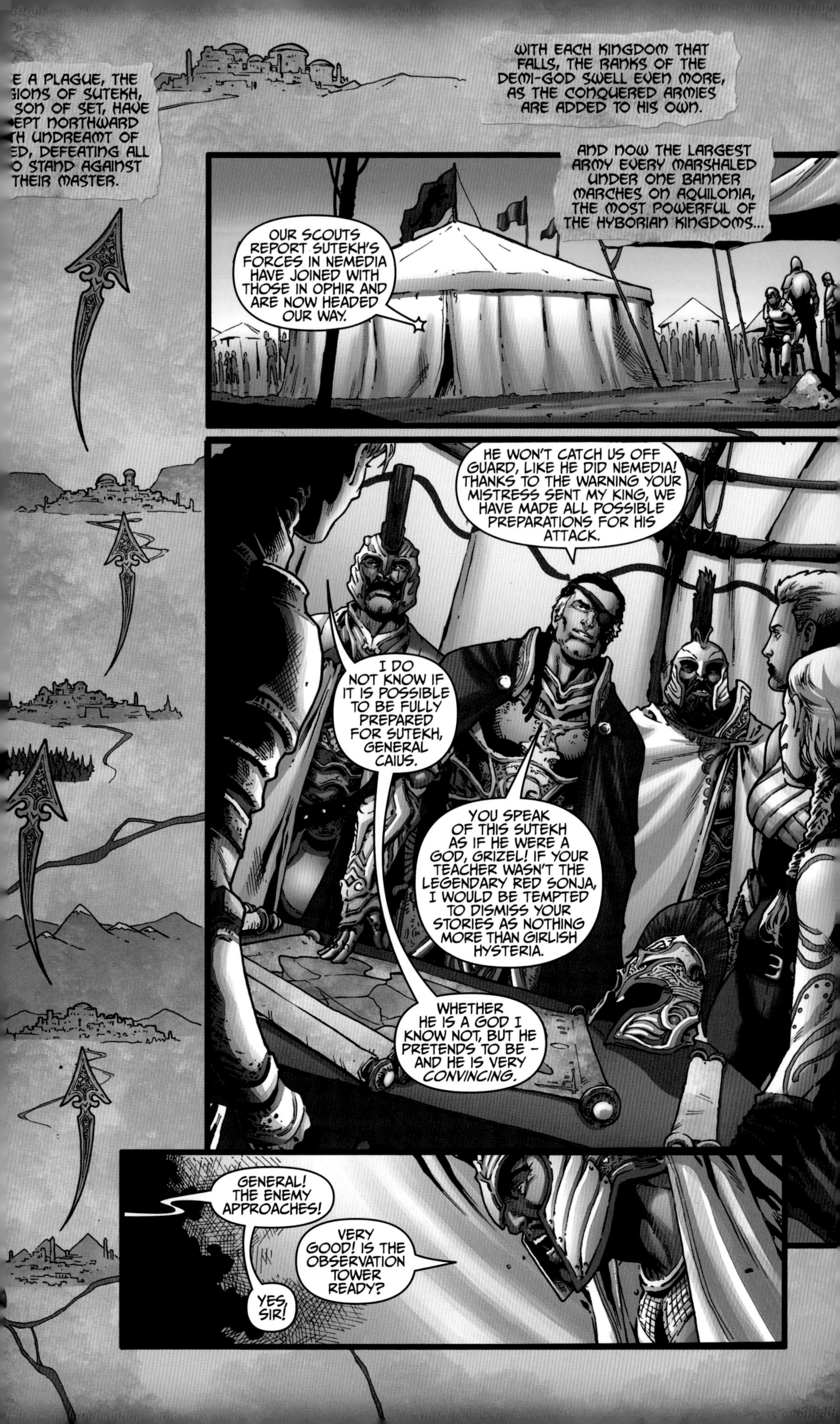
E A PLAGUE, THE
GIONS OF SUTEKH,
SON OF SET, HAVE
EPT NORTHWARD
TH UNDREAMT OF
ED, DEFEATING ALL
O STAND AGAINST
THEIR MASTER.
WITH EACH KINGDOM THAT FALLS, THE RANKS OF THE DEMI-GOD SWELL EVEN MORE, AS THE CONQUERED ARMIES ARE ADDED TO HIS OWN.
AND NOW THE LARGEST ARMY EVERY MARSHALED UNDER ONE BANNER MARCHES ON AQUILONIA, THE MOST POWERFUL OF THE HYBORIAN KINGDOMS...
OUR SCOUTS REPORT SUTEKH'S FORCES IN NEMEDIA HAVE JOINED WITH THOSE IN OPHIR AND ARE NOW HEADED OUR WAY.
HE WON'T CATCH US OFF GUARD, LIKE HE DID NEMEDIA! THANKS TO THE WARNING YOUR MISTRESS SENT MY KING, WE HAVE MADE ALL POSSIBLE PREPARATIONS FOR HIS ATTACK.
I DO NOT KNOW IF IT IS POSSIBLE TO BE FULLY PREPARED FOR SUTEKH, GENERAL CAIUS.
YOU SPEAK OF THIS SUTEKH AS IF HE WERE A GOD, GRIZEL! IF YOUR TEACHER WASN'T THE LEGENDARY RED SONJA, I WOULD BE TEMPTED TO DISMISS YOUR STORIES AS NOTHING MORE THAN GIRLISH HYSTERIA.
WHETHER HE IS A GOD I KNOW NOT, BUT HE PRETENDS TO BE – AND HE IS VERY CONVINCING.
GENERAL! THE ENEMY APPROACHES!
VERY GOOD! IS THE OBSERVATION TOWER READY?
YES, SIR!

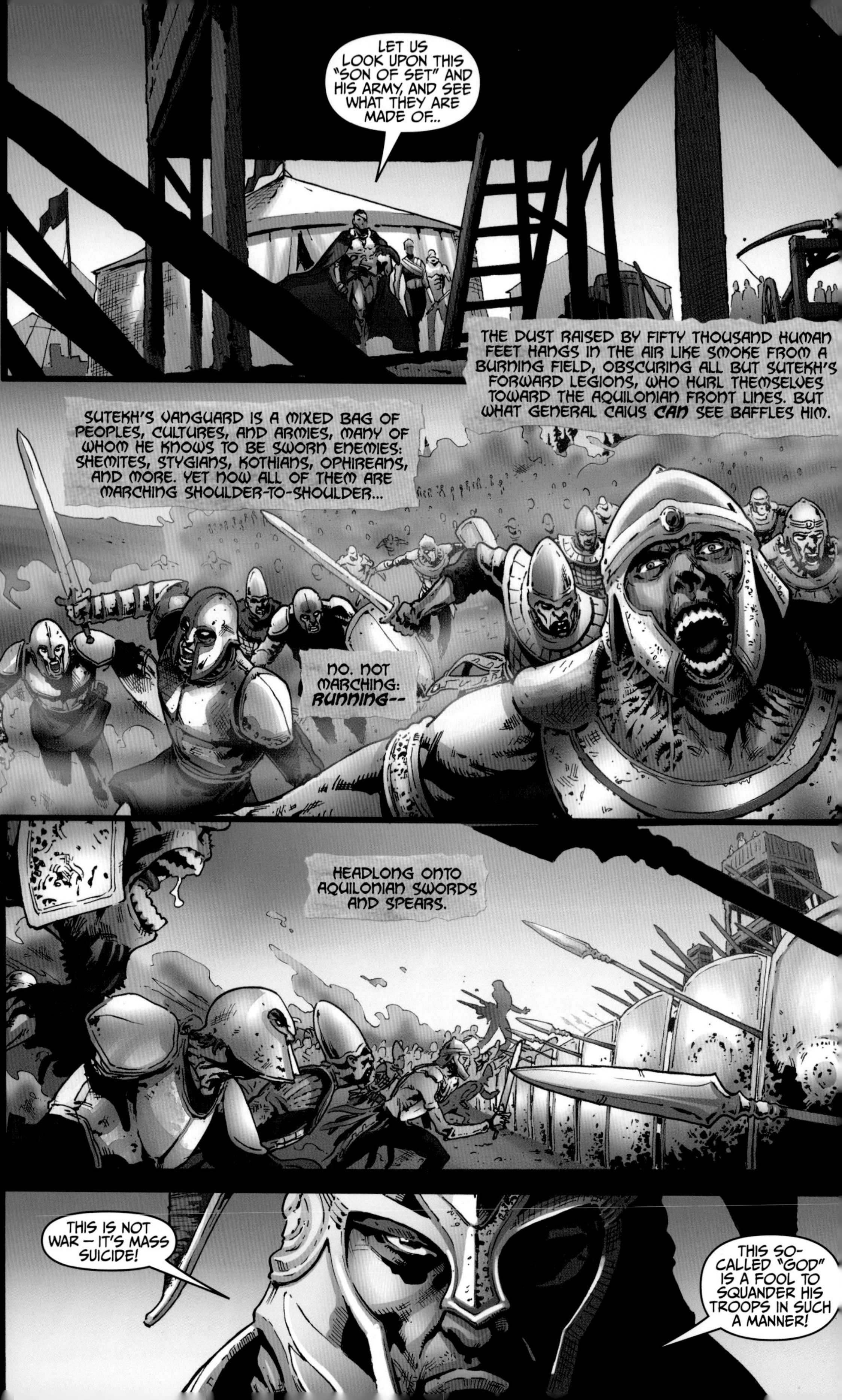
LET US LOOK UPON THIS "SON OF SET" AND HIS ARMY, AND SEE WHAT THEY ARE MADE OF...
THE DUST RAISED BY FIFTY THOUSAND HUMAN FEET HANGS IN THE AIR LIKE SMOKE FROM A BURNING FIELD, OBSCURING ALL BUT SUTEKH'S FORWARD LEGIONS, WHO HURL THEMSELVES TOWARD THE AQUILONIAN FRONT LINES. BUT WHAT GENERAL CAIUS CAN SEE BAFFLES HIM.
SUTEKH'S VANGUARD IS A MIXED BAG OF PEOPLES, CULTURES, AND ARMIES, MANY OF WHOM HE KNOWS TO BE SWORN ENEMIES: SHEMITES, STYGIANS, KOTHIANS, OPHIREANS, AND MORE. YET NOW ALL OF THEM ARE MARCHING SHOULDER-TO-SHOULDER...
NO. NOT MARCHING: RUNNING--
HEADLONG ONTO AQUILONIAN SWORDS AND SPEARS.
THIS IS NOT WAR — IT'S MASS SUICIDE!
THIS SO-CALLED "GOD" IS A FOOL TO SQUANDER HIS TROOPS IN SUCH A MANNER!

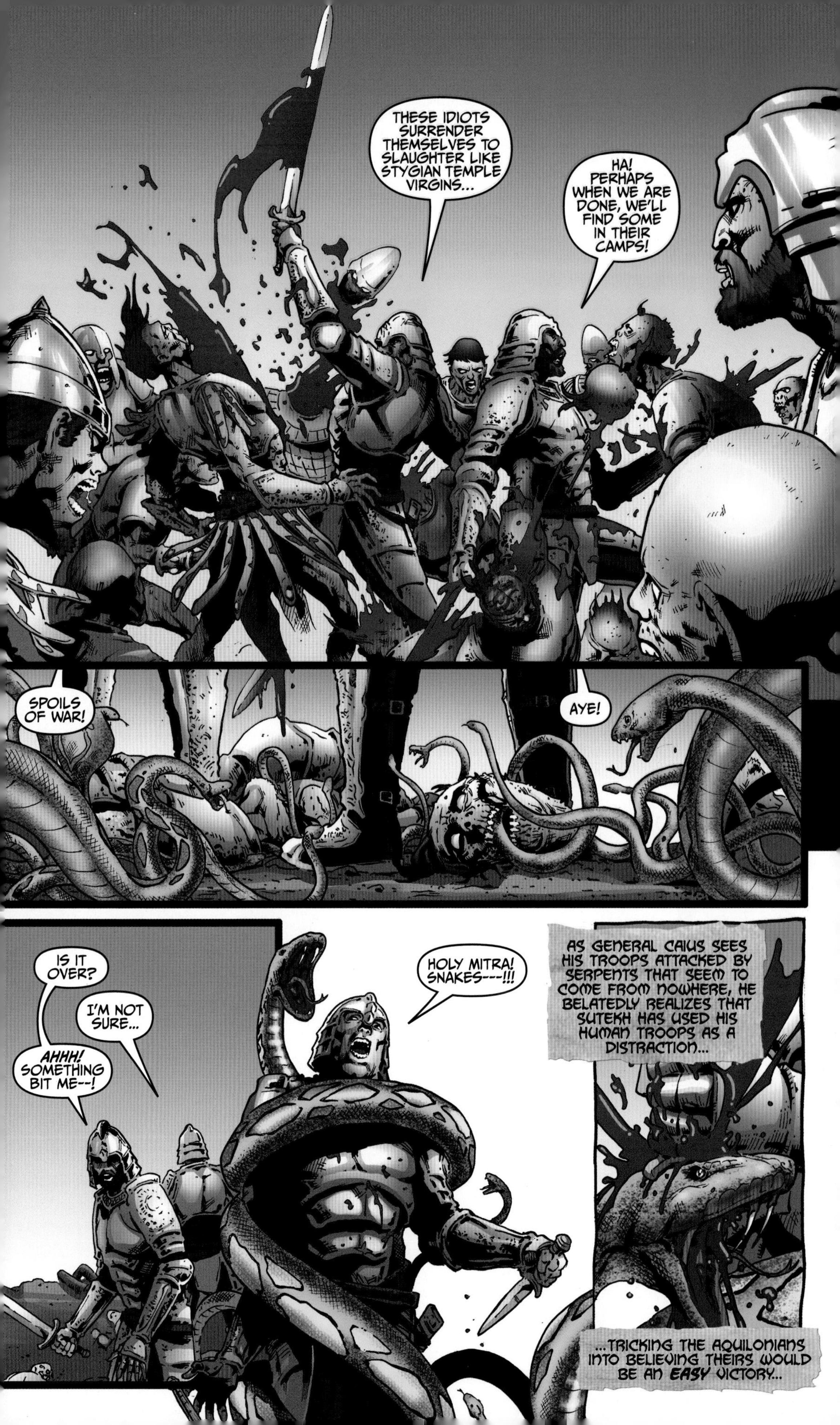

THESE IDIOTS SURRENDER THEMSELVES TO SLAUGHTER LIKE STYGIAN TEMPLE VIRGINS...
HA! PERHAPS WHEN WE ARE DONE, WE'LL FIND SOME IN THEIR CAMPS!
SPOILS OF WAR!
AYE!
IS IT OVER?
I'M NOT SURE...
AHHH! SOMETHING BIT ME--!
HOLY MITRA! SNAKES---!!!
AS GENERAL CAIUS SEES HIS TROOPS ATTACKED BY SERPENTS THAT SEEM TO COME FROM NOWHERE, HE BELATEDLY REALIZES THAT SUTEKH HAS USED HIS HUMAN TROOPS AS A DISTRACTION...
...TRICKING THE AQUILONIANS INTO BELIEVING THEIRS WOULD BE AN EASY VICTORY...

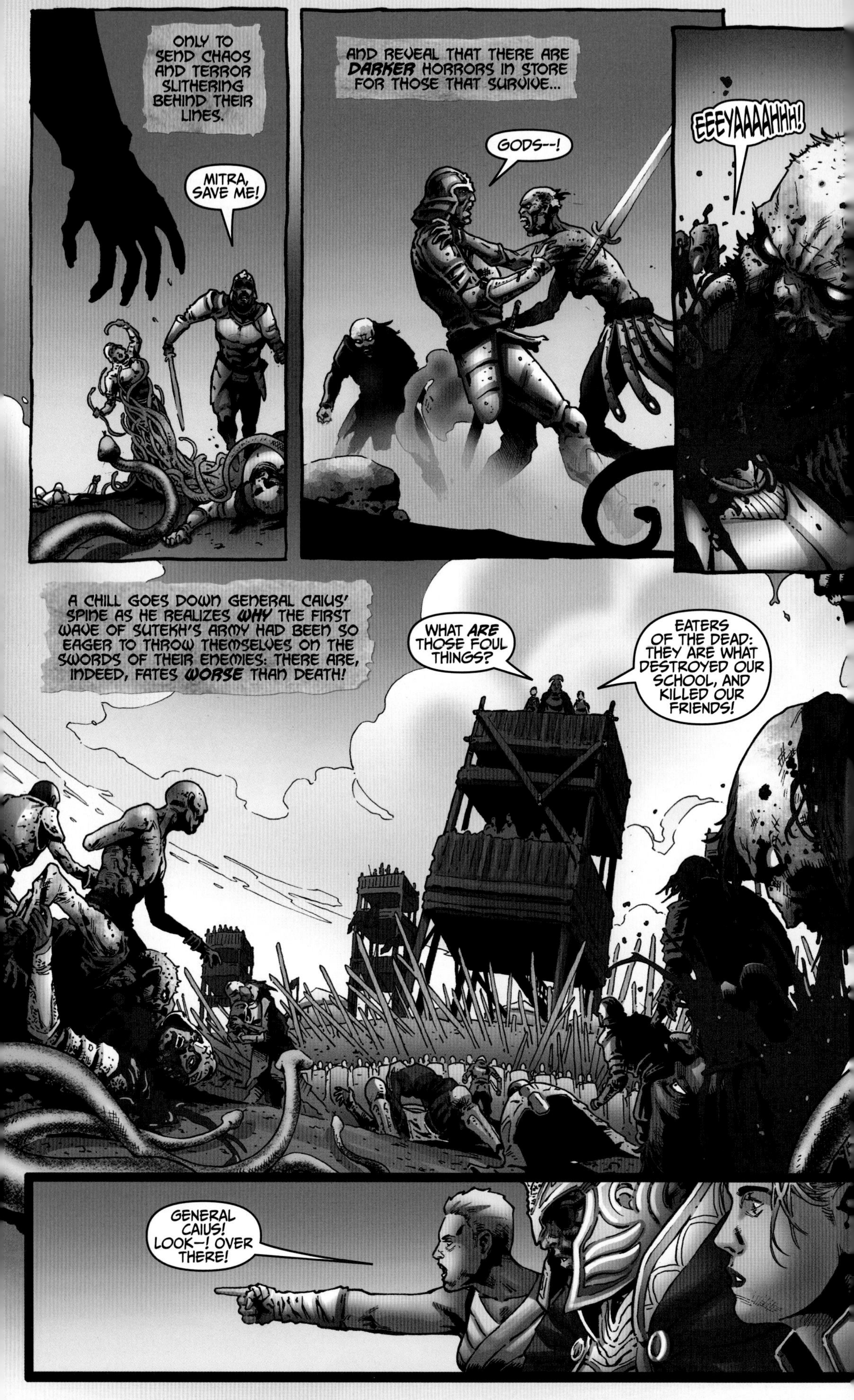

ONLY TO SEND CHAOS AND TERROR SLITHERING BEHIND THEIR LINES.
MITRA, SAVE ME!
AND REVEAL THAT THERE ARE DARKER HORRORS IN STORE FOR THOSE THAT SURVIVE...
GODS--!
EEEYAAAAHHH!
A CHILL GOES DOWN GENERAL CAIUS' SPINE AS HE REALIZES WHY THE FIRST WAVE OF SUTEKH'S ARMY HAD BEEN SO EAGER TO THROW THEMSELVES ON THE SWORDS OF THEIR ENEMIES: THERE ARE, INDEED, FATES WORSE THAN DEATH!
WHAT ARE THOSE FOUL THINGS?
EATERS OF THE DEAD: THEY ARE WHAT DESTROYED OUR SCHOOL, AND KILLED OUR FRIENDS!
GENERAL CAIUS! LOOK--! OVER THERE!

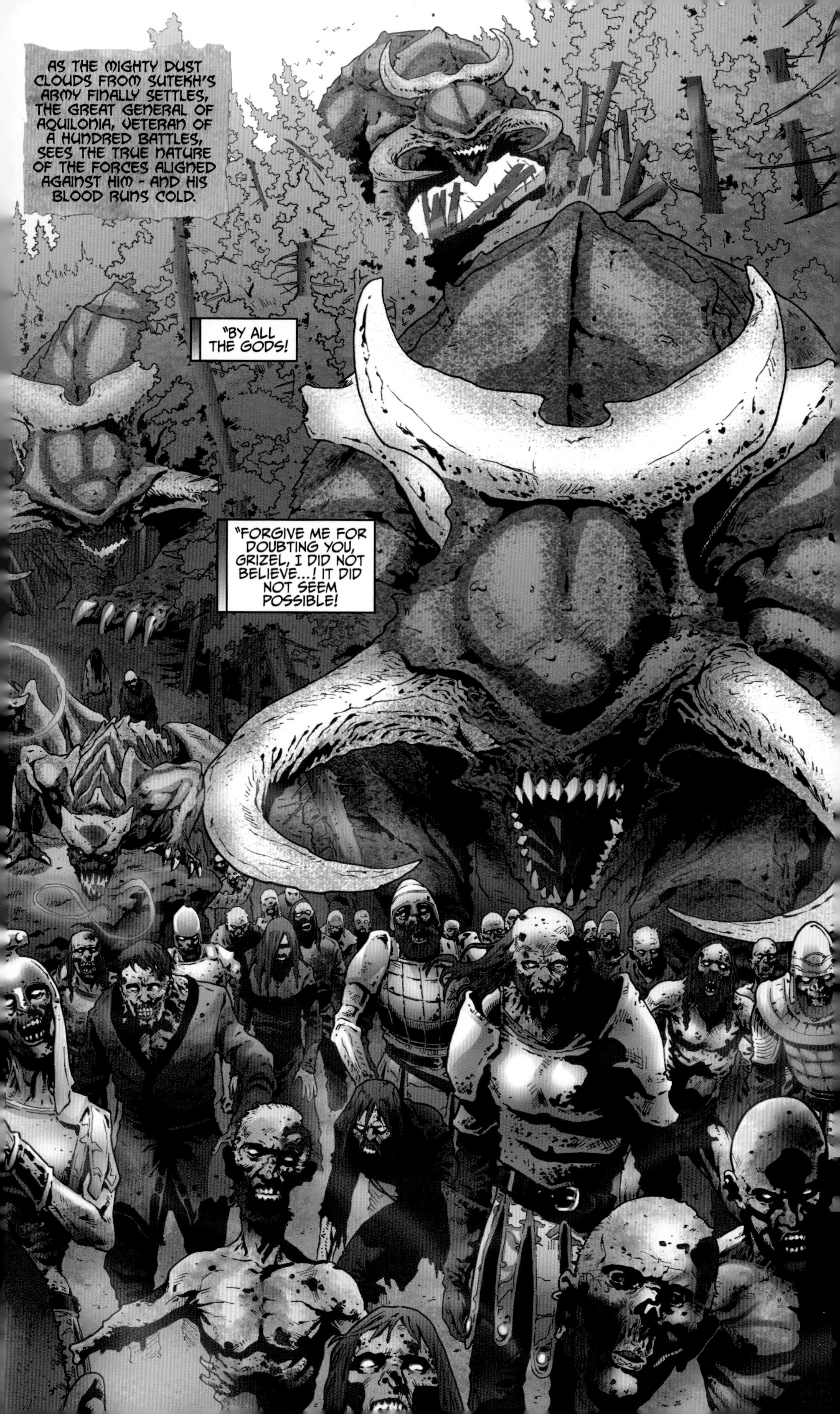
AS THE MIGHTY DUST CLOUDS FROM SUTEKH'S ARMY FINALLY SETTLES, THE GREAT GENERAL OF AQUILONIA, VETERAN OF A HUNDRED BATTLES, SEES THE TRUE NATURE OF THE FORCES ALIGNED AGAINST HIM - AND HIS BLOOD RUNS COLD.
"BY ALL THE GODS!
"FORGIVE ME FOR DOUBTING YOU, GRIZEL, I DID NOT BELIEVE...! IT DID NOT SEEM POSSIBLE!

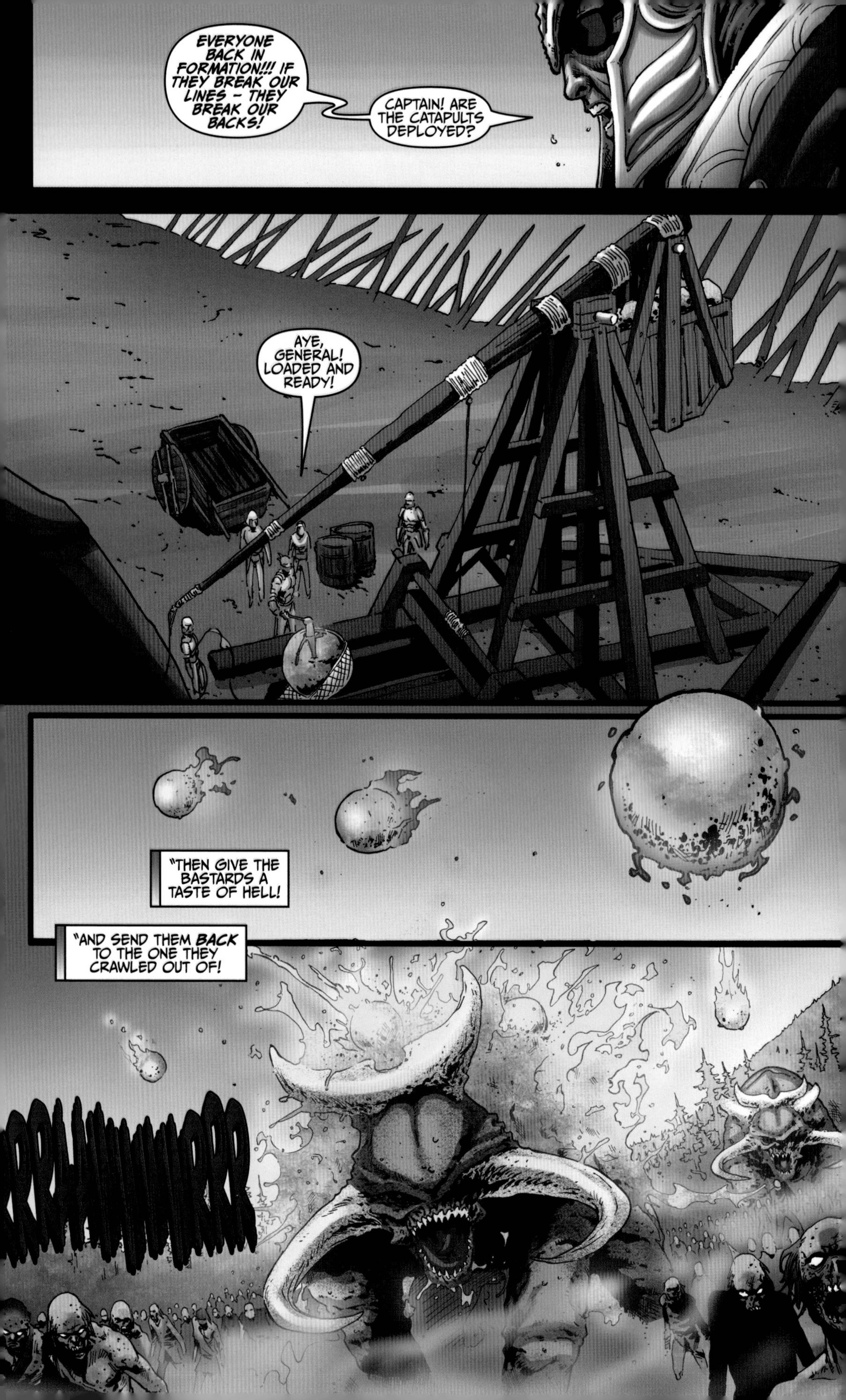
EVERYONE BACK IN FORMATION!!! IF THEY BREAK OUR LINES - THEY BREAK OUR BACKS!
CAPTAIN! ARE THE CATAPULTS DEPLOYED?
AYE, GENERAL! LOADED AND READY!
"THEN GIVE THE BASTARDS A TASTE OF HELL!
"AND SEND THEM BACK TO THE ONE THEY CRAWLED OUT OF!
RRRAWWWRRR

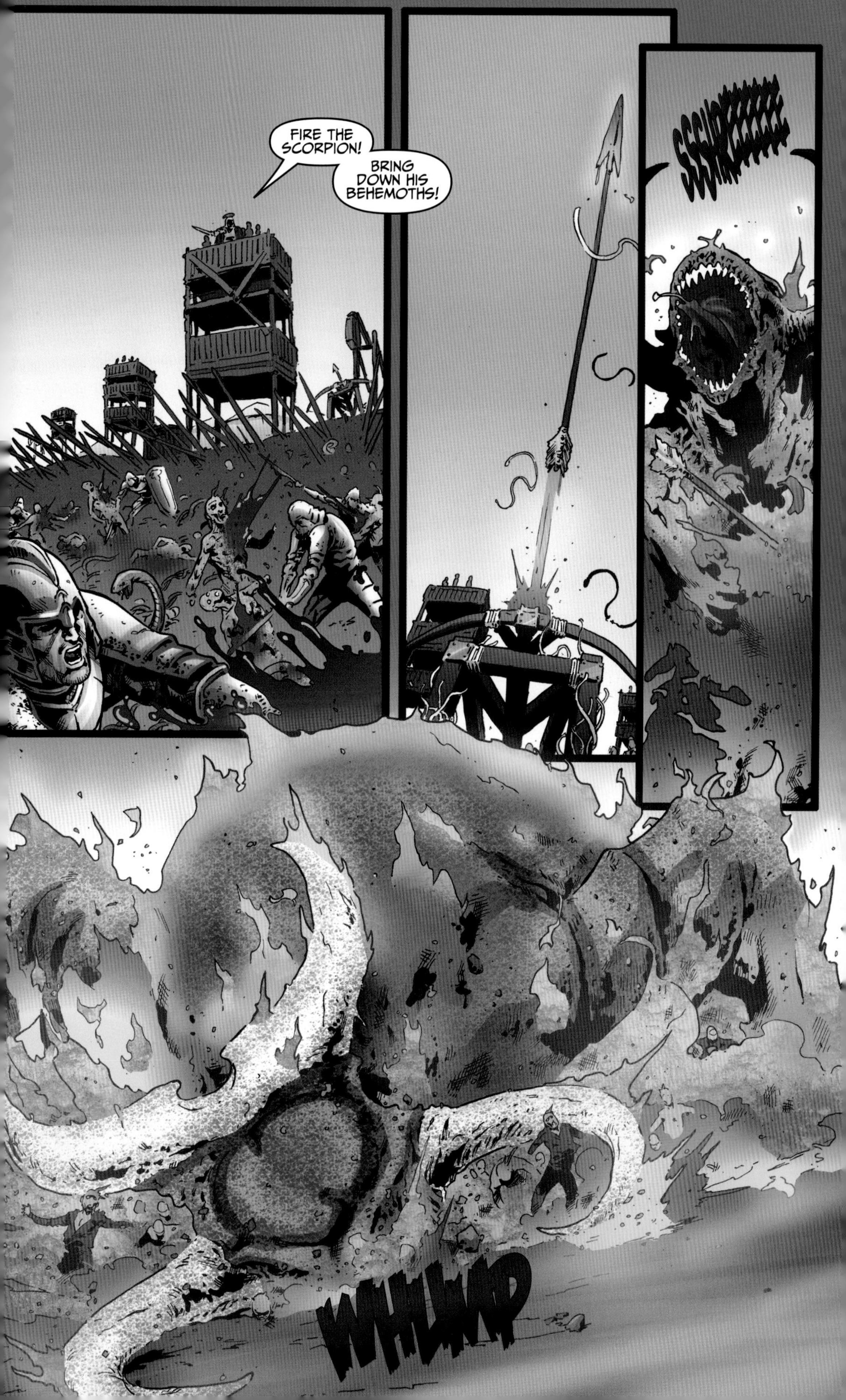
FIRE THE SCORPION!
BRING DOWN HIS BEHEMOTHS!
WHUMP

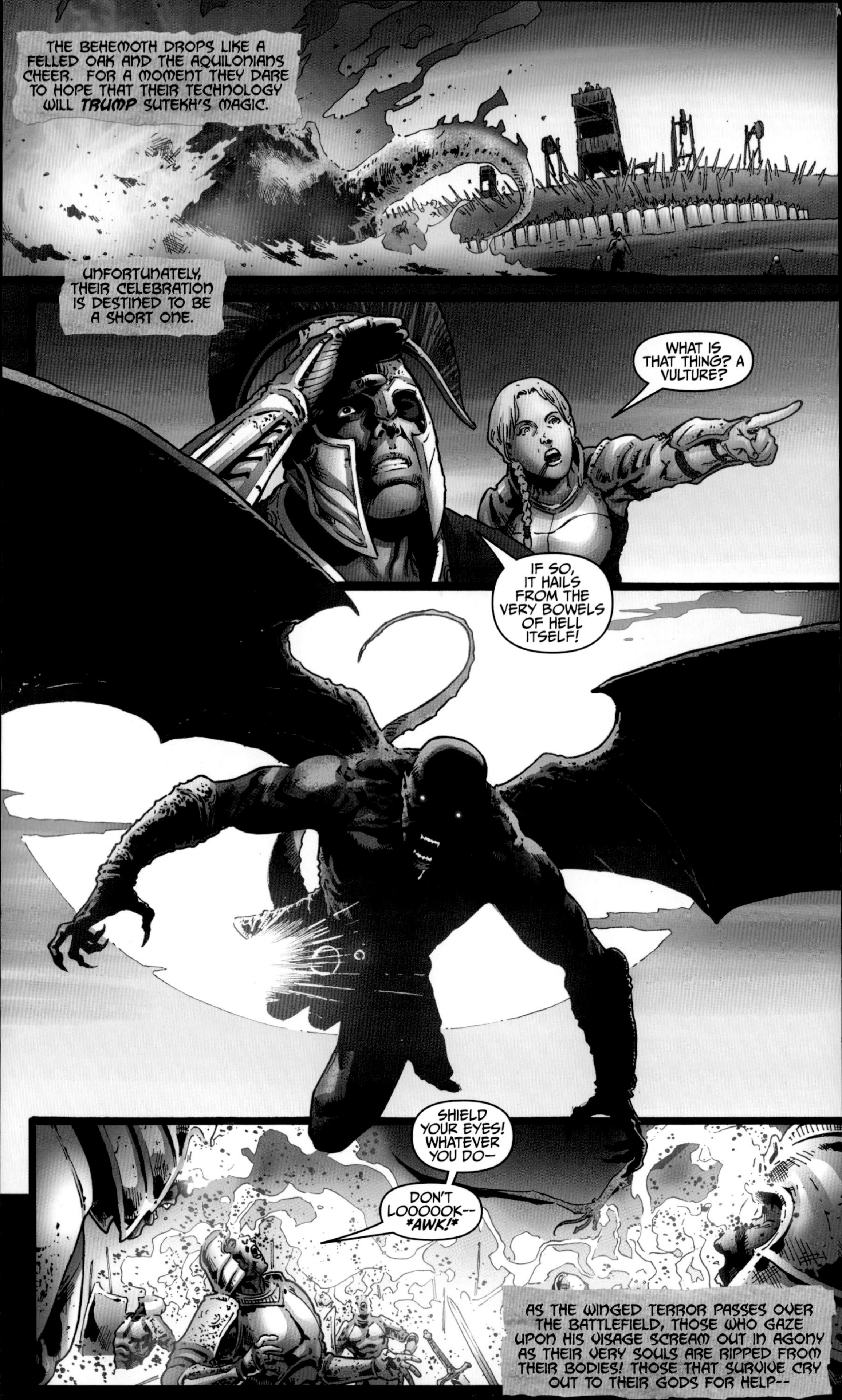
THE BEHEMOTH DROPS LIKE A FELLED OAK AND THE AQUILONIANS CHEER. FOR A MOMENT THEY DARE TO HOPE THAT THEIR TECHNOLOGY WILL TRUMP SUTEKH'S MAGIC.
UNFORTUNATELY, THEIR CELEBRATION IS DESTINED TO BE A SHORT ONE.
WHAT IS THAT THING? A VULTURE?
IF SO, IT HAILS FROM THE VERY BOWELS OF HELL ITSELF!
SHIELD YOUR EYES! WHATEVER YOU DO—
DON'T LOOOOOK-- *AWK!*
AS THE WINGED TERROR PASSES OVER THE BATTLEFIELD, THOSE WHO GAZE UPON HIS VISAGE SCREAM OUT IN AGONY AS THEIR VERY SOULS ARE RIPPED FROM THEIR BODIES! THOSE THAT SURVIVE CRY OUT TO THEIR GODS FOR HELP--

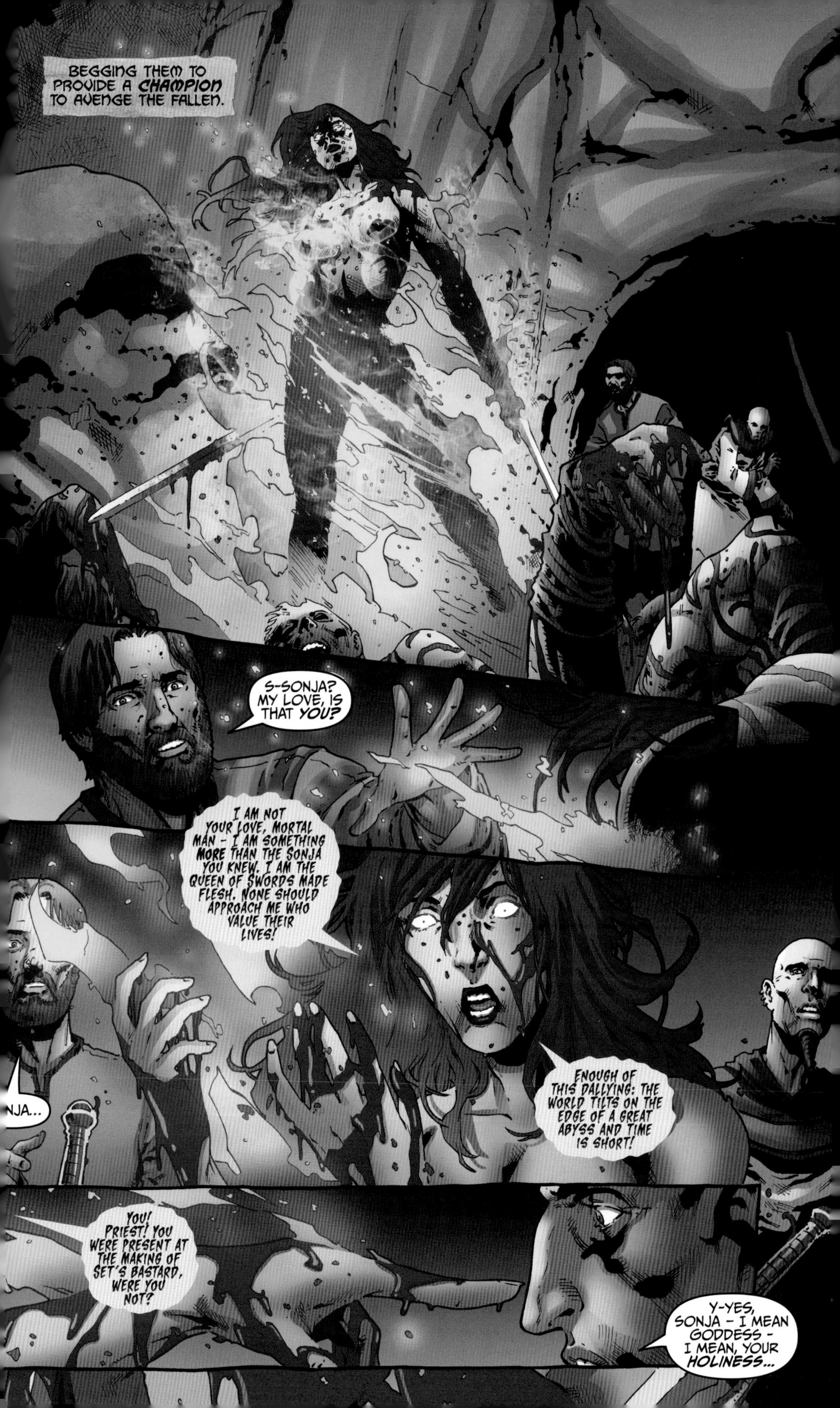
BEGGING THEM TO PROVIDE A CHAMPION TO AVENGE THE FALLEN.
S-SONJA? MY LOVE, IS THAT YOU?
I AM NOT YOUR LOVE, MORTAL MAN - I AM SOMETHING MORE THAN THE SONJA YOU KNEW. I AM THE QUEEN OF SWORDS MADE FLESH. NONE SHOULD APPROACH ME WHO VALUE THEIR LIVES!
NJA...
ENOUGH OF THIS DALLYING: THE WORLD TILTS ON THE EDGE OF A GREAT ABYSS AND TIME IS SHORT!
YOU! PRIEST! YOU WERE PRESENT AT THE MAKING OF SET'S BASTARD, WERE YOU NOT?
Y-YES, SONJA - I MEAN GODDESS - I MEAN, YOUR HOLINESS...

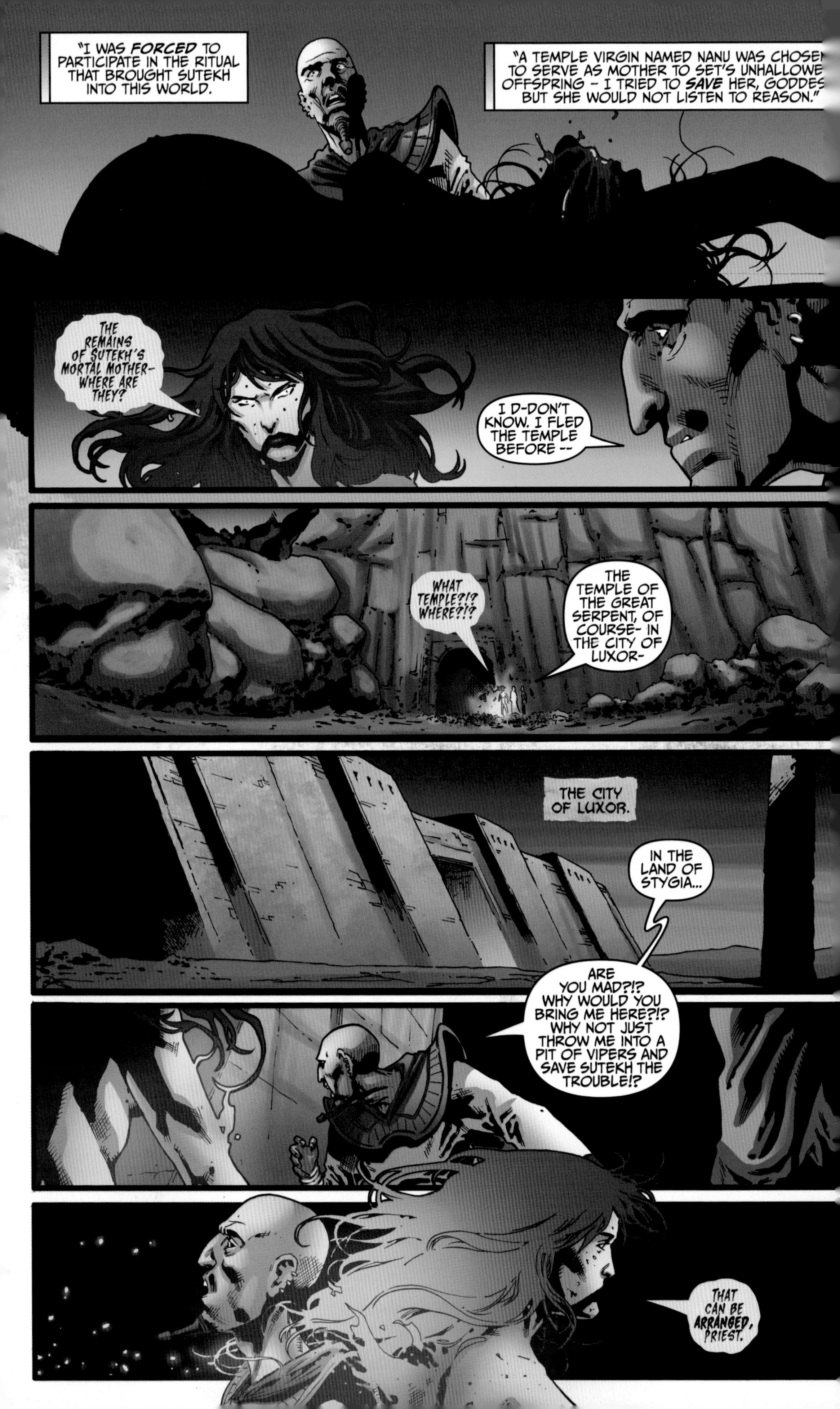
"I WAS FORCED TO PARTICIPATE IN THE RITUAL THAT BROUGHT SUTEKH INTO THIS WORLD.
"A TEMPLE VIRGIN NAMED NANU WAS CHOSEN TO SERVE AS MOTHER TO SET'S UNHALLOWED OFFSPRING - I TRIED TO SAVE HER, GODDESS BUT SHE WOULD NOT LISTEN TO REASON."
THE REMAINS OF SUTEKH'S MORTAL MOTHER-WHERE ARE THEY?
I D-DON'T KNOW. I FLED THE TEMPLE BEFORE --
WHAT TEMPLE?!? WHERE?!?
THE TEMPLE OF THE GREAT SERPENT, OF COURSE- IN THE CITY OF LUXOR-
THE CITY OF LUXOR.
IN THE LAND OF STYGIA...
ARE YOU MAD?!? WHY WOULD YOU BRING ME HERE?!? WHY NOT JUST THROW ME INTO A PIT OF VIPERS AND SAVE SUTEKH THE TROUBLE!?
THAT CAN BE ARRANGED, PRIEST.

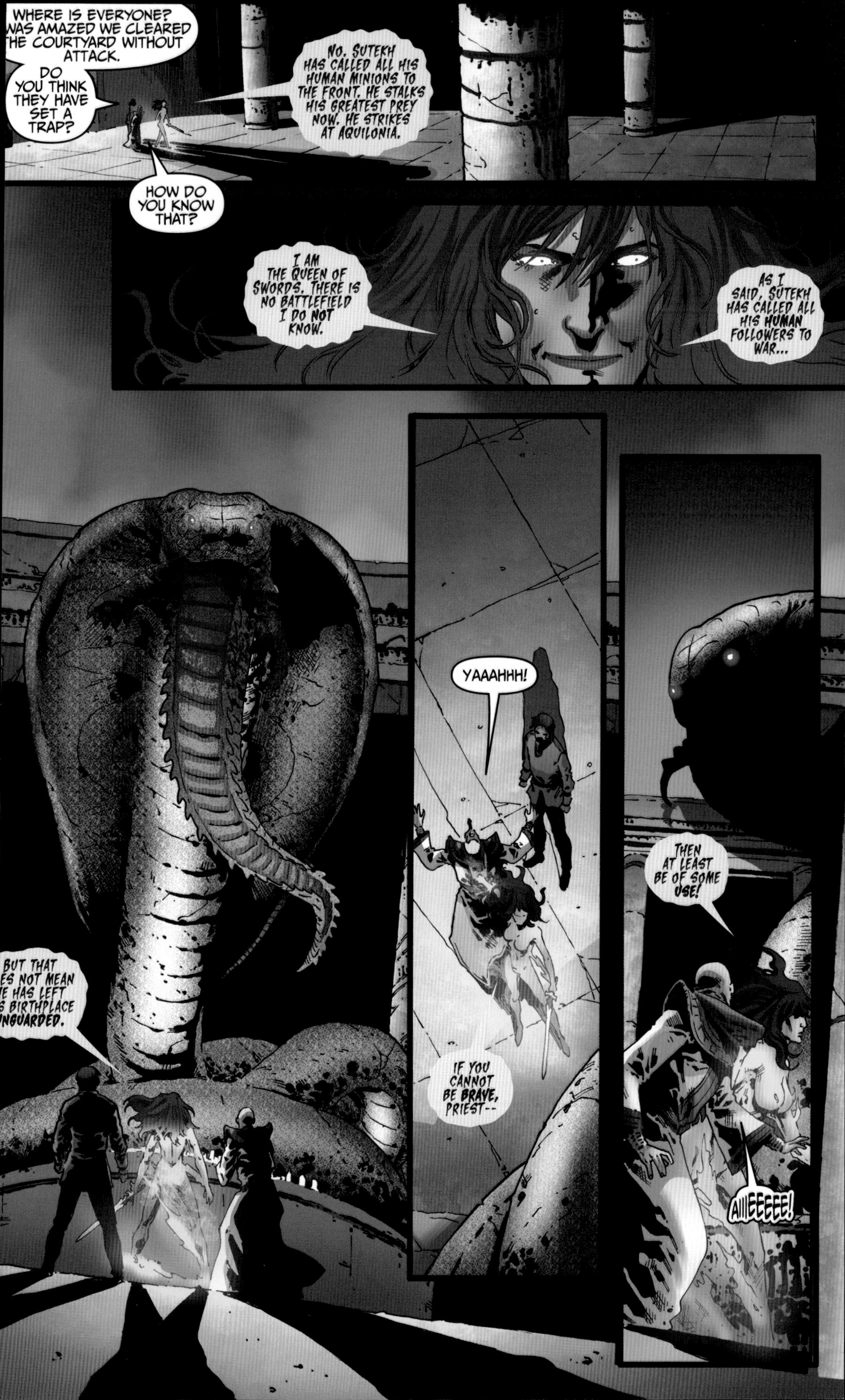
WHERE IS EVERYONE? I WAS AMAZED WE CLEARED THE COURTYARD WITHOUT ATTACK.
DO YOU THINK THEY HAVE SET A TRAP?
NO. SUTEKH HAS CALLED ALL HIS HUMAN MINIONS TO THE FRONT. HE STALKS HIS GREATEST PREY NOW. HE STRIKES AT AQUILONIA.
HOW DO YOU KNOW THAT?
I AM THE QUEEN OF SWORDS. THERE IS NO BATTLEFIELD I DO NOT KNOW.
AS I SAID, SUTEKH HAS CALLED ALL HIS HUMAN FOLLOWERS TO WAR...
BUT THAT ES NOT MEAN E HAS LEFT S BIRTHPLACE UNGUARDED.
YAAAHHH!
IF YOU CANNOT BE BRAVE, PRIEST--
THEN AT LEAST BE OF SOME USE!
AIIIEEEEE!

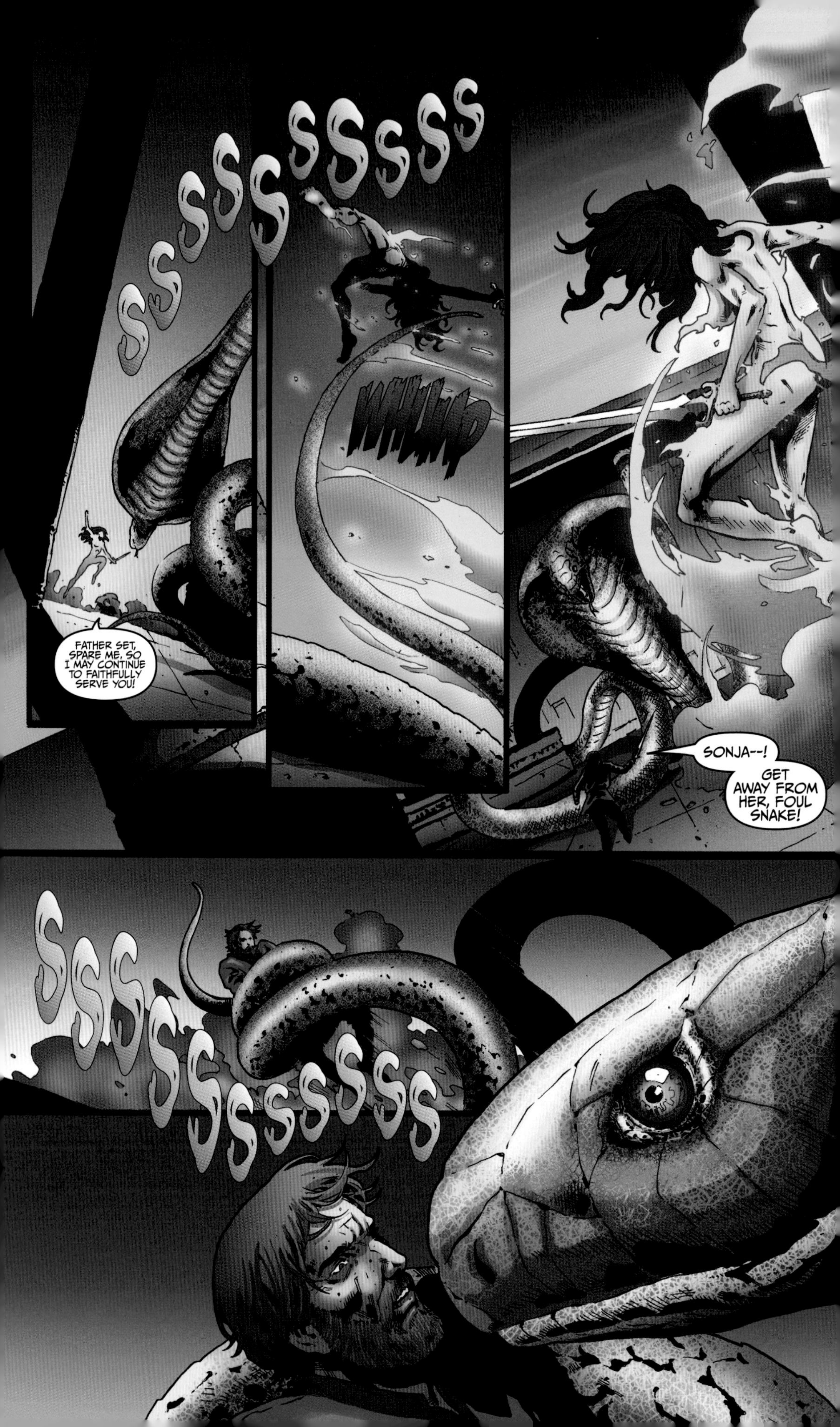
SSSSSSSSSSSS
WHUMP
FATHER SET, SPARE ME, SO I MAY CONTINUE TO FAITHFULLY SERVE YOU!
SONJA--!
GET AWAY FROM HER, FOUL SNAKE!
SSSSSSSSSSS

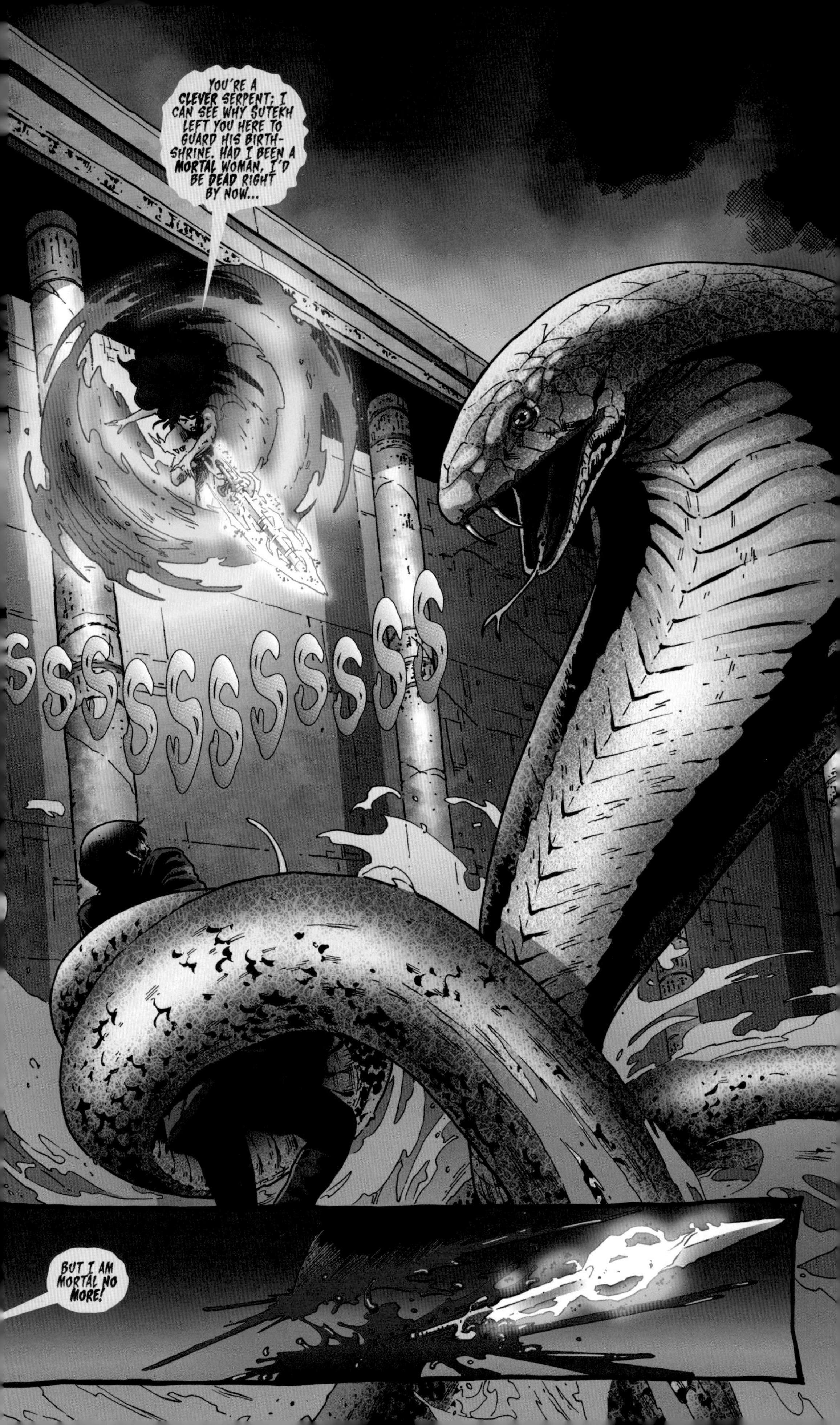
YOU'RE A CLEVER SERPENT; I CAN SEE WHY SUTEKH LEFT YOU HERE TO GUARD HIS BIRTH-SHRINE. HAD I BEEN A MORTAL WOMAN, I'D BE DEAD RIGHT BY NOW...
SSSSSSSSSSS
BUT I AM MORTAL NO MORE!

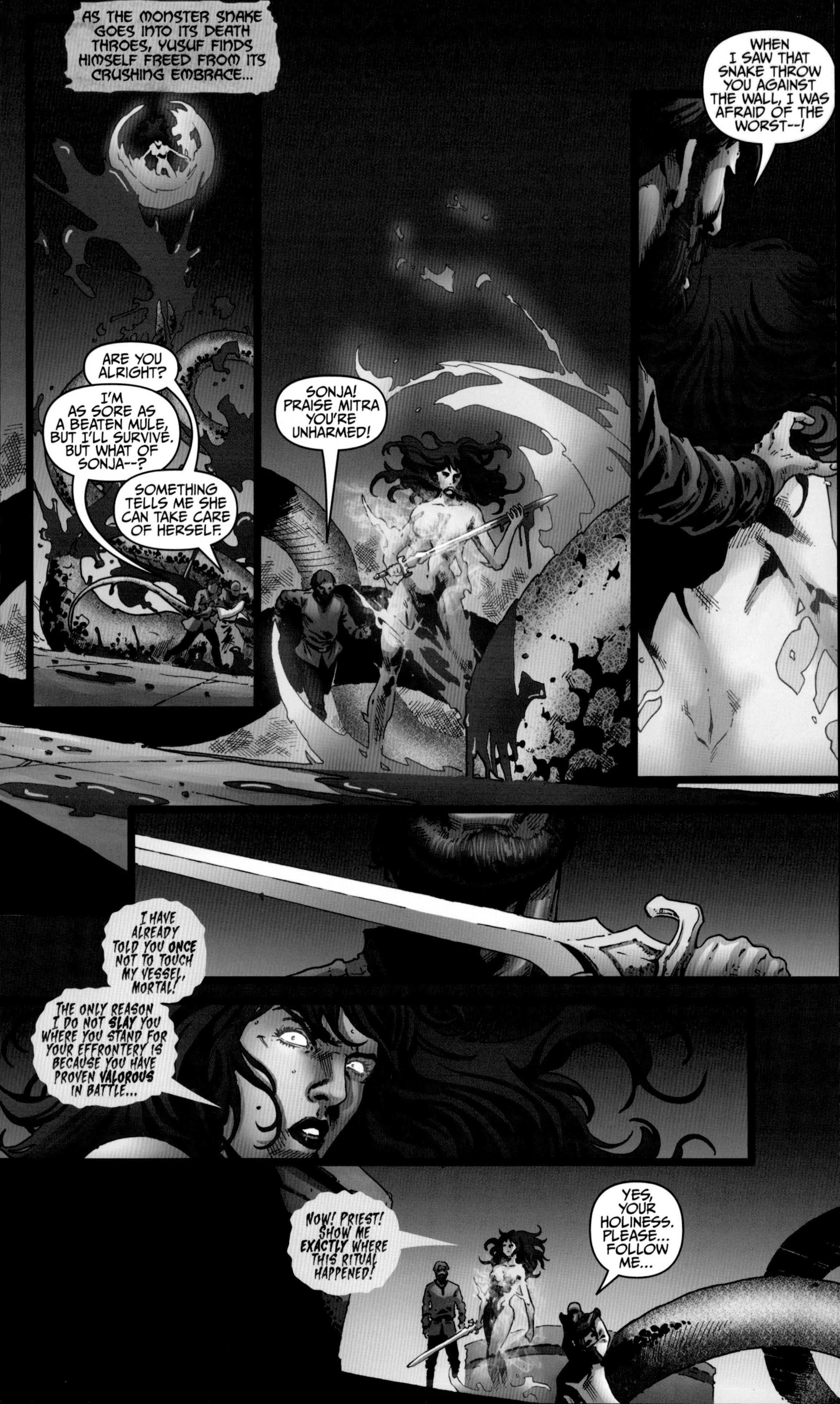
AS THE MONSTER SNAKE GOES INTO ITS DEATH THROES, YUSUF FINDS HIMSELF FREED FROM ITS CRUSHING EMBRACE...
ARE YOU ALRIGHT?
I'M AS SORE AS A BEATEN MULE, BUT I'LL SURVIVE. BUT WHAT OF SONJA--?
SOMETHING TELLS ME SHE CAN TAKE CARE OF HERSELF.
SONJA! PRAISE MITRA YOU'RE UNHARMED!
WHEN I SAW THAT SNAKE THROW YOU AGAINST THE WALL, I WAS AFRAID OF THE WORST--!
I HAVE ALREADY TOLD YOU ONCE NOT TO TOUCH MY VESSEL, MORTAL!
THE ONLY REASON I DO NOT SLAY YOU WHERE YOU STAND FOR YOUR EFFRONTERY IS BECAUSE YOU HAVE PROVEN VALOROUS IN BATTLE...
NOW! PRIEST! SHOW ME EXACTLY WHERE THIS RITUAL HAPPENED!
YES, YOUR HOLINESS. PLEASE... FOLLOW ME...

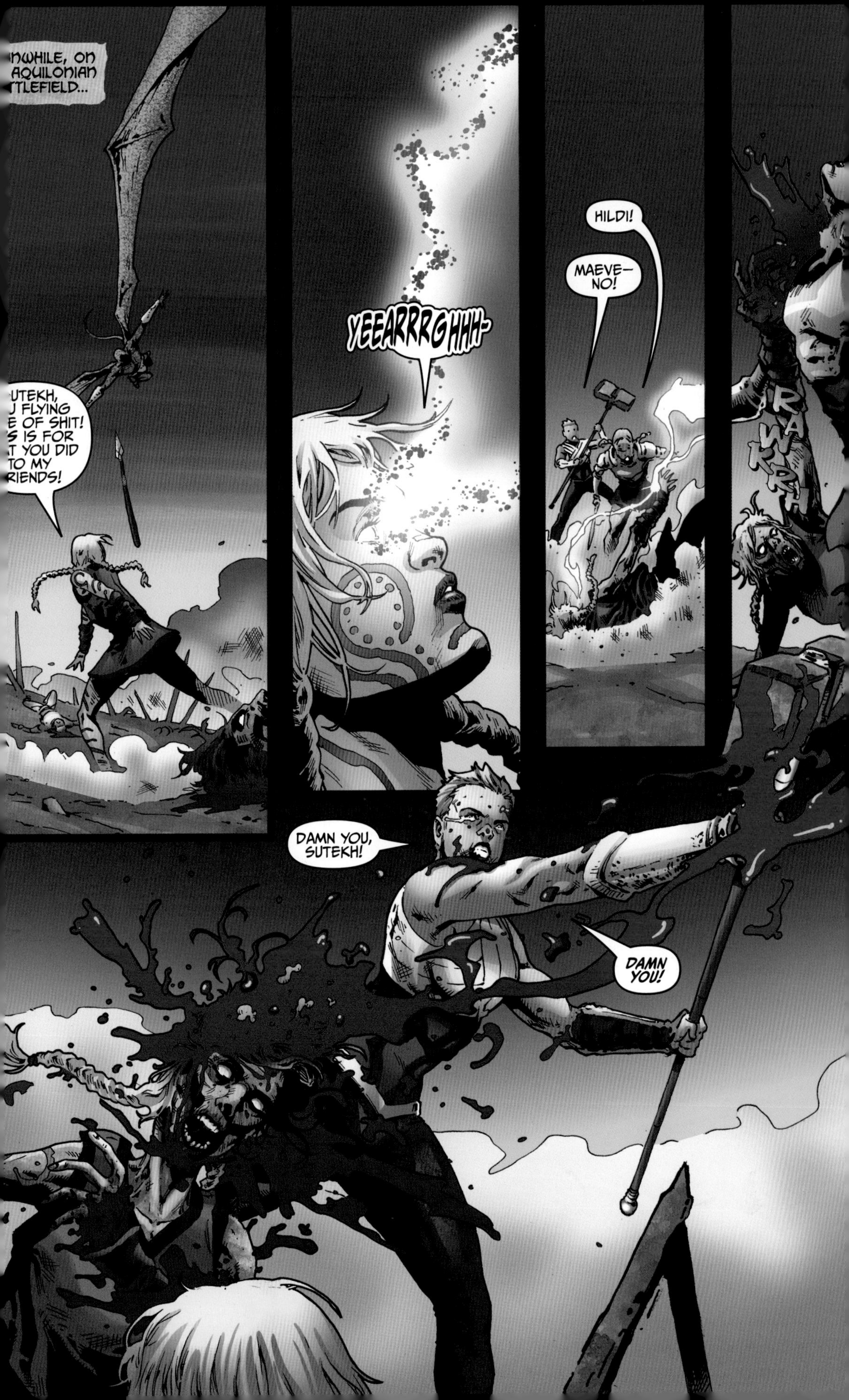

NWHILE, ON AQUILONIAN TTLEFIELD...
UTEKH, U FLYING E OF SHIT! S IS FOR T YOU DID TO MY RIENDS!
YEEARRRGHHH-
HILDI!
MAEVE-NO!
RAWKRH
DAMN YOU, SUTEKH!
DAMN YOU!

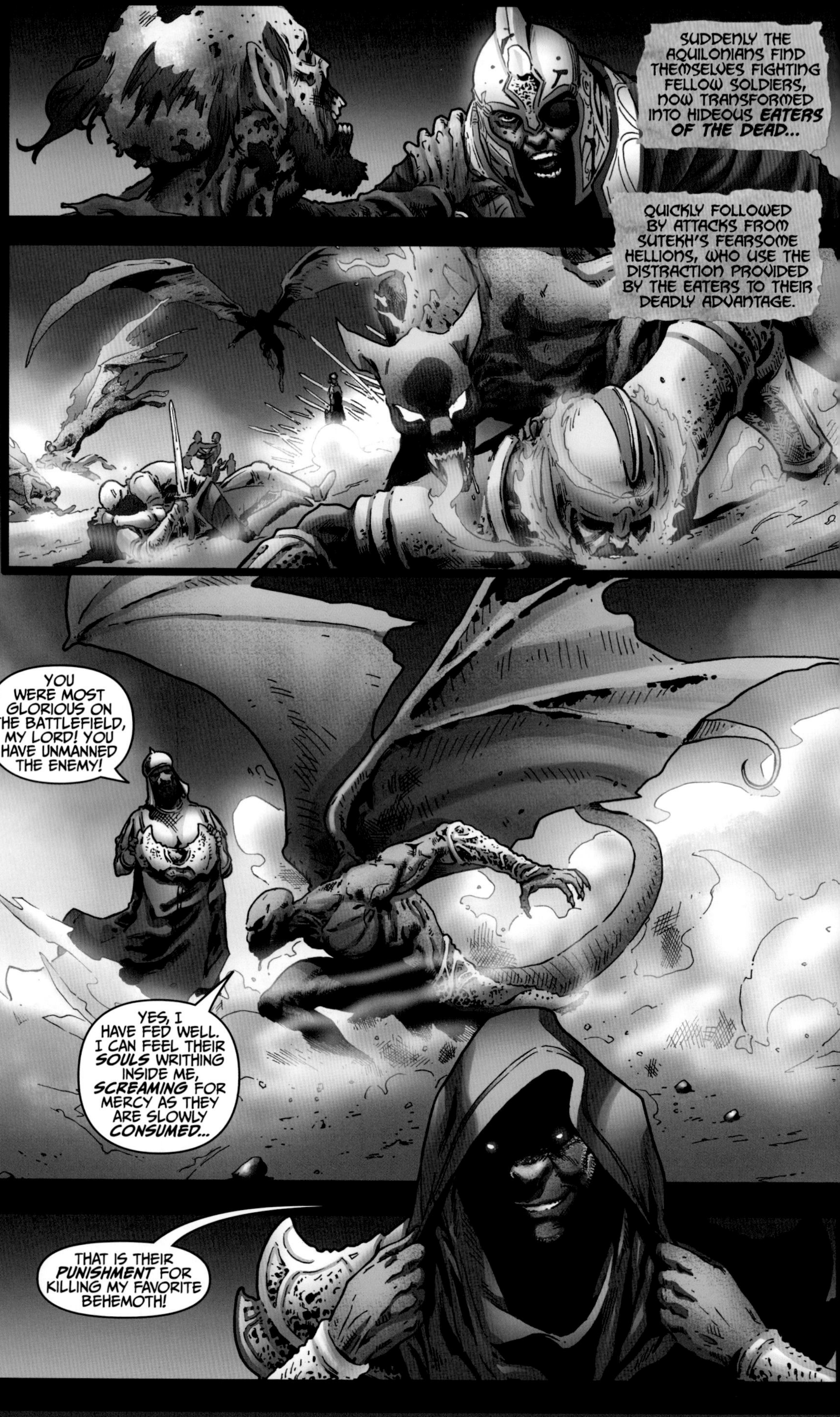
SUDDENLY THE AQUILONIANS FIND THEMSELVES FIGHTING FELLOW SOLDIERS, NOW TRANSFORMED INTO HIDEOUS EATERS OF THE DEAD...
QUICKLY FOLLOWED BY ATTACKS FROM SUTEKH'S FEARSOME HELLIONS, WHO USE THE DISTRACTION PROVIDED BY THE EATERS TO THEIR DEADLY ADVANTAGE.
YOU WERE MOST GLORIOUS ON THE BATTLEFIELD, MY LORD! YOU HAVE UNMANNED THE ENEMY!
YES, I HAVE FED WELL. I CAN FEEL THEIR SOULS WRITHING INSIDE ME, SCREAMING FOR MERCY AS THEY ARE SLOWLY CONSUMED...
THAT IS THEIR PUNISHMENT FOR KILLING MY FAVORITE BEHEMOTH!

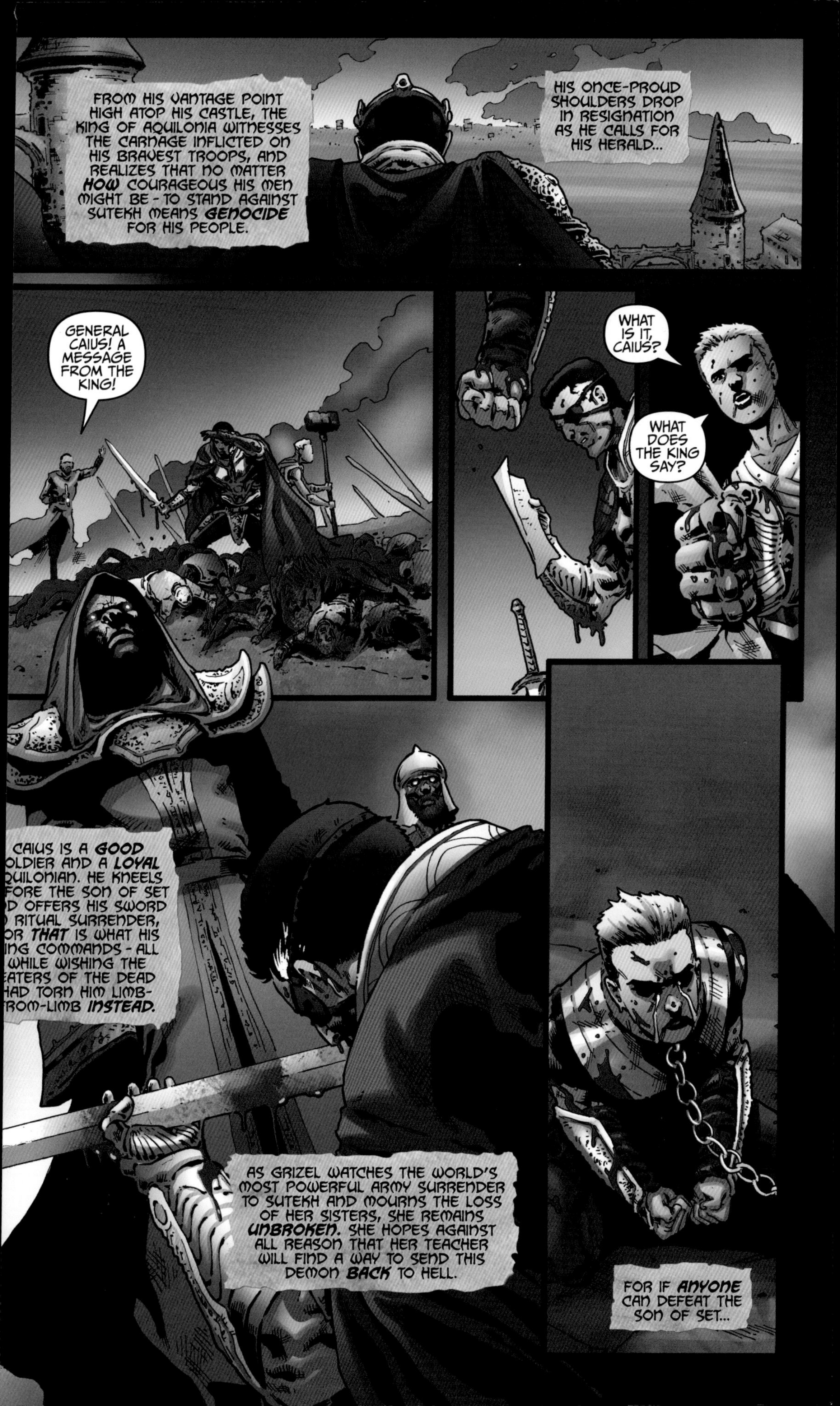

FROM HIS VANTAGE POINT HIGH ATOP HIS CASTLE, THE KING OF AQUILONIA WITNESSES THE CARNAGE INFLICTED ON HIS BRAVEST TROOPS, AND REALIZES THAT NO MATTER HOW COURAGEOUS HIS MEN MIGHT BE - TO STAND AGAINST SUTEKH MEANS GENOCIDE FOR HIS PEOPLE.
HIS ONCE-PROUD SHOULDERS DROP IN RESIGNATION AS HE CALLS FOR HIS HERALD...
GENERAL CAIUS! A MESSAGE FROM THE KING!
WHAT IS IT, CAIUS?
WHAT DOES THE KING SAY?
CAIUS IS A GOOD OLDIER AND A LOYAL QUILONIAN. HE KNEELS FORE THE SON OF SET D OFFERS HIS SWORD RITUAL SURRENDER, OR THAT IS WHAT HIS ING COMMANDS - ALL WHILE WISHING THE EATERS OF THE DEAD HAD TORN HIM LIMB-ROM-LIMB INSTEAD.
AS GRIZEL WATCHES THE WORLD'S MOST POWERFUL ARMY SURRENDER TO SUTEKH AND MOURNS THE LOSS OF HER SISTERS, SHE REMAINS UNBROKEN. SHE HOPES AGAINST ALL REASON THAT HER TEACHER WILL FIND A WAY TO SEND THIS DEMON BACK TO HELL.
FOR IF ANYONE CAN DEFEAT THE SON OF SET...

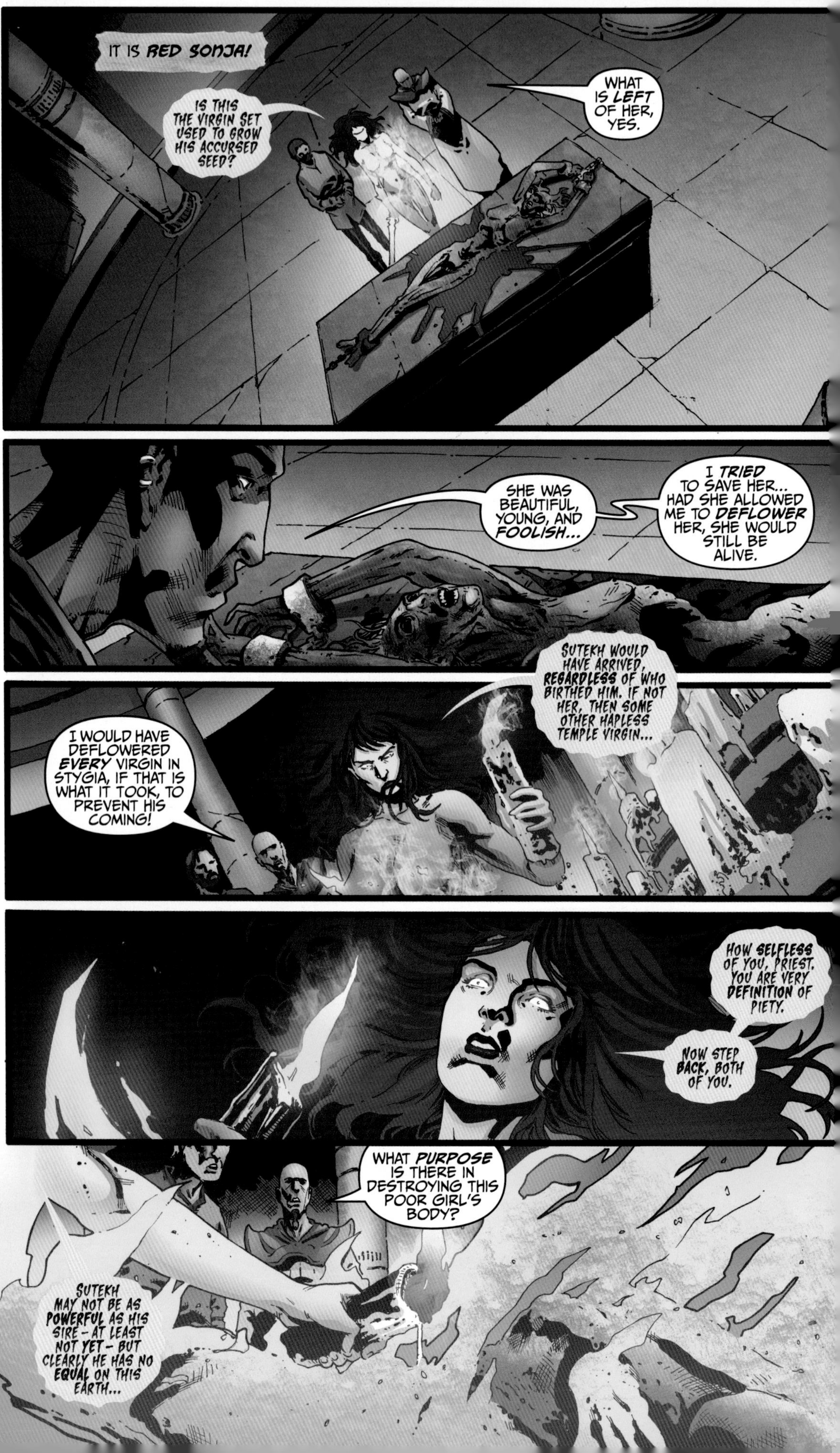
IT IS RED SONJA!
IS THIS THE VIRGIN SET USED TO GROW HIS ACCURSED SEED?
WHAT IS LEFT OF HER, YES.
SHE WAS BEAUTIFUL, YOUNG, AND FOOLISH...
I TRIED TO SAVE HER... HAD SHE ALLOWED ME TO DEFLOWER HER, SHE WOULD STILL BE ALIVE.
SUTEKH WOULD HAVE ARRIVED, REGARDLESS OF WHO BIRTHED HIM. IF NOT HER, THEN SOME OTHER HAPLESS TEMPLE VIRGIN...
I WOULD HAVE DEFLOWERED EVERY VIRGIN IN STYGIA, IF THAT IS WHAT IT TOOK, TO PREVENT HIS COMING!
HOW SELFLESS OF YOU, PRIEST. YOU ARE VERY DEFINITION OF PIETY.
NOW STEP BACK, BOTH OF YOU.
WHAT PURPOSE IS THERE IN DESTROYING THIS POOR GIRL'S BODY?
SUTEKH MAY NOT BE AS POWERFUL AS HIS SIRE - AT LEAST NOT YET - BUT CLEARLY HE HAS NO EQUAL ON THIS EARTH...

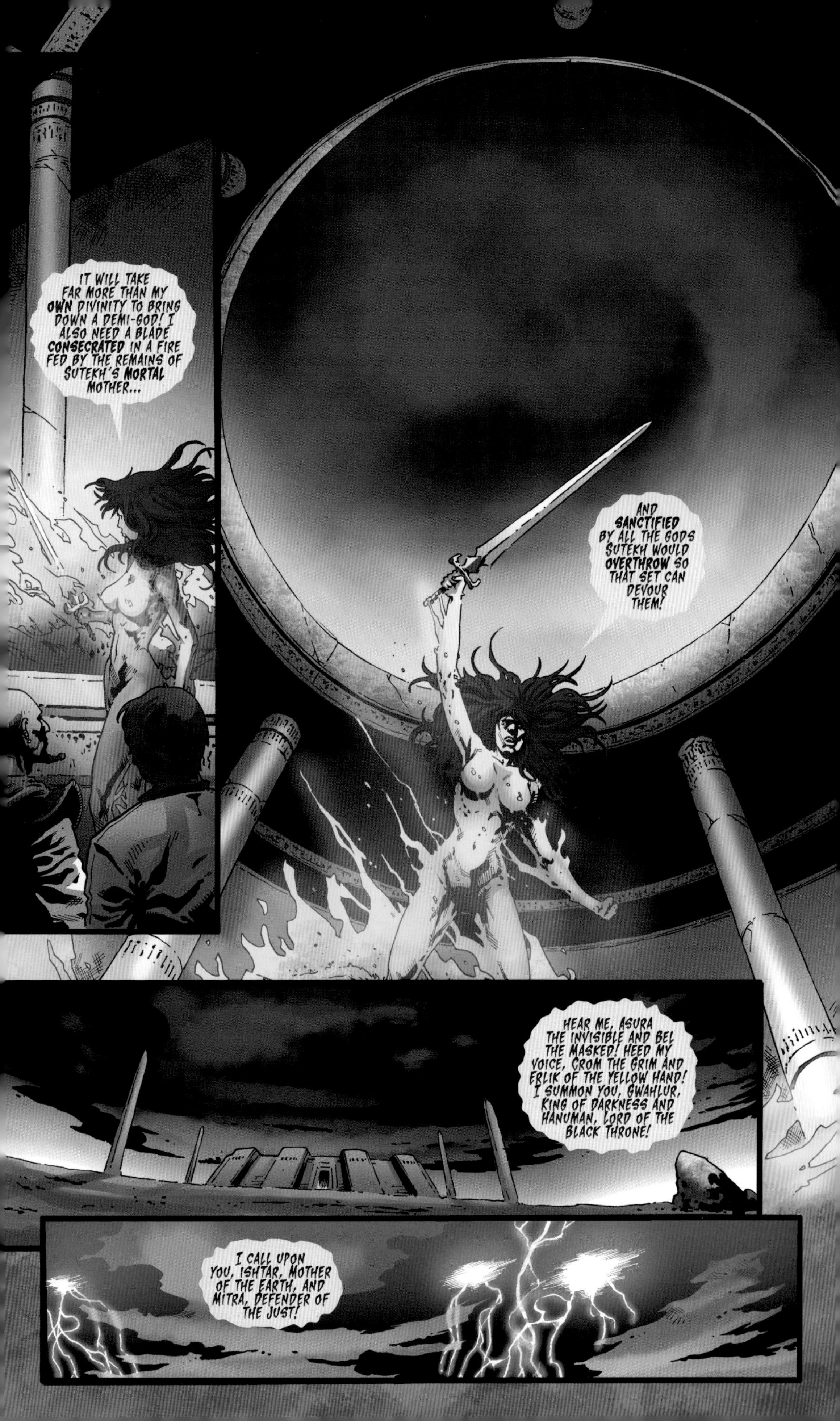
IT WILL TAKE FAR MORE THAN MY OWN DIVINITY TO BRING DOWN A DEMI-GOD! I ALSO NEED A BLADE CONSECRATED IN A FIRE FED BY THE REMAINS OF SUTEKH'S MORTAL MOTHER...
AND SANCTIFIED BY ALL THE GODS SUTEKH WOULD OVERTHROW SO THAT SET CAN DEVOUR THEM!
HEAR ME, ASURA THE INVISIBLE AND BEL THE MASKED! HEED MY VOICE, CROM THE GRIM AND ERLIK OF THE YELLOW HAND! I SUMMON YOU, GWAHLUR, KING OF DARKNESS AND HANUMAN, LORD OF THE BLACK THRONE!
I CALL UPON YOU, ISHTAR, MOTHER OF THE EARTH, AND MITRA, DEFENDER OF THE JUST!

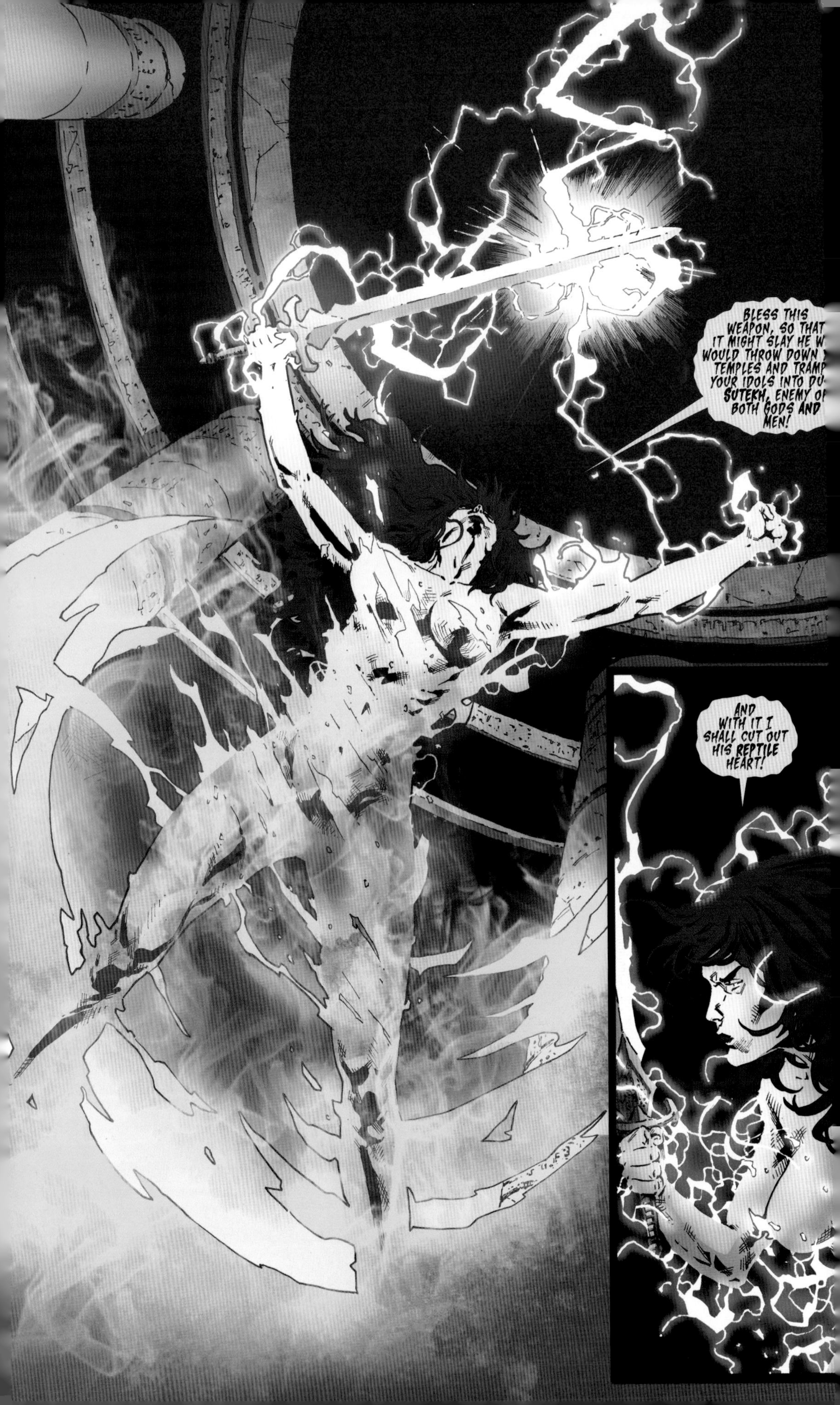
BLESS THIS WEAPON, SO THAT IT MIGHT SLAY HE W WOULD THROW DOWN Y TEMPLES AND TRAMP YOUR IDOLS INTO DU SUTEKH, ENEMY OF BOTH GODS AND MEN!
AND WITH IT I SHALL CUT OUT HIS REPTILE HEART!

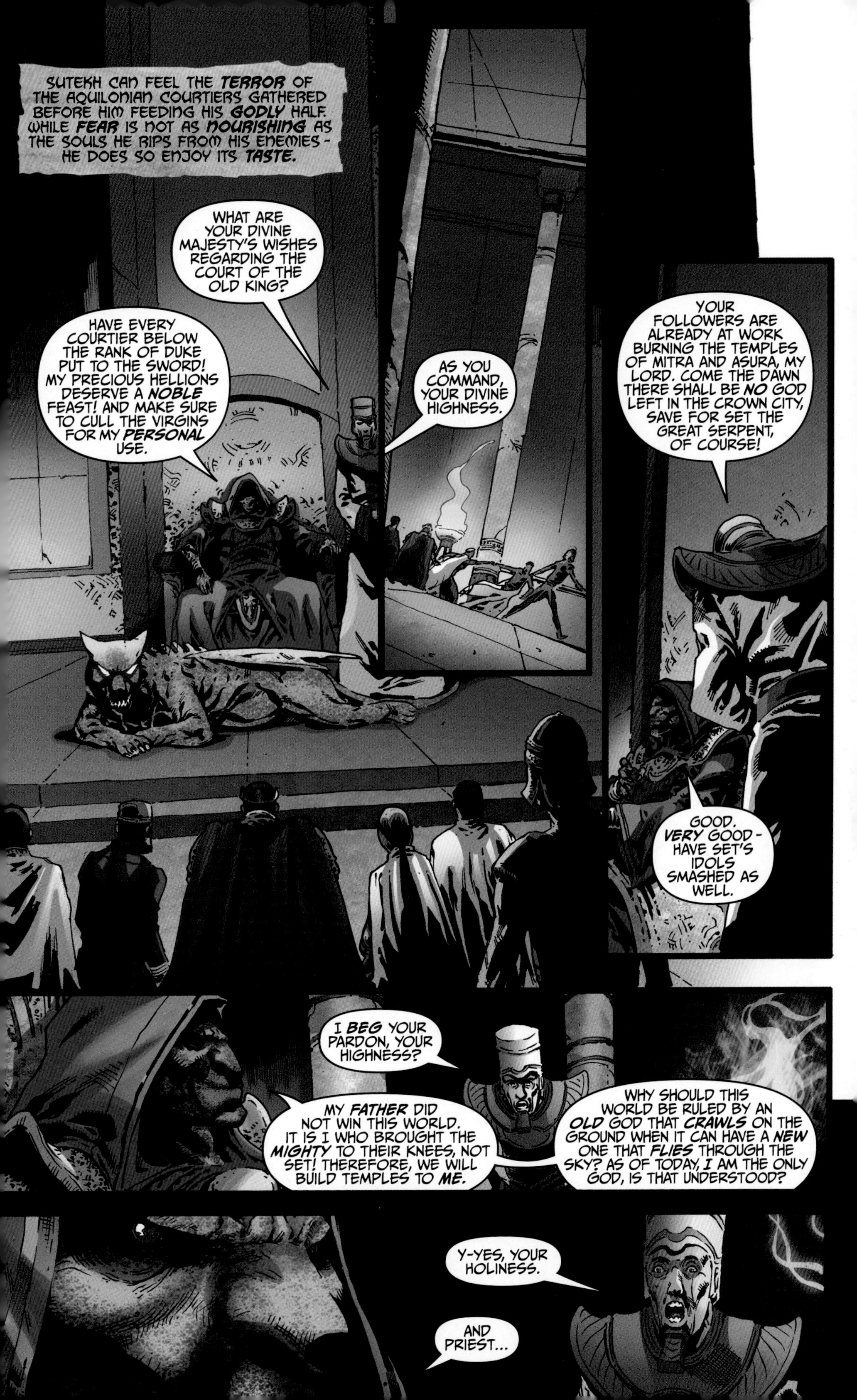

SUTEKH CAN FEEL THE TERROR OF THE AQUILONIAN COURTIERS GATHERED BEFORE HIM FEEDING HIS GODLY HALF. WHILE FEAR IS NOT AS NOURISHING AS THE SOULS HE RIPS FROM HIS ENEMIES - HE DOES SO ENJOY ITS TASTE.
WHAT ARE YOUR DIVINE MAJESTY'S WISHES REGARDING THE COURT OF THE OLD KING?
HAVE EVERY COURTIER BELOW THE RANK OF DUKE PUT TO THE SWORD! MY PRECIOUS HELLIONS DESERVE A NOBLE FEAST! AND MAKE SURE TO CULL THE VIRGINS FOR MY PERSONAL USE.
AS YOU COMMAND, YOUR DIVINE HIGHNESS.
YOUR FOLLOWERS ARE ALREADY AT WORK BURNING THE TEMPLES OF MITRA AND ASURA, MY LORD. COME THE DAWN THERE SHALL BE NO GOD LEFT IN THE CROWN CITY, SAVE FOR SET THE GREAT SERPENT, OF COURSE!
GOOD. VERY GOOD - HAVE SET'S IDOLS SMASHED AS WELL.
I BEG YOUR PARDON, YOUR HIGHNESS?
MY FATHER DID NOT WIN THIS WORLD. IT IS I WHO BROUGHT THE MIGHTY TO THEIR KNEES, NOT SET! THEREFORE, WE WILL BUILD TEMPLES TO ME.
WHY SHOULD THIS WORLD BE RULED BY AN OLD GOD THAT CRAWLS ON THE GROUND WHEN IT CAN HAVE A NEW ONE THAT FLIES THROUGH THE SKY? AS OF TODAY, I AM THE ONLY GOD, IS THAT UNDERSTOOD?
Y-YES, YOUR HOLINESS.
AND PRIEST...

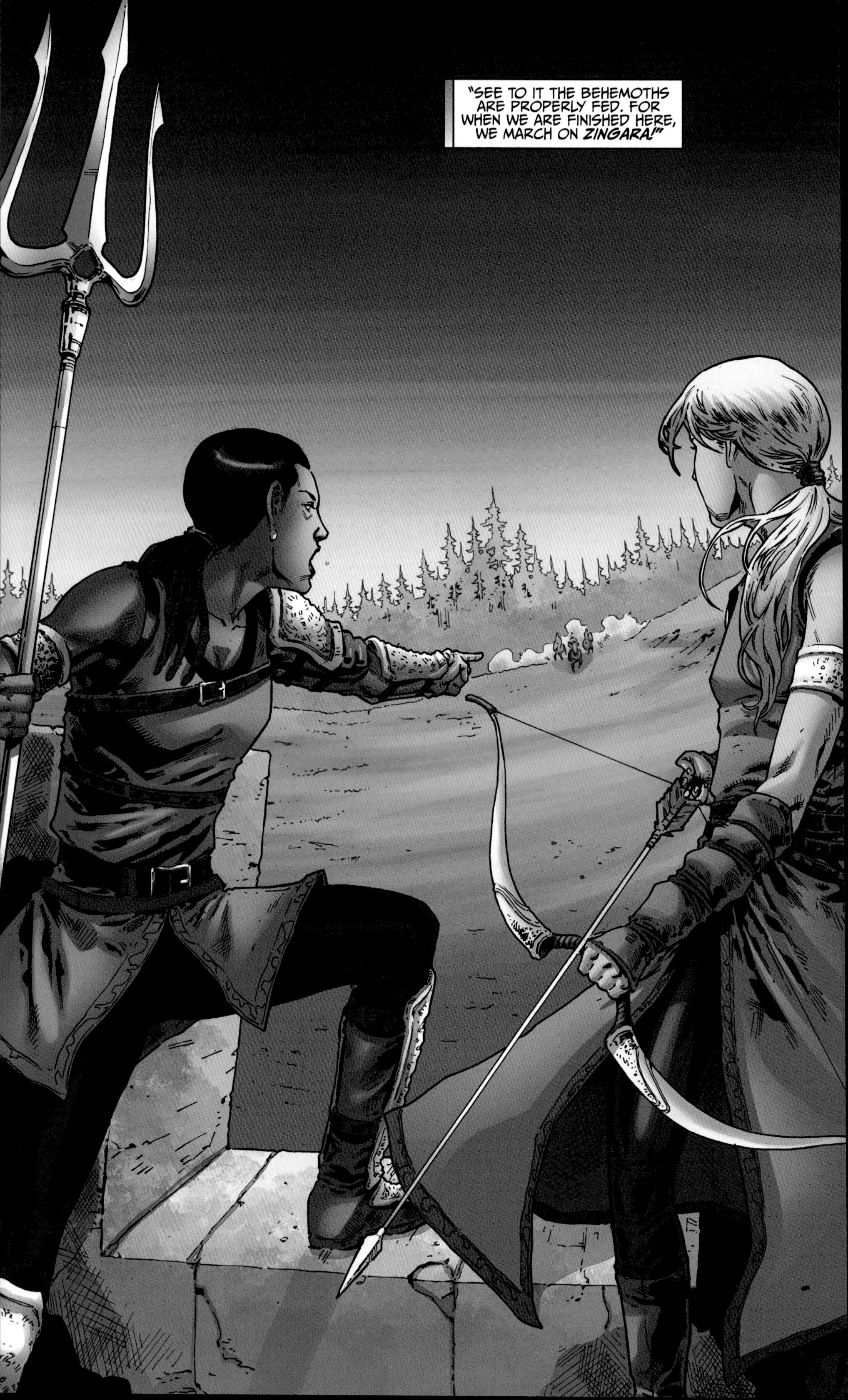
"SEE TO IT THE BEHEMOTHS ARE PROPERLY FED. FOR WHEN WE ARE FINISHED HERE, WE MARCH ON ZINGARA!"

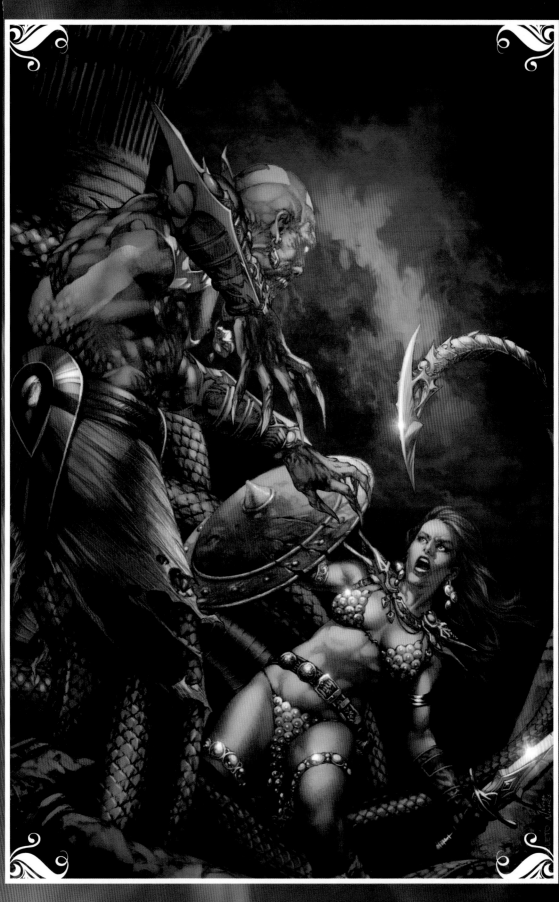

ISSUE FIVE
cover art by Jay Anacleto and Ivan Nunes

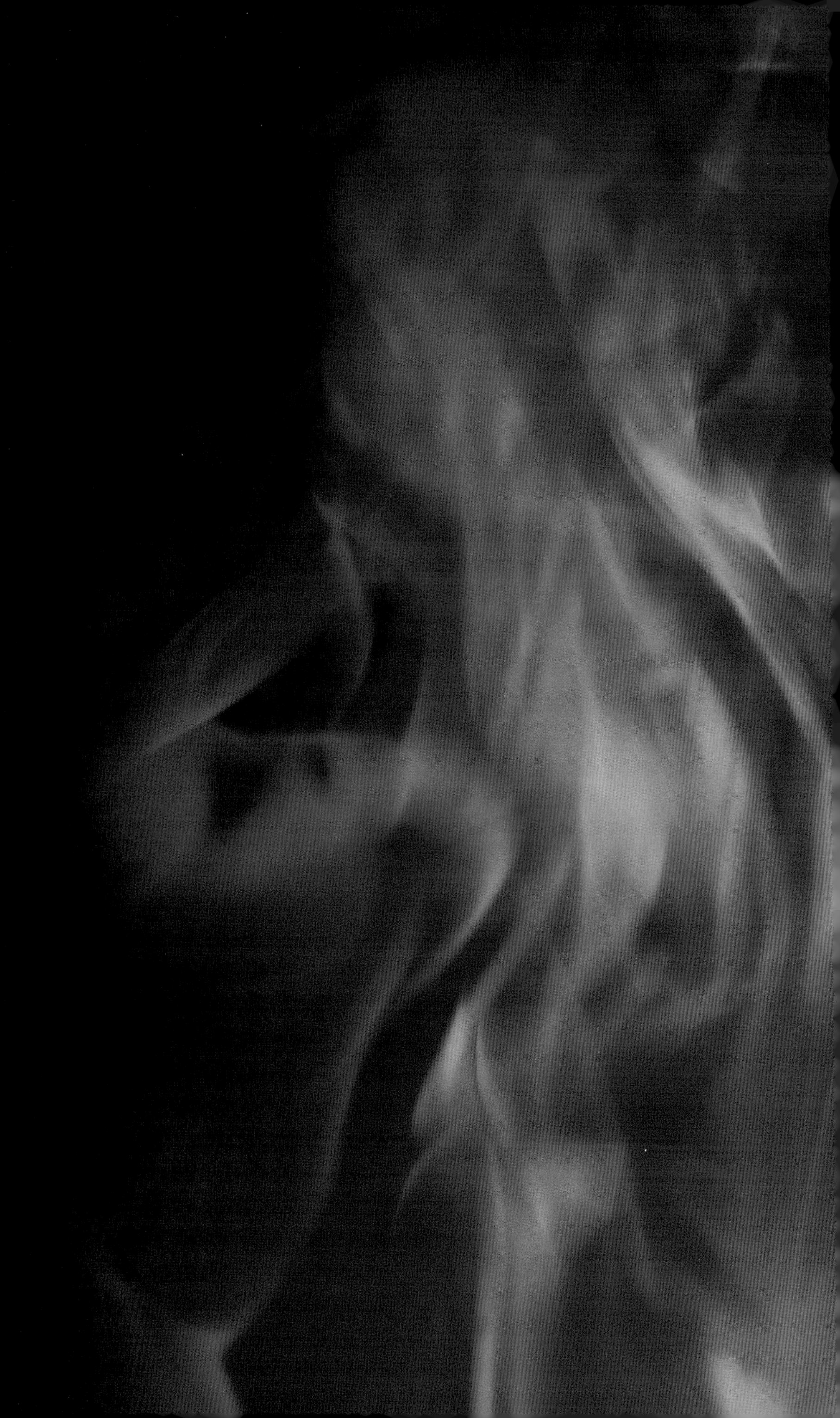

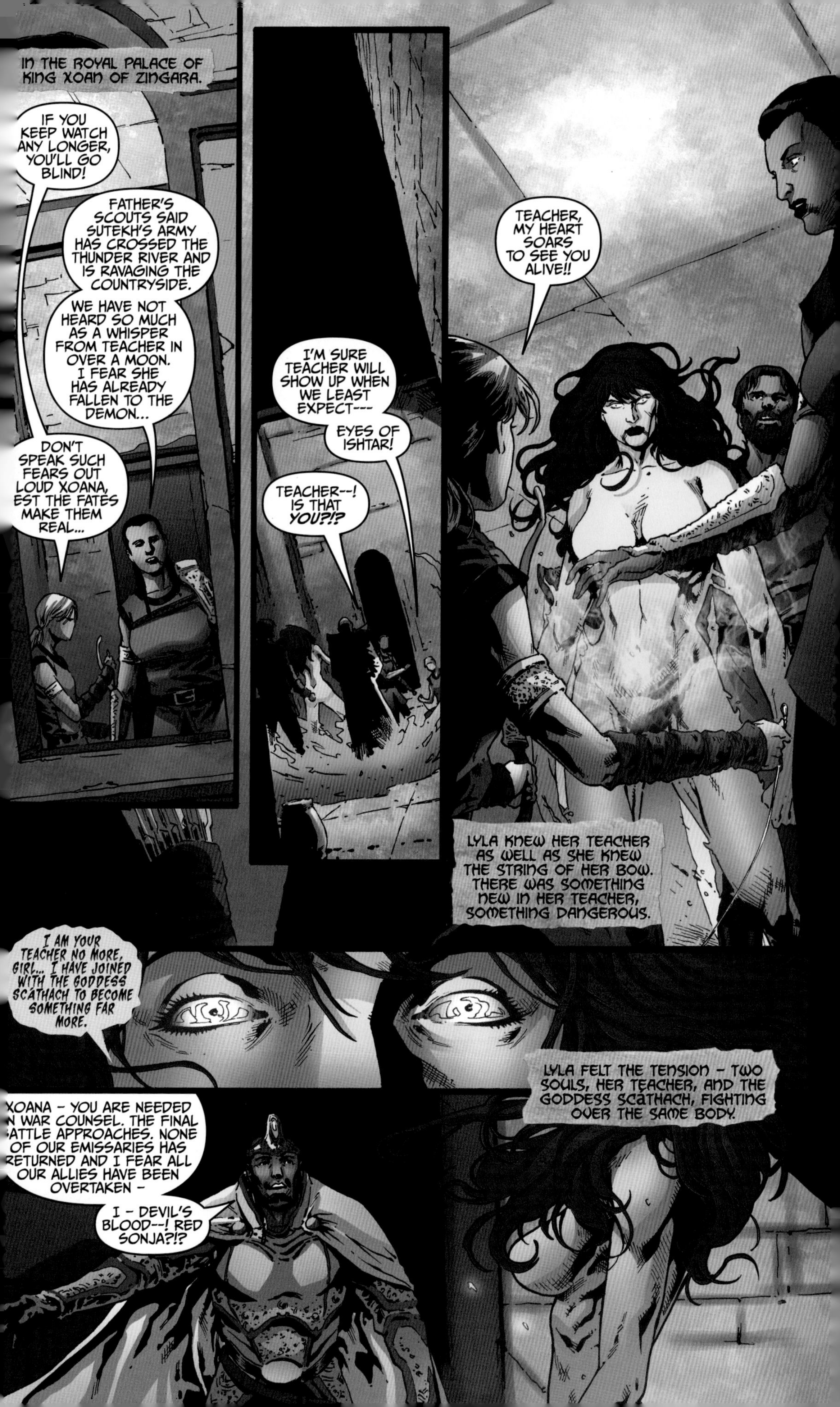

IN THE ROYAL PALACE OF KING XOAN OF ZINGARA.
IF YOU KEEP WATCH ANY LONGER, YOU'LL GO BLIND!
FATHER'S SCOUTS SAID SUTEKH'S ARMY HAS CROSSED THE THUNDER RIVER AND IS RAVAGING THE COUNTRYSIDE.
WE HAVE NOT HEARD SO MUCH AS A WHISPER FROM TEACHER IN OVER A MOON. I FEAR SHE HAS ALREADY FALLEN TO THE DEMON...
DON'T SPEAK SUCH FEARS OUT LOUD XOANA, EST THE FATES MAKE THEM REAL...
I'M SURE TEACHER WILL SHOW UP WHEN WE LEAST EXPECT---
EYES OF ISHTAR!
TEACHER--! IS THAT YOU?!?
TEACHER, MY HEART SOARS TO SEE YOU ALIVE!!
LYLA KNEW HER TEACHER AS WELL AS SHE KNEW THE STRING OF HER BOW. THERE WAS SOMETHING NEW IN HER TEACHER, SOMETHING DANGEROUS.
I AM YOUR TEACHER NO MORE, GIRL... I HAVE JOINED WITH THE GODDESS SCATHACH TO BECOME SOMETHING FAR MORE.
LYLA FELT THE TENSION - TWO SOULS, HER TEACHER, AND THE GODDESS SCATHACH, FIGHTING OVER THE SAME BODY.
XOANA - YOU ARE NEEDED N WAR COUNSEL. THE FINAL ATTLE APPROACHES. NONE OF OUR EMISSARIES HAS RETURNED AND I FEAR ALL OUR ALLIES HAVE BEEN OVERTAKEN -
I - DEVIL'S BLOOD--! RED SONJA?!?

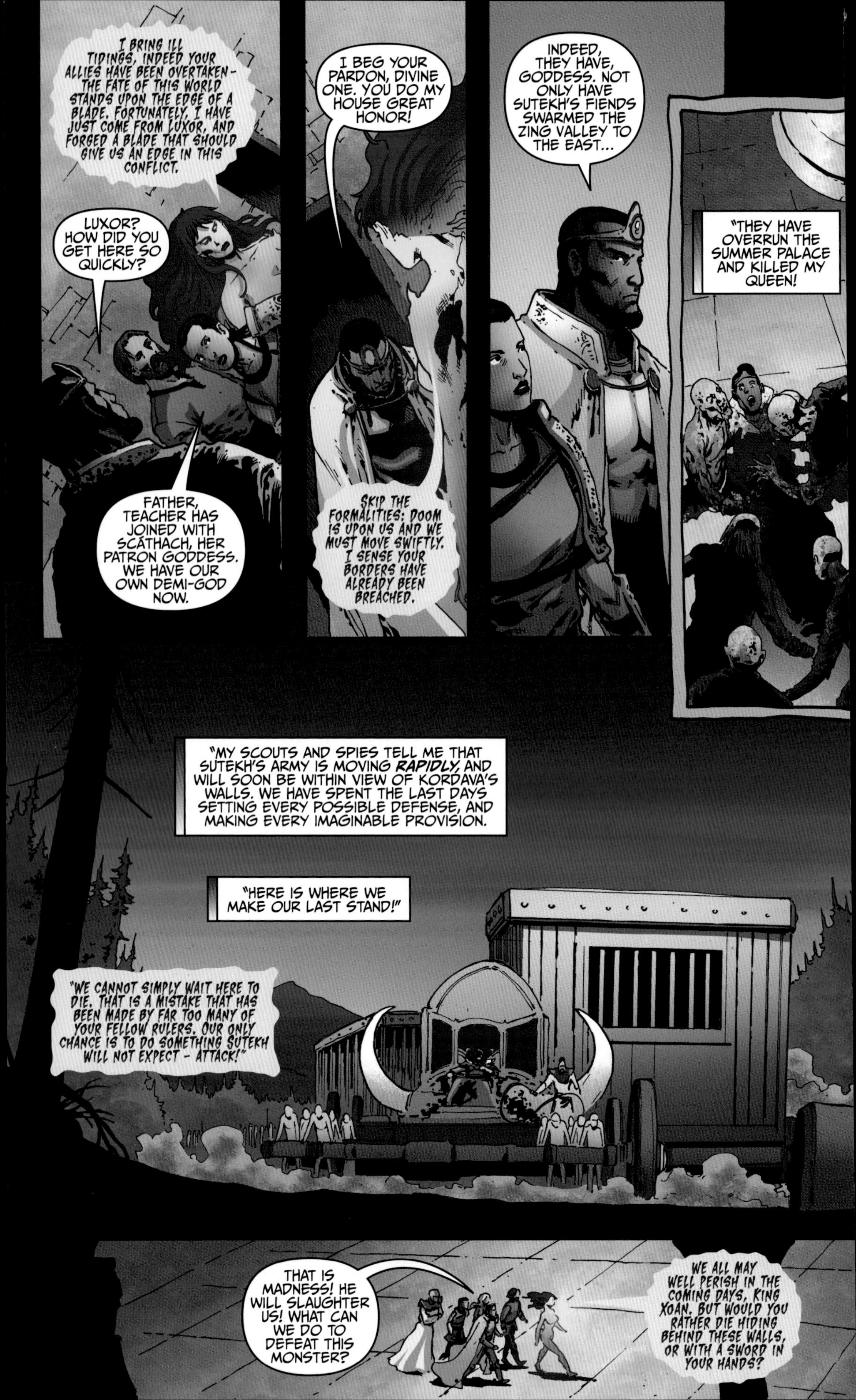

I BRING ILL TIDINGS, INDEED YOUR ALLIES HAVE BEEN OVERTAKEN - THE FATE OF THIS WORLD STANDS UPON THE EDGE OF A BLADE. FORTUNATELY, I HAVE JUST COME FROM LUXOR, AND FORGED A BLADE THAT SHOULD GIVE US AN EDGE IN THIS CONFLICT.
LUXOR? HOW DID YOU GET HERE SO QUICKLY?
FATHER, TEACHER HAS JOINED WITH SCÁTHACH, HER PATRON GODDESS. WE HAVE OUR OWN DEMI-GOD NOW.
I BEG YOUR PARDON, DIVINE ONE. YOU DO MY HOUSE GREAT HONOR!
SKIP THE FORMALITIES: DOOM IS UPON US AND WE MUST MOVE SWIFTLY. I SENSE YOUR BORDERS HAVE ALREADY BEEN BREACHED.
INDEED, THEY HAVE, GODDESS. NOT ONLY HAVE SUTEKH'S FIENDS SWARMED THE ZING VALLEY TO THE EAST...
"THEY HAVE OVERRUN THE SUMMER PALACE AND KILLED MY QUEEN!
"MY SCOUTS AND SPIES TELL ME THAT SUTEKH'S ARMY IS MOVING *RAPIDLY,* AND WILL SOON BE WITHIN VIEW OF KORDAVA'S WALLS. WE HAVE SPENT THE LAST DAYS SETTING EVERY POSSIBLE DEFENSE, AND MAKING EVERY IMAGINABLE PROVISION.
"HERE IS WHERE WE MAKE OUR LAST STAND!"
"WE CANNOT SIMPLY WAIT HERE TO DIE. THAT IS A MISTAKE THAT HAS BEEN MADE BY FAR TOO MANY OF YOUR FELLOW RULERS. OUR ONLY CHANCE IS TO DO SOMETHING SUTEKH WILL NOT EXPECT - ATTACK!"
THAT IS MADNESS! HE WILL SLAUGHTER US! WHAT CAN WE DO TO DEFEAT THIS MONSTER?
WE ALL MAY WELL PERISH IN THE COMING DAYS, KING XOAN. BUT WOULD YOU RATHER DIE HIDING BEHIND THESE WALLS, OR WITH A SWORD IN YOUR HANDS?

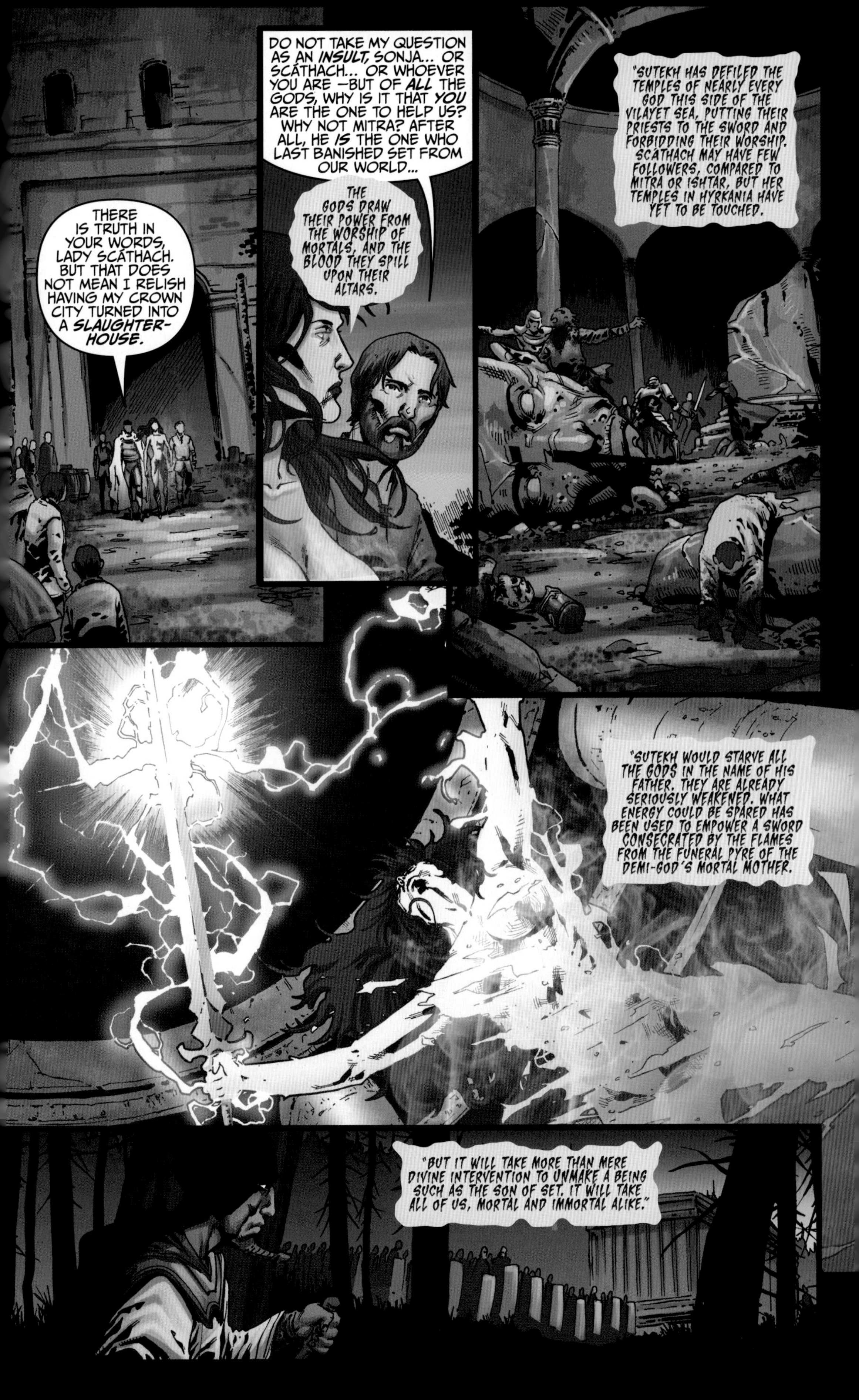
DO NOT TAKE MY QUESTION AS AN *INSULT,* SONJA... OR SCÁTHACH... OR WHOEVER YOU ARE —BUT OF *ALL* THE GODS, WHY IS IT THAT *YOU* ARE THE ONE TO HELP US? WHY NOT MITRA? AFTER ALL, HE *IS* THE ONE WHO LAST BANISHED SET FROM OUR WORLD...
THE GODS DRAW THEIR POWER FROM THE WORSHIP OF MORTALS, AND THE BLOOD THEY SPILL UPON THEIR ALTARS.
THERE IS TRUTH IN YOUR WORDS, LADY SCÁTHACH. BUT THAT DOES NOT MEAN I RELISH HAVING MY CROWN CITY TURNED INTO A *SLAUGHTER-HOUSE.*
"SUTEKH HAS DEFILED THE TEMPLES OF NEARLY EVERY GOD THIS SIDE OF THE VILAYET SEA, PUTTING THEIR PRIESTS TO THE SWORD AND FORBIDDING THEIR WORSHIP. SCÁTHACH MAY HAVE FEW FOLLOWERS, COMPARED TO MITRA OR ISHTAR, BUT HER TEMPLES IN HYRKANIA HAVE YET TO BE TOUCHED.
"SUTEKH WOULD STARVE ALL THE GODS IN THE NAME OF HIS FATHER. THEY ARE ALREADY SERIOUSLY WEAKENED. WHAT ENERGY COULD BE SPARED HAS BEEN USED TO EMPOWER A SWORD CONSECRATED BY THE FLAMES FROM THE FUNERAL PYRE OF THE DEMI-GOD'S MORTAL MOTHER.
"BUT IT WILL TAKE MORE THAN MERE DIVINE INTERVENTION TO UNMAKE A BEING SUCH AS THE SON OF SET. IT WILL TAKE ALL OF US, MORTAL AND IMMORTAL ALIKE."

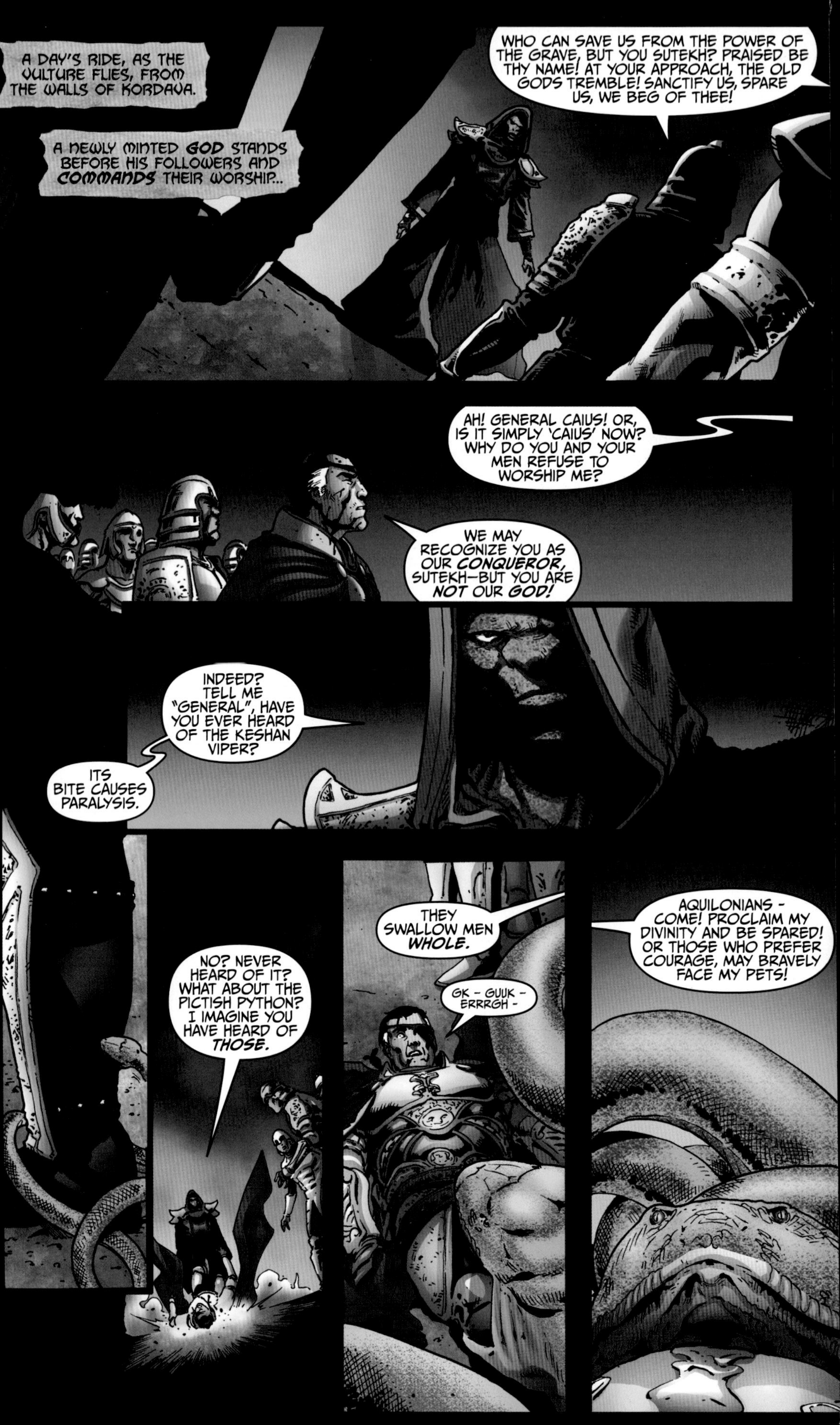
A DAY'S RIDE, AS THE VULTURE FLIES, FROM THE WALLS OF KORDAVA.
A NEWLY MINTED GOD STANDS BEFORE HIS FOLLOWERS AND COMMANDS THEIR WORSHIP...
WHO CAN SAVE US FROM THE POWER OF THE GRAVE, BUT YOU SUTEKH? PRAISED BE THY NAME! AT YOUR APPROACH, THE OLD GODS TREMBLE! SANCTIFY US, SPARE US, WE BEG OF THEE!
AH! GENERAL CAIUS! OR, IS IT SIMPLY 'CAIUS' NOW? WHY DO YOU AND YOUR MEN REFUSE TO WORSHIP ME?
WE MAY RECOGNIZE YOU AS OUR CONQUEROR, SUTEKH—BUT YOU ARE NOT OUR GOD!
INDEED? TELL ME "GENERAL", HAVE YOU EVER HEARD OF THE KESHAN VIPER?
ITS BITE CAUSES PARALYSIS.
NO? NEVER HEARD OF IT? WHAT ABOUT THE PICTISH PYTHON? I IMAGINE YOU HAVE HEARD OF THOSE.
THEY SWALLOW MEN WHOLE.
GK - GUUK - ERRRGH -
AQUILONIANS - COME! PROCLAIM MY DIVINITY AND BE SPARED! OR THOSE WHO PREFER COURAGE, MAY BRAVELY FACE MY PETS!

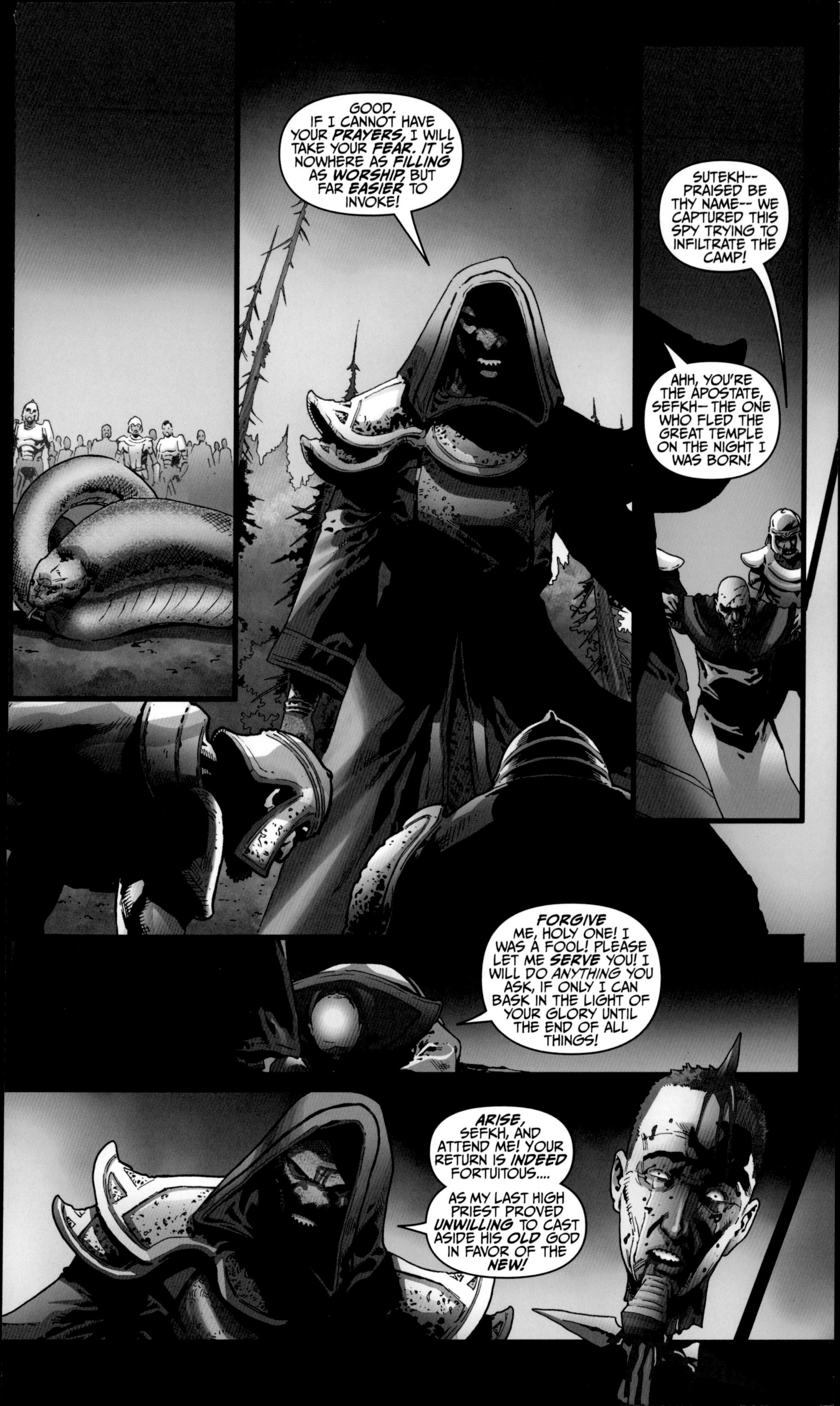
GOOD. IF I CANNOT HAVE YOUR PRAYERS, I WILL TAKE YOUR FEAR. IT IS NOWHERE AS FILLING AS WORSHIP, BUT FAR EASIER TO INVOKE!
SUTEKH-- PRAISED BE THY NAME-- WE CAPTURED THIS SPY TRYING TO INFILTRATE THE CAMP!
AHH, YOU'RE THE APOSTATE, SEFKH-- THE ONE WHO FLED THE GREAT TEMPLE ON THE NIGHT I WAS BORN!
FORGIVE ME, HOLY ONE! I WAS A FOOL! PLEASE LET ME SERVE YOU! I WILL DO ANYTHING YOU ASK, IF ONLY I CAN BASK IN THE LIGHT OF YOUR GLORY UNTIL THE END OF ALL THINGS!
ARISE, SEFKH, AND ATTEND ME! YOUR RETURN IS INDEED FORTUITOUS....
AS MY LAST HIGH PRIEST PROVED UNWILLING TO CAST ASIDE HIS OLD GOD IN FAVOR OF THE NEW!

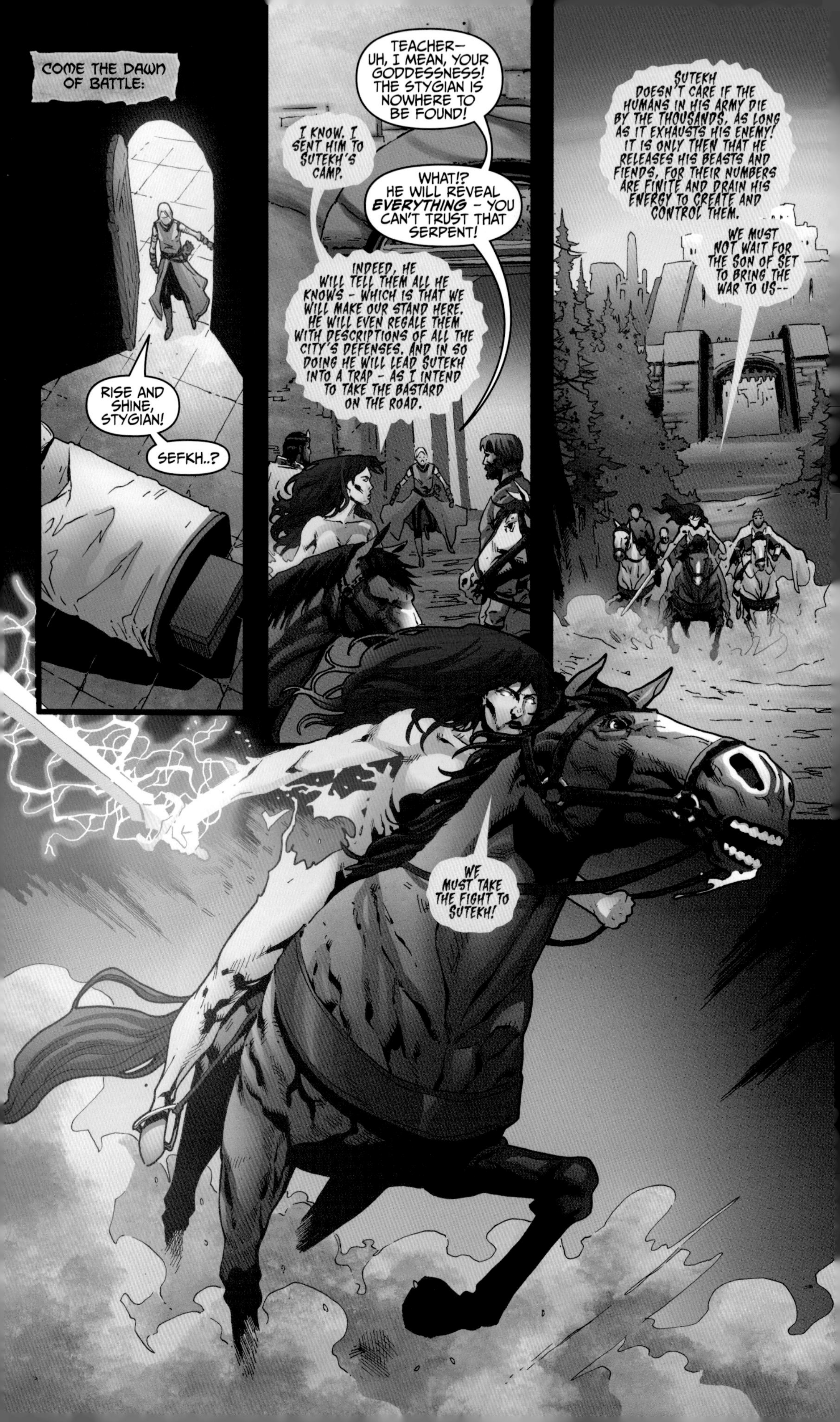
COME THE DAWN OF BATTLE:
RISE AND SHINE, STYGIAN!
SEFKH..?
TEACHER— UH, I MEAN, YOUR GODDESSNESS! THE STYGIAN IS NOWHERE TO BE FOUND!
I KNOW. I SENT HIM TO SUTEKH'S CAMP.
WHAT!? HE WILL REVEAL EVERYTHING - YOU CAN'T TRUST THAT SERPENT!
INDEED, HE WILL TELL THEM ALL HE KNOWS - WHICH IS THAT WE WILL MAKE OUR STAND HERE. HE WILL EVEN REGALE THEM WITH DESCRIPTIONS OF ALL THE CITY'S DEFENSES. AND IN SO DOING HE WILL LEAD SUTEKH INTO A TRAP - AS I INTEND TO TAKE THE BASTARD ON THE ROAD.
SUTEKH DOESN'T CARE IF THE HUMANS IN HIS ARMY DIE BY THE THOUSANDS, AS LONG AS IT EXHAUSTS HIS ENEMY! IT IS ONLY THEN THAT HE RELEASES HIS BEASTS AND FIENDS, FOR THEIR NUMBERS ARE FINITE AND DRAIN HIS ENERGY TO CREATE AND CONTROL THEM.
WE MUST NOT WAIT FOR THE SON OF SET TO BRING THE WAR TO US--
WE MUST TAKE THE FIGHT TO SUTEKH!

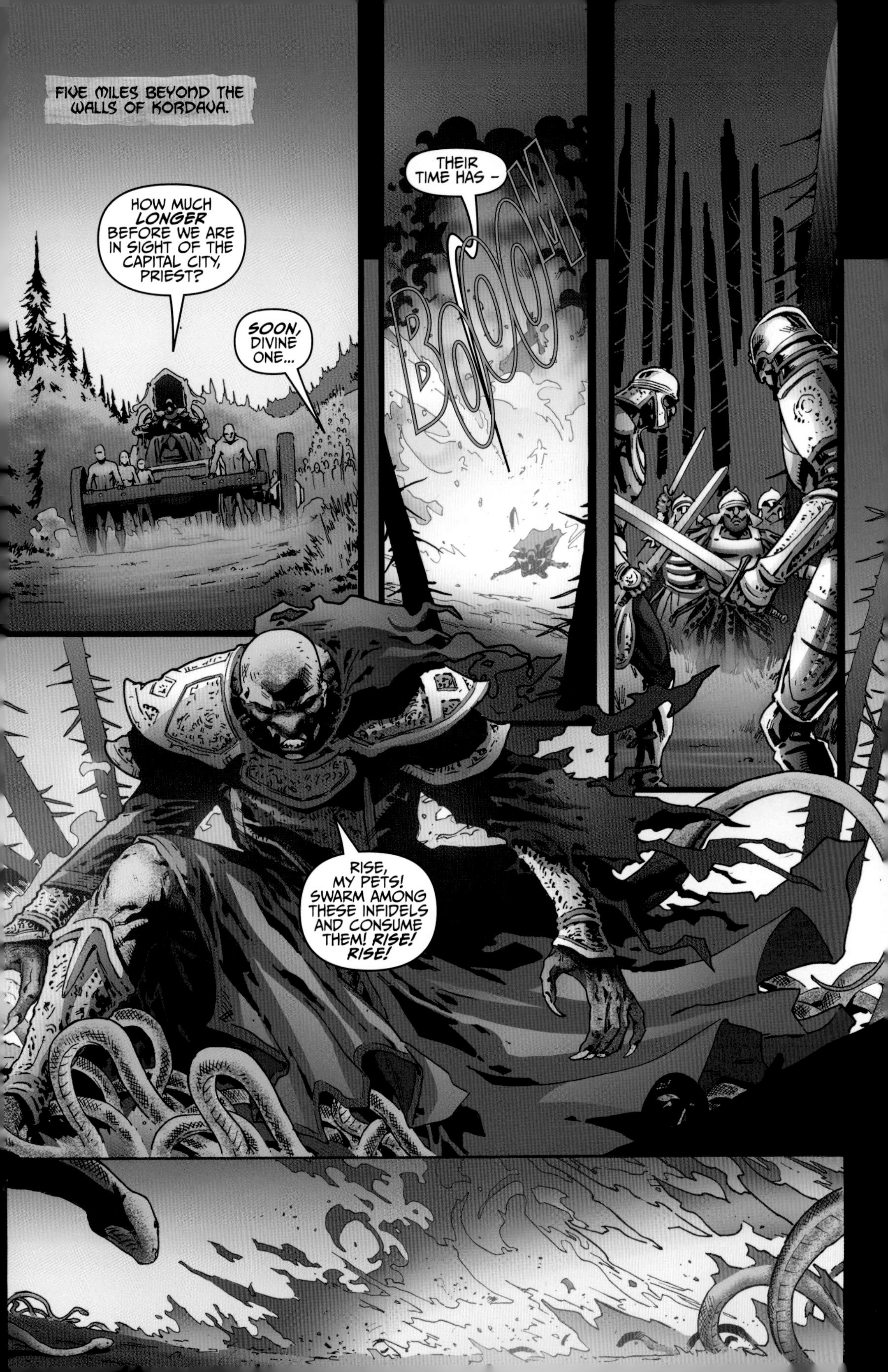
FIVE MILES BEYOND THE WALLS OF KORDAVA.
HOW MUCH LONGER BEFORE WE ARE IN SIGHT OF THE CAPITAL CITY, PRIEST?
SOON, DIVINE ONE...
THEIR TIME HAS –
BOOOOM!
RISE, MY PETS! SWARM AMONG THESE INFIDELS AND CONSUME THEM! RISE! RISE!

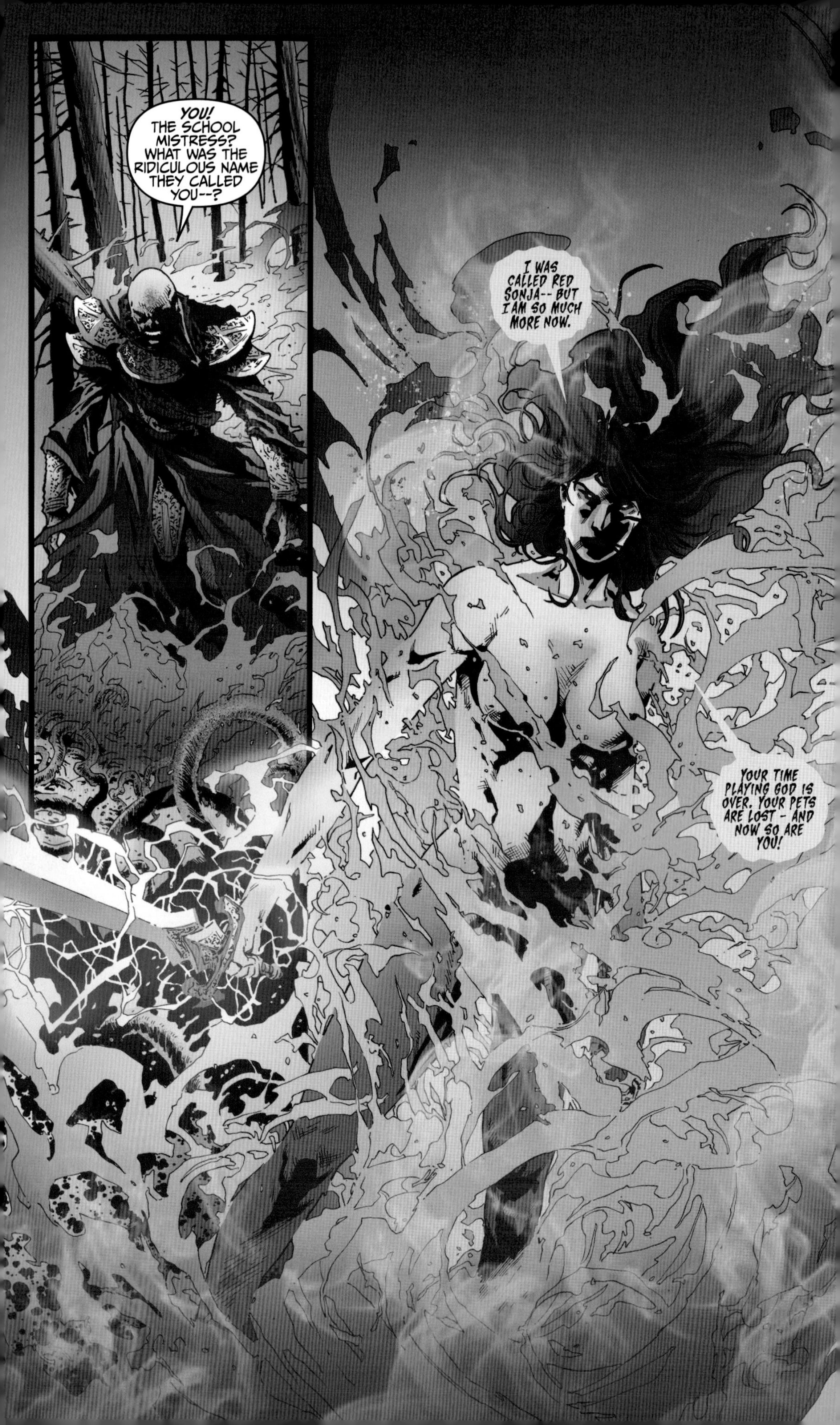
YOU! THE SCHOOL MISTRESS? WHAT WAS THE RIDICULOUS NAME THEY CALLED YOU--?
I WAS CALLED RED SONJA-- BUT I AM SO MUCH MORE NOW.
YOUR TIME PLAYING GOD IS OVER. YOUR PETS ARE LOST - AND NOW SO ARE YOU!

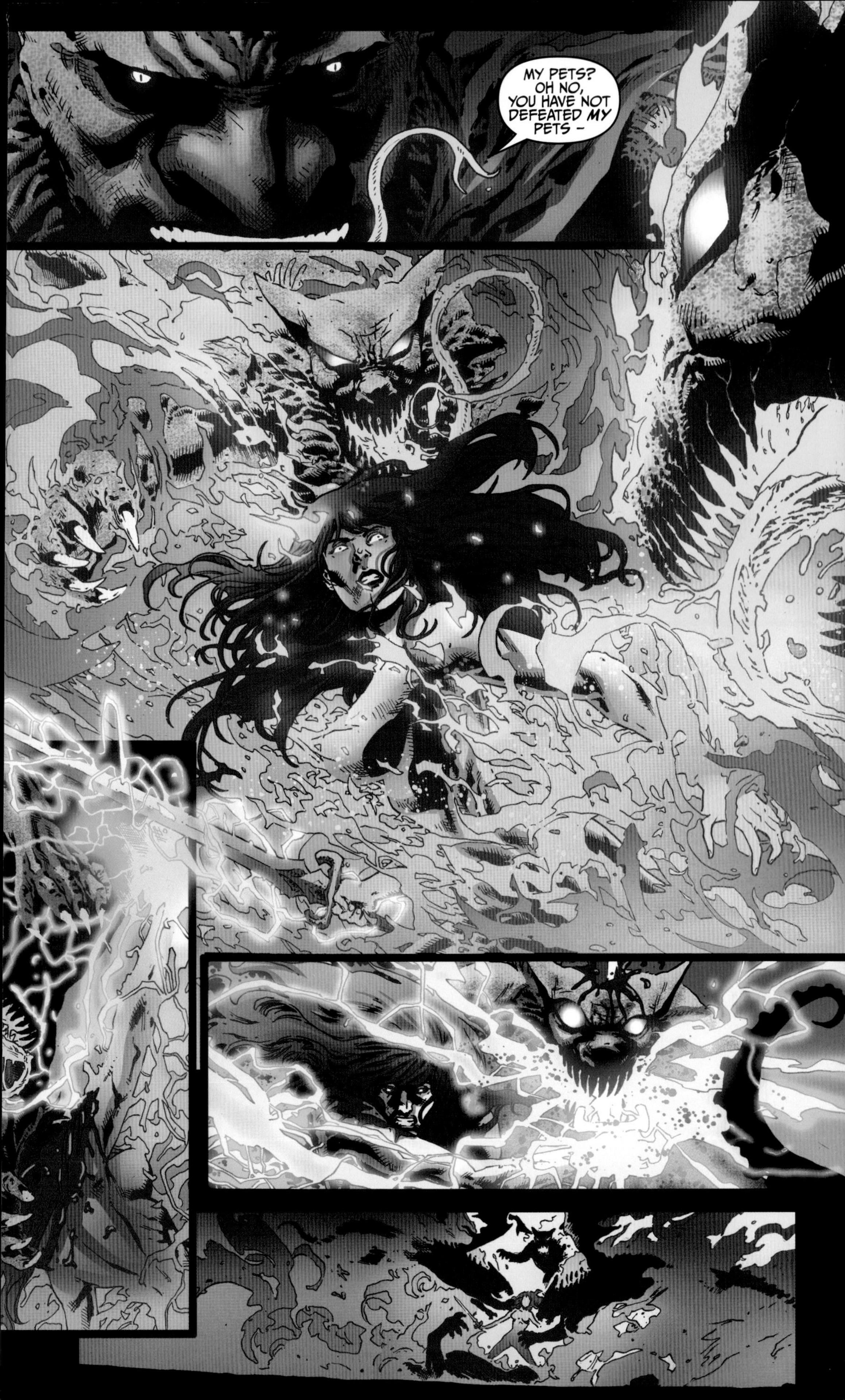
MY PETS? OH NO, YOU HAVE NOT DEFEATED MY PETS –

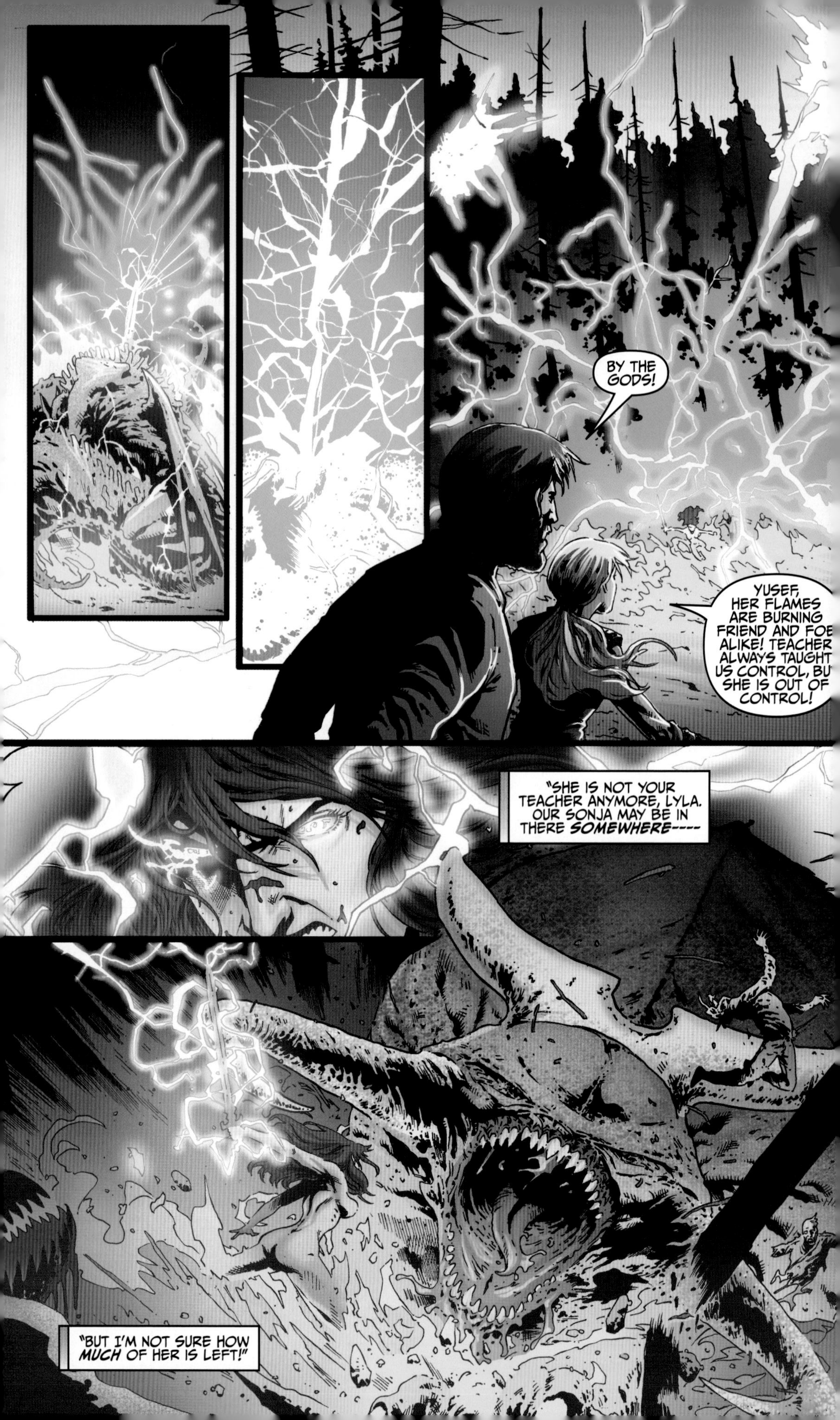
BY THE GODS!
YUSEF, HER FLAMES ARE BURNING FRIEND AND FOE ALIKE! TEACHER ALWAYS TAUGHT US CONTROL, BUT SHE IS OUT OF CONTROL!
"SHE IS NOT YOUR TEACHER ANYMORE, LYLA. OUR SONJA MAY BE IN THERE SOMEWHERE----
"BUT I'M NOT SURE HOW MUCH OF HER IS LEFT!"

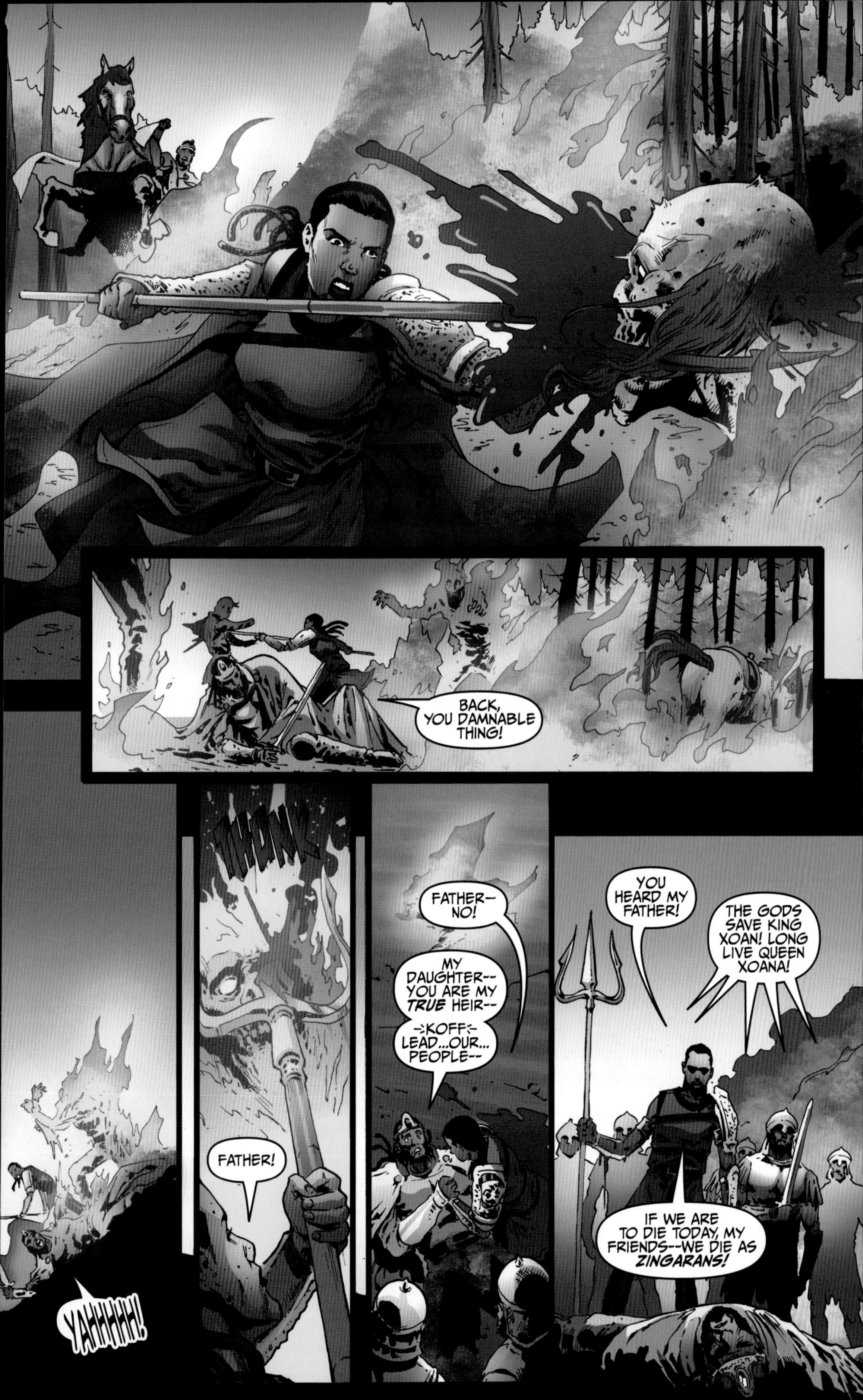
BACK, YOU DAMNABLE THING!
YAHHHHH!
THONK
FATHER!
FATHER-- NO!
MY DAUGHTER-- YOU ARE MY TRUE HEIR--
-KOFF- LEAD...OUR... PEOPLE--
YOU HEARD MY FATHER!
THE GODS SAVE KING XOAN! LONG LIVE QUEEN XOANA!
IF WE ARE TO DIE TODAY, MY FRIENDS--WE DIE AS ZINGARANS!

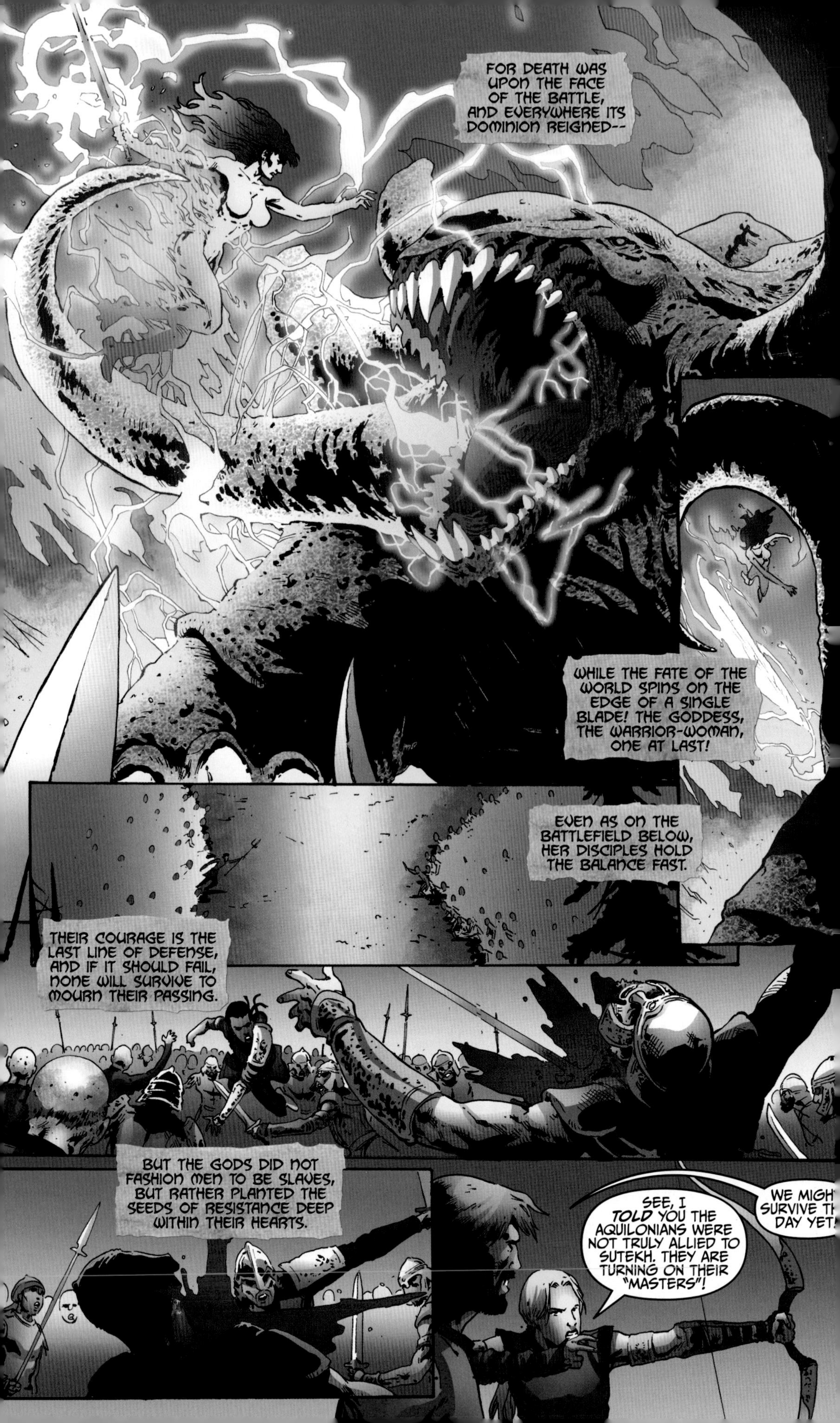

FOR DEATH WAS UPON THE FACE OF THE BATTLE, AND EVERYWHERE ITS DOMINION REIGNED--
WHILE THE FATE OF THE WORLD SPINS ON THE EDGE OF A SINGLE BLADE! THE GODDESS, THE WARRIOR-WOMAN, ONE AT LAST!
EVEN AS ON THE BATTLEFIELD BELOW, HER DISCIPLES HOLD THE BALANCE FAST.
THEIR COURAGE IS THE LAST LINE OF DEFENSE, AND IF IT SHOULD FAIL, NONE WILL SURVIVE TO MOURN THEIR PASSING.
BUT THE GODS DID NOT FASHION MEN TO BE SLAVES, BUT RATHER PLANTED THE SEEDS OF RESISTANCE DEEP WITHIN THEIR HEARTS.
SEE, I *TOLD* YOU THE AQUILONIANS WERE NOT TRULY ALLIED TO SUTEKH. THEY ARE TURNING ON THEIR "MASTERS"!

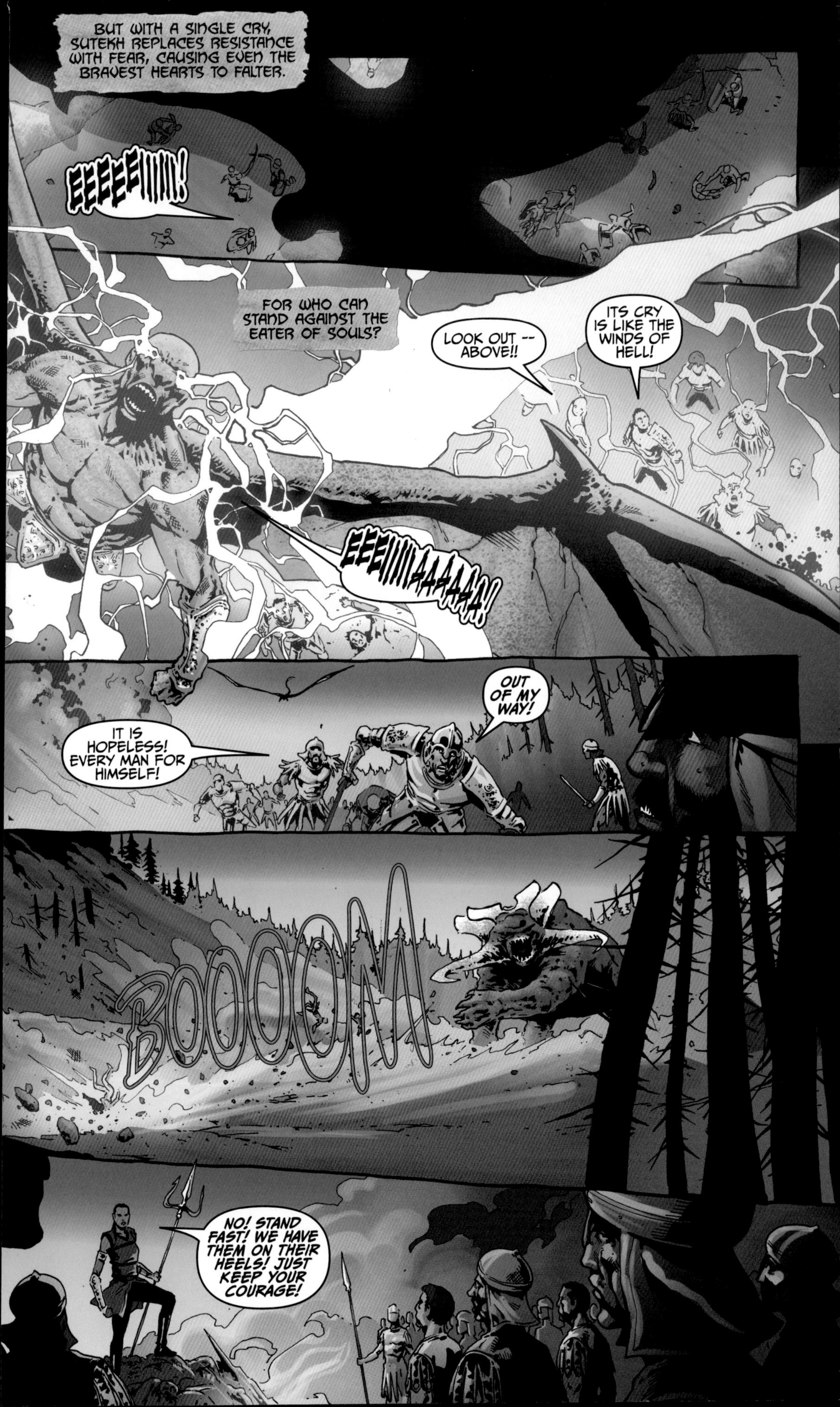

BUT WITH A SINGLE CRY, SUTEKH REPLACES RESISTANCE WITH FEAR, CAUSING EVEN THE BRAVEST HEARTS TO FALTER.
EEEEEIIIIII!
FOR WHO CAN STAND AGAINST THE EATER OF SOULS?
LOOK OUT -- ABOVE!!
ITS CRY IS LIKE THE WINDS OF HELL!
EEEIIIIIIAAAAAA!
IT IS HOPELESS! EVERY MAN FOR HIMSELF!
OUT OF MY WAY!
BOOOOOM
NO! STAND FAST! WE HAVE THEM ON THEIR HEELS! JUST KEEP YOUR COURAGE!

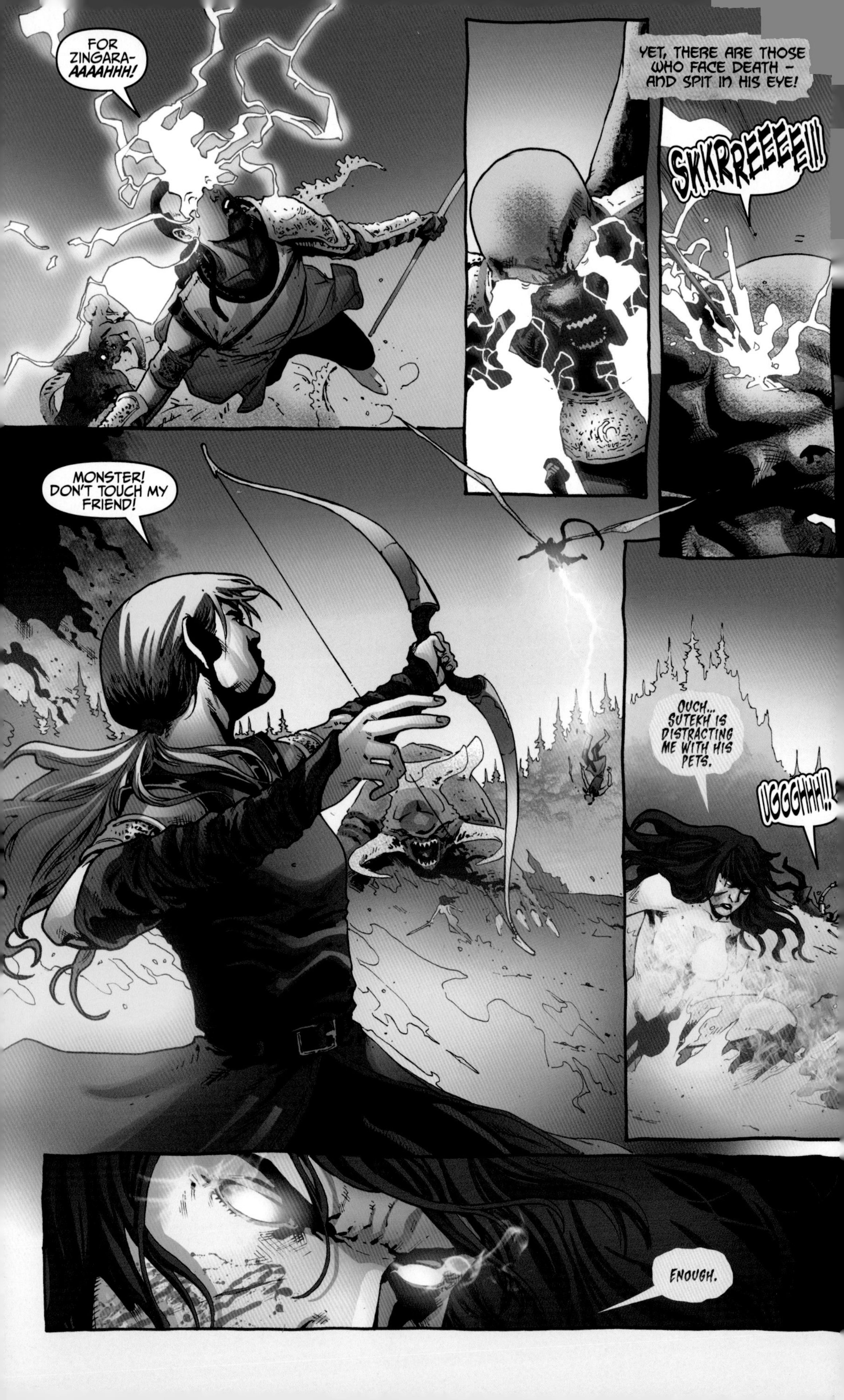
FOR ZINGARA-AAAAHHH!
YET, THERE ARE THOSE WHO FACE DEATH - AND SPIT IN HIS EYE!
SKKRREEEEE!!!
MONSTER! DON'T TOUCH MY FRIEND!
OUCH... SUTEKH IS DISTRACTING ME WITH HIS PETS.
UGGGHH!!
ENOUGH.

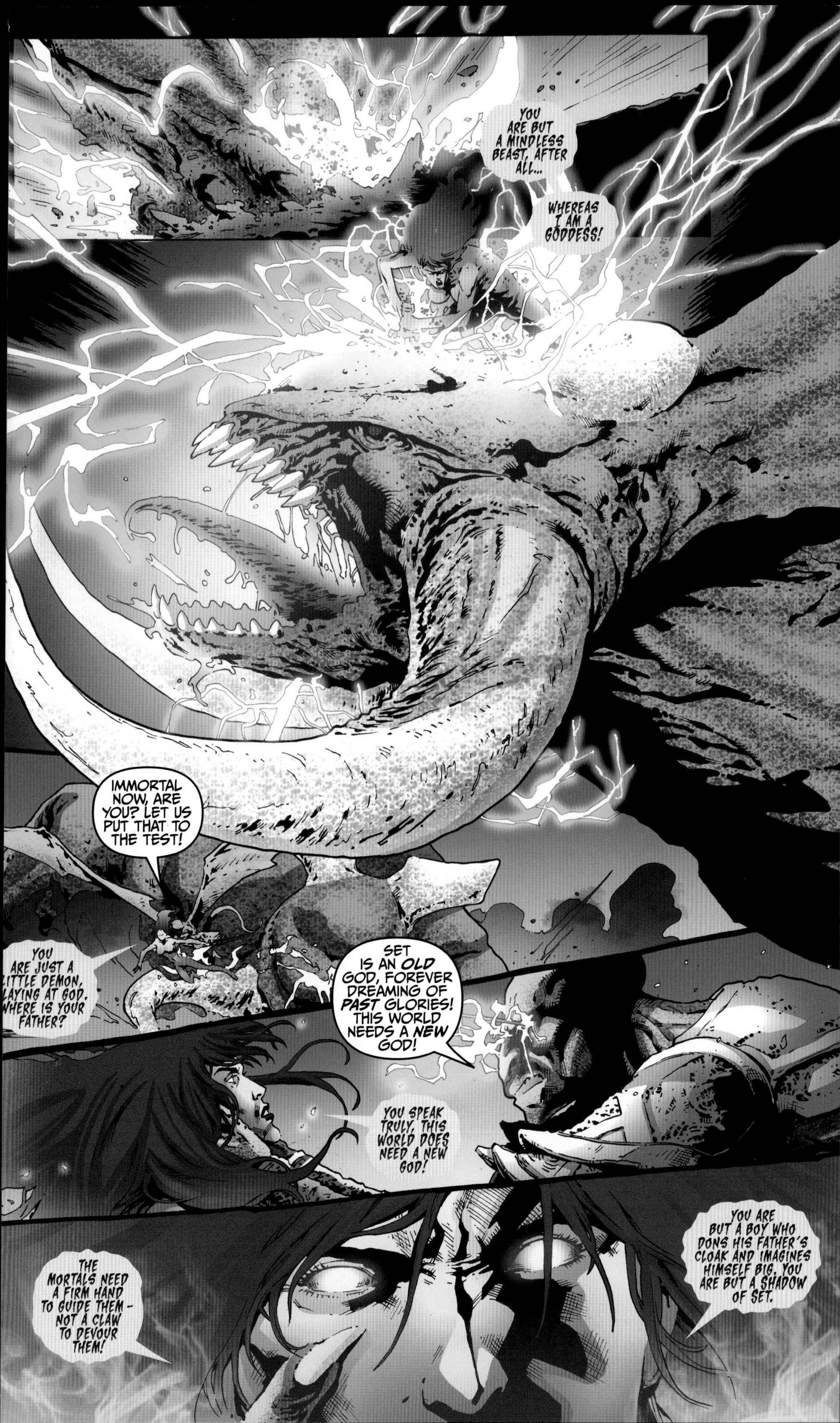
YOU ARE BUT A MINDLESS BEAST, AFTER ALL...
WHEREAS I AM A GODDESS!
IMMORTAL NOW, ARE YOU? LET US PUT THAT TO THE TEST!
YOU ARE JUST A LITTLE DEMON, PLAYING AT GOD. WHERE IS YOUR FATHER?
SET IS AN OLD GOD, FOREVER DREAMING OF PAST GLORIES! THIS WORLD NEEDS A NEW GOD!
YOU SPEAK TRULY, THIS WORLD DOES NEED A NEW GOD!
THE MORTALS NEED A FIRM HAND TO GUIDE THEM - NOT A CLAW TO DEVOUR THEM!
YOU ARE BUT A BOY WHO DONS HIS FATHER'S CLOAK AND IMAGINES HIMSELF BIG. YOU ARE BUT A SHADOW OF SET.

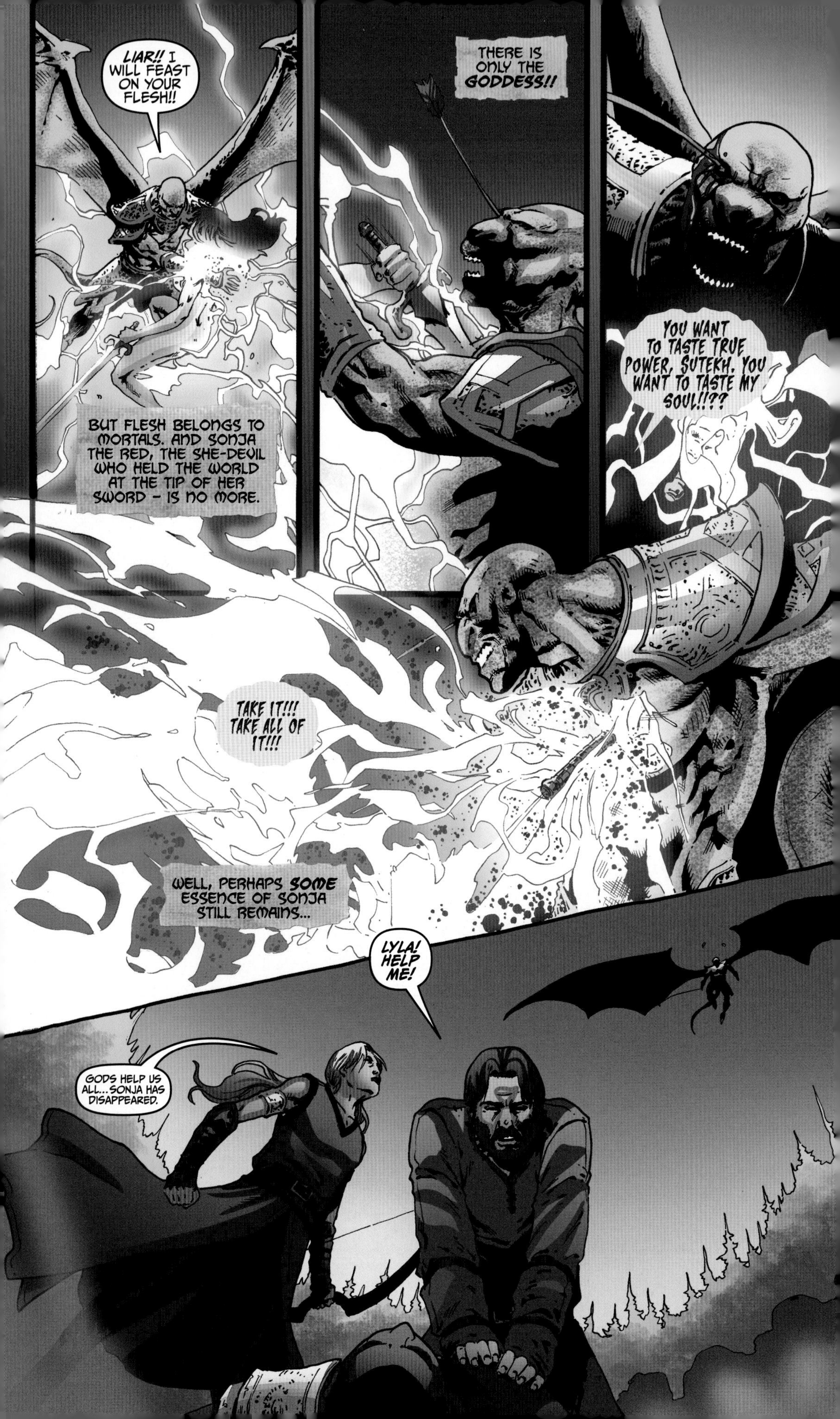
LIAR!! I WILL FEAST ON YOUR FLESH!!
THERE IS ONLY THE GODDESS!!
YOU WANT TO TASTE TRUE POWER, SUTEKH. YOU WANT TO TASTE MY SOUL!!??
BUT FLESH BELONGS TO MORTALS. AND SONJA THE RED, THE SHE-DEVIL WHO HELD THE WORLD AT THE TIP OF HER SWORD – IS NO MORE.
TAKE IT!!! TAKE ALL OF IT!!!
WELL, PERHAPS SOME ESSENCE OF SONJA STILL REMAINS...
LYLA! HELP ME!
GODS HELP US ALL...SONJA HAS DISAPPEARED.

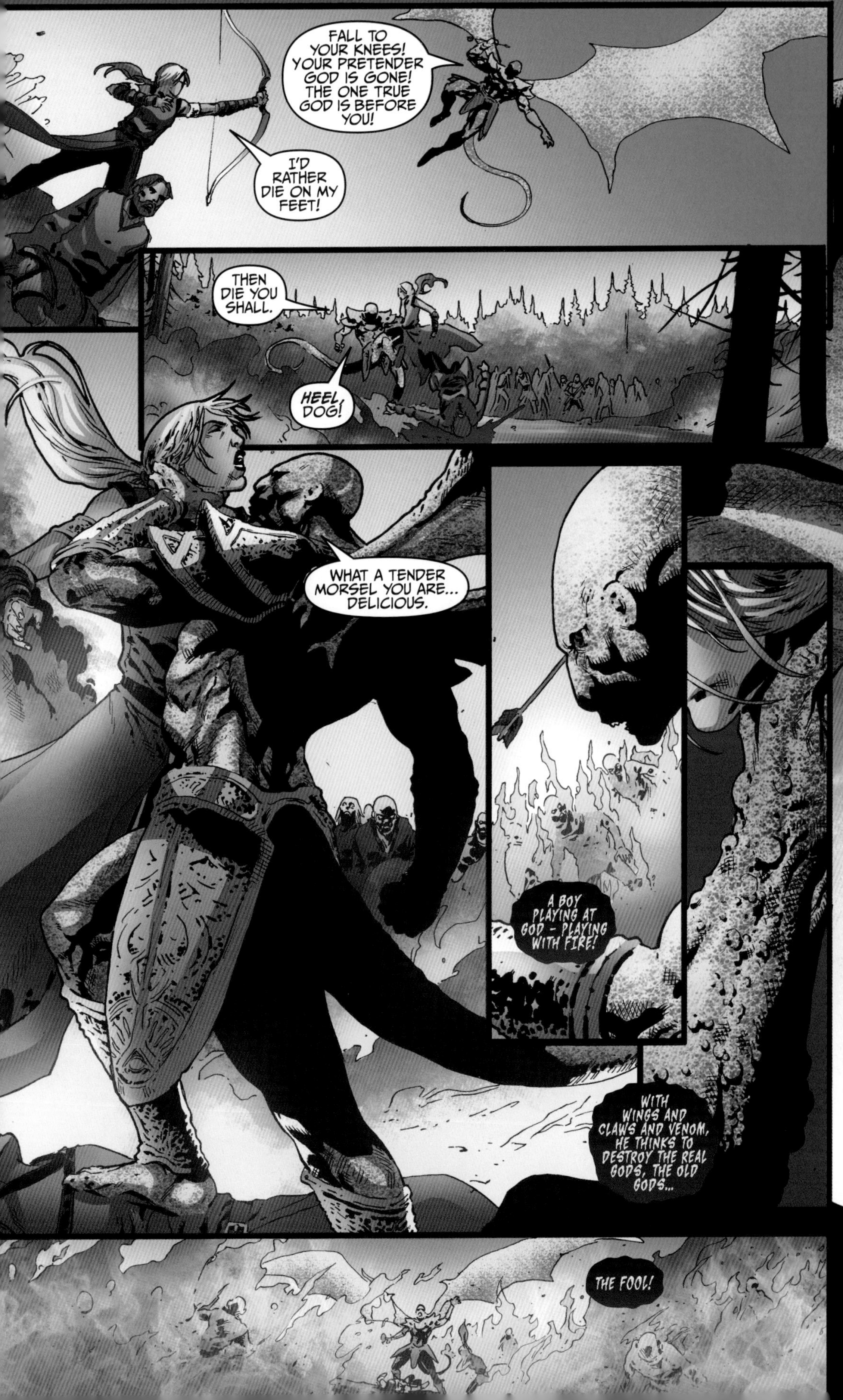
FALL TO YOUR KNEES! YOUR PRETENDER GOD IS GONE! THE ONE TRUE GOD IS BEFORE YOU!
I'D RATHER DIE ON MY FEET!
THEN DIE YOU SHALL.
HEEL, DOG!
WHAT A TENDER MORSEL YOU ARE... DELICIOUS.
A BOY PLAYING AT GOD - PLAYING WITH FIRE!
WITH WINGS AND CLAWS AND VENOM, HE THINKS TO DESTROY THE REAL GODS, THE OLD GODS...
THE FOOL!

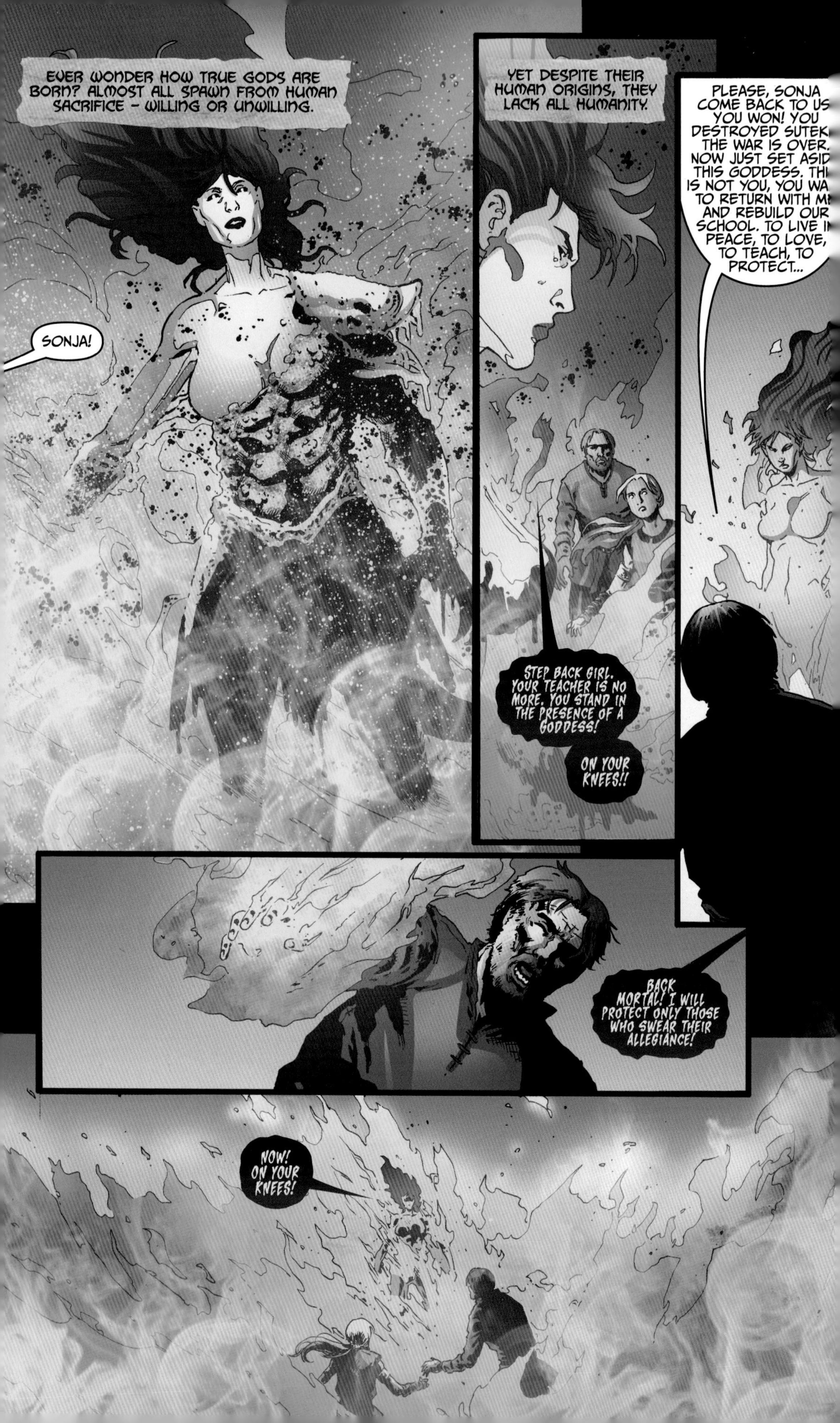
EVER WONDER HOW TRUE GODS ARE BORN? ALMOST ALL SPAWN FROM HUMAN SACRIFICE - WILLING OR UNWILLING.
SONJA!
YET DESPITE THEIR HUMAN ORIGINS, THEY LACK ALL HUMANITY.
PLEASE, SONJA COME BACK TO US YOU WON! YOU DESTROYED SUTEK THE WAR IS OVER. NOW JUST SET ASID THIS GODDESS. TH IS NOT YOU, YOU WA TO RETURN WITH M AND REBUILD OUR SCHOOL. TO LIVE I PEACE, TO LOVE, TO TEACH, TO PROTECT...
STEP BACK GIRL. YOUR TEACHER IS NO MORE. YOU STAND IN THE PRESENCE OF A GODDESS!
ON YOUR KNEES!!
BACK MORTAL! I WILL PROTECT ONLY THOSE WHO SWEAR THEIR ALLEGIANCE!
NOW! ON YOUR KNEES!

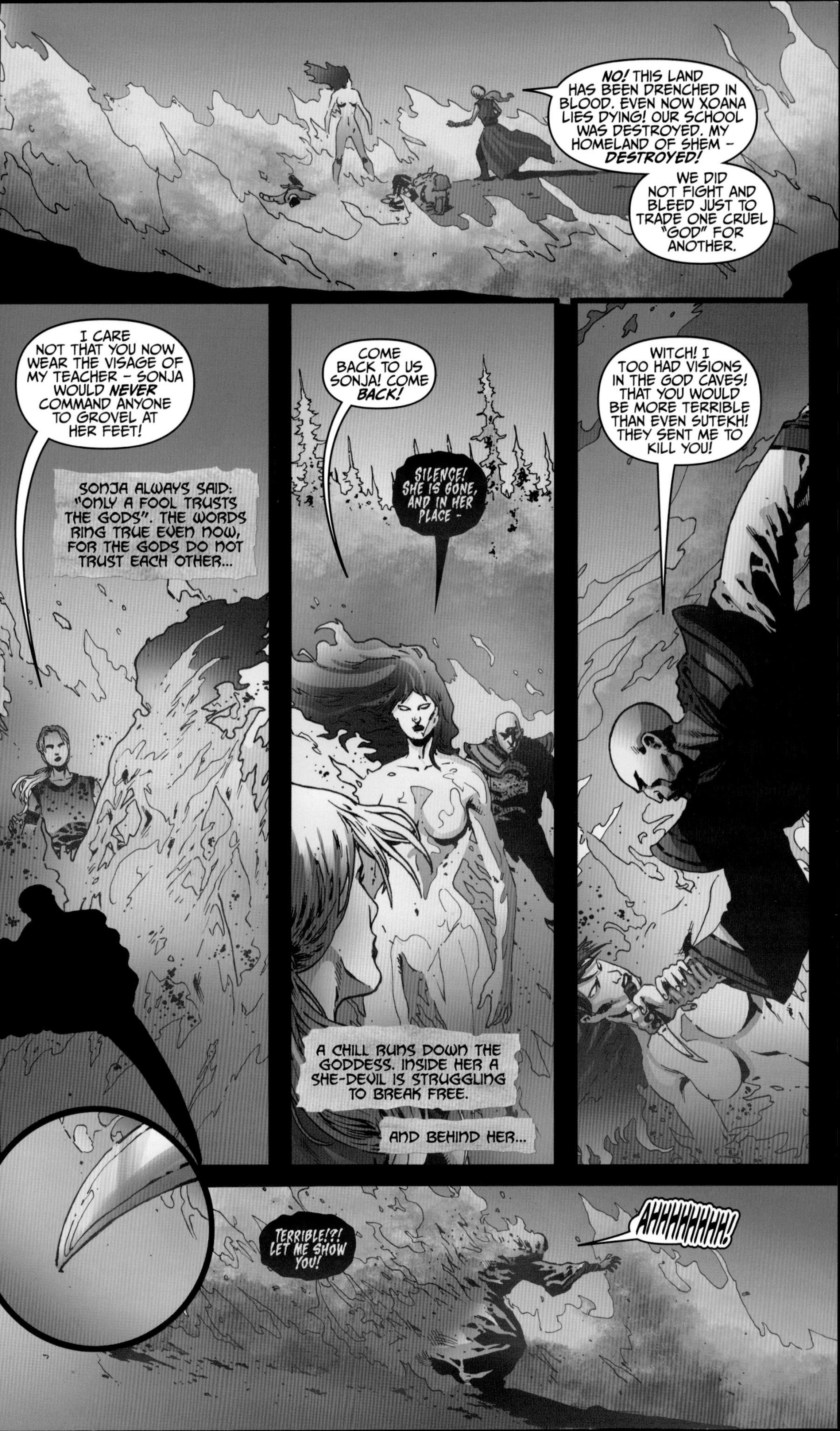

NO! THIS LAND HAS BEEN DRENCHED IN BLOOD. EVEN NOW XOANA LIES DYING! OUR SCHOOL WAS DESTROYED. MY HOMELAND OF SHEM - DESTROYED!
WE DID NOT FIGHT AND BLEED JUST TO TRADE ONE CRUEL "GOD" FOR ANOTHER.
I CARE NOT THAT YOU NOW WEAR THE VISAGE OF MY TEACHER - SONJA WOULD NEVER COMMAND ANYONE TO GROVEL AT HER FEET!
SONJA ALWAYS SAID: "ONLY A FOOL TRUSTS THE GODS". THE WORDS RING TRUE EVEN NOW, FOR THE GODS DO NOT TRUST EACH OTHER...
COME BACK TO US SONJA! COME BACK!
SILENCE! SHE IS GONE, AND IN HER PLACE -
A CHILL RUNS DOWN THE GODDESS. INSIDE HER A SHE-DEVIL IS STRUGGLING TO BREAK FREE.
AND BEHIND HER...
WITCH! I TOO HAD VISIONS IN THE GOD CAVES! THAT YOU WOULD BE MORE TERRIBLE THAN EVEN SUTEKH! THEY SENT ME TO KILL YOU!
TERRIBLE!?! LET ME SHOW YOU!
AHHHHHHHH!

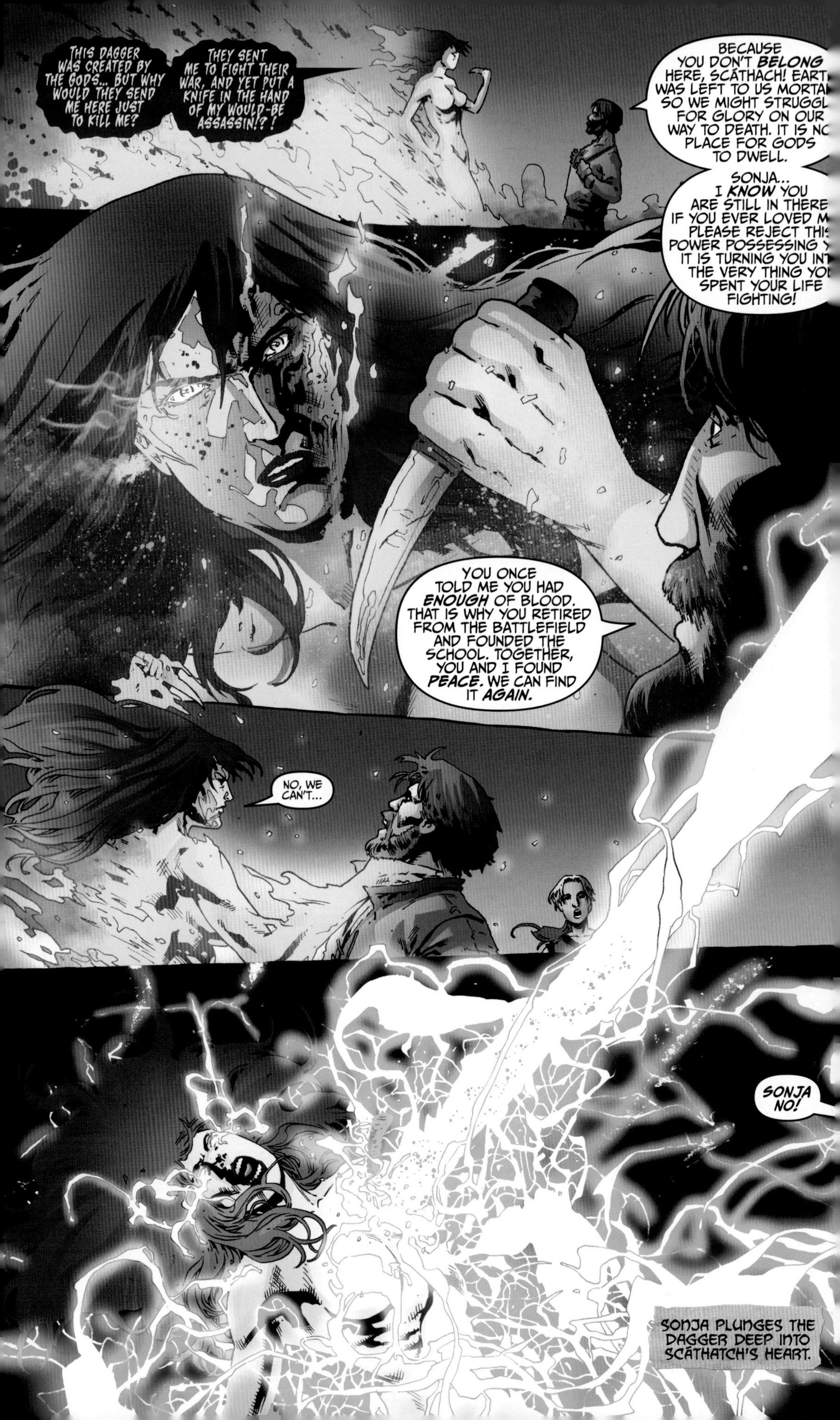
THIS DAGGER WAS CREATED BY THE GODS... BUT WHY WOULD THEY SEND ME HERE JUST TO KILL ME?
THEY SENT ME TO FIGHT THEIR WAR, AND YET PUT A KNIFE IN THE HAND OF MY WOULD-BE ASSASSIN!?!
BECAUSE YOU DON'T BELONG HERE, SCÁTHACH! EARTH WAS LEFT TO US MORTALS SO WE MIGHT STRUGGLE FOR GLORY ON OUR WAY TO DEATH. IT IS NO PLACE FOR GODS TO DWELL.
SONJA... I KNOW YOU ARE STILL IN THERE. IF YOU EVER LOVED ME PLEASE REJECT THIS POWER POSSESSING YOU. IT IS TURNING YOU INTO THE VERY THING YOU SPENT YOUR LIFE FIGHTING!
YOU ONCE TOLD ME YOU HAD ENOUGH OF BLOOD. THAT IS WHY YOU RETIRED FROM THE BATTLEFIELD AND FOUNDED THE SCHOOL. TOGETHER, YOU AND I FOUND PEACE. WE CAN FIND IT AGAIN.
NO, WE CAN'T...
SONJA NO!
SONJA PLUNGES THE DAGGER DEEP INTO SCÁTHATCH'S HEART.

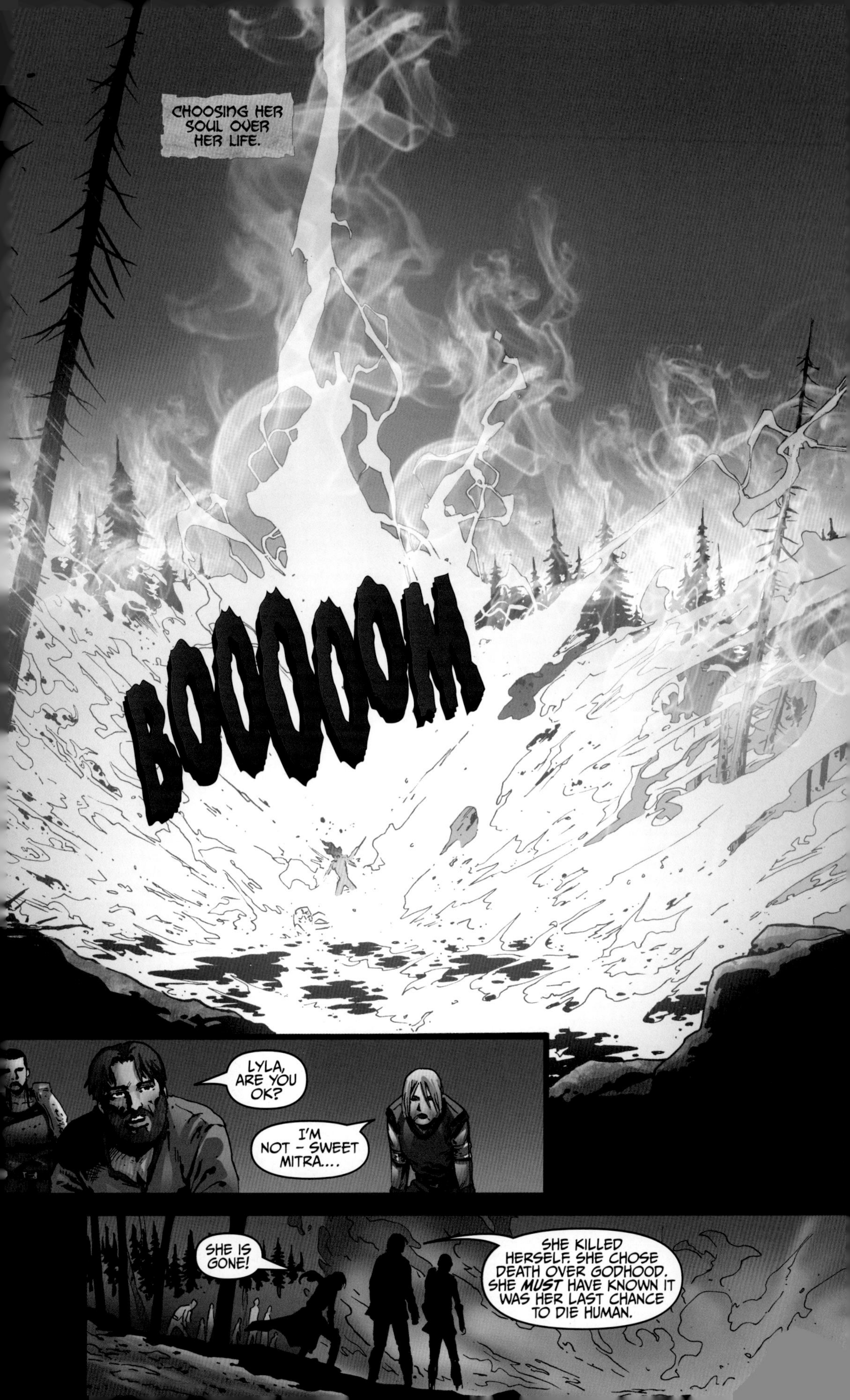
CHOOSING HER SOUL OVER HER LIFE.
BOOOOOM
LYLA, ARE YOU OK?
I'M NOT – SWEET MITRA...
SHE IS GONE!
SHE KILLED HERSELF. SHE CHOSE DEATH OVER GODHOOD. SHE *MUST* HAVE KNOWN IT WAS HER LAST CHANCE TO DIE HUMAN.

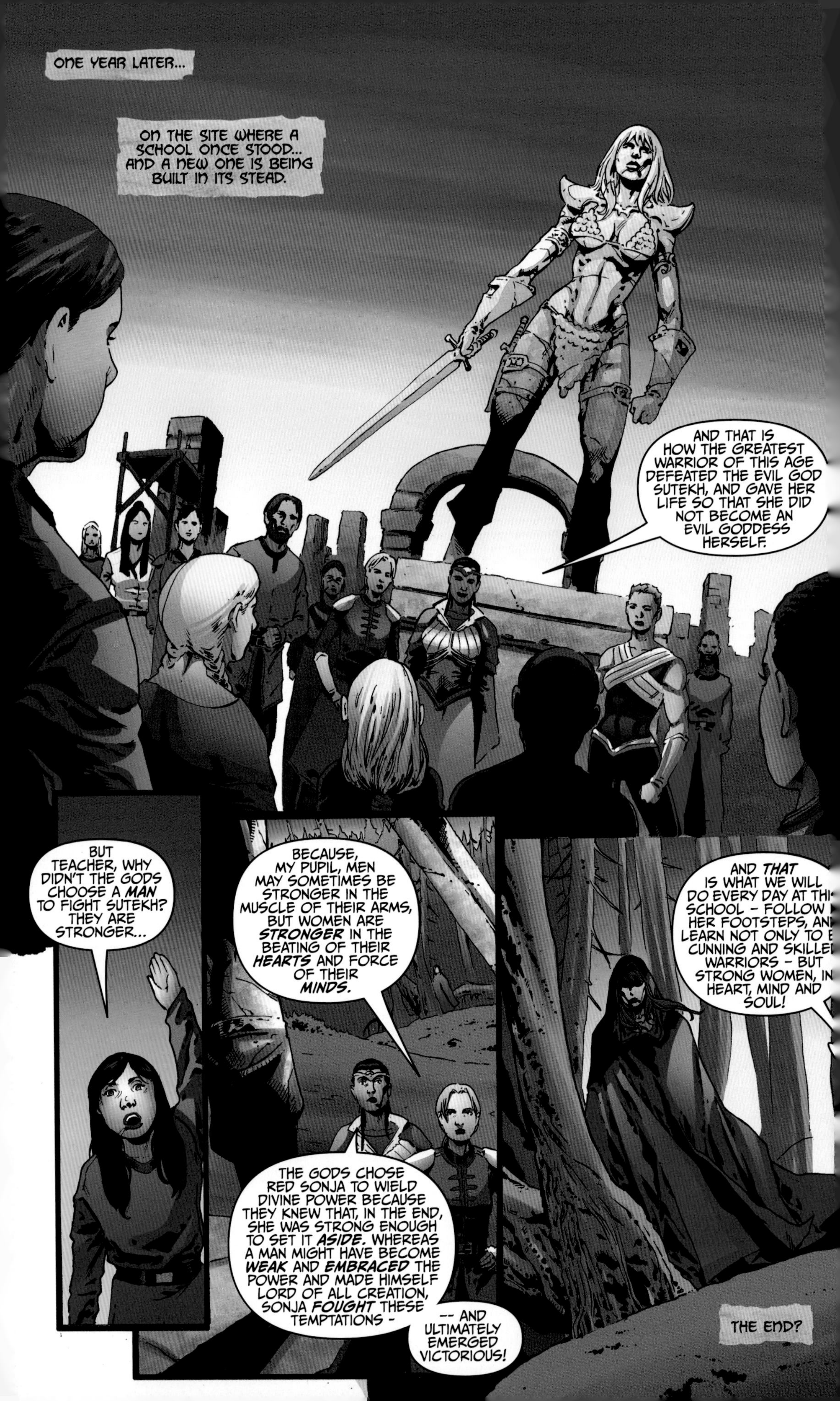
ONE YEAR LATER...
ON THE SITE WHERE A SCHOOL ONCE STOOD... AND A NEW ONE IS BEING BUILT IN ITS STEAD.
AND THAT IS HOW THE GREATEST WARRIOR OF THIS AGE DEFEATED THE EVIL GOD SUTEKH, AND GAVE HER LIFE SO THAT SHE DID NOT BECOME AN EVIL GODDESS HERSELF.
BUT TEACHER, WHY DIDN'T THE GODS CHOOSE A MAN TO FIGHT SUTEKH? THEY ARE STRONGER...
BECAUSE, MY PUPIL, MEN MAY SOMETIMES BE STRONGER IN THE MUSCLE OF THEIR ARMS, BUT WOMEN ARE STRONGER IN THE BEATING OF THEIR HEARTS AND FORCE OF THEIR MINDS.
THE GODS CHOSE RED SONJA TO WIELD DIVINE POWER BECAUSE THEY KNEW THAT, IN THE END, SHE WAS STRONG ENOUGH TO SET IT ASIDE. WHEREAS A MAN MIGHT HAVE BECOME WEAK AND EMBRACED THE POWER AND MADE HIMSELF LORD OF ALL CREATION, SONJA FOUGHT THESE TEMPTATIONS -
-- AND ULTIMATELY EMERGED VICTORIOUS!
AND THAT IS WHAT WE WILL DO EVERY DAY AT THI SCHOOL - FOLLOW HER FOOTSTEPS, AN LEARN NOT ONLY TO B CUNNING AND SKILLE WARRIORS - BUT STRONG WOMEN, IN HEART, MIND AND SOUL!
THE END?

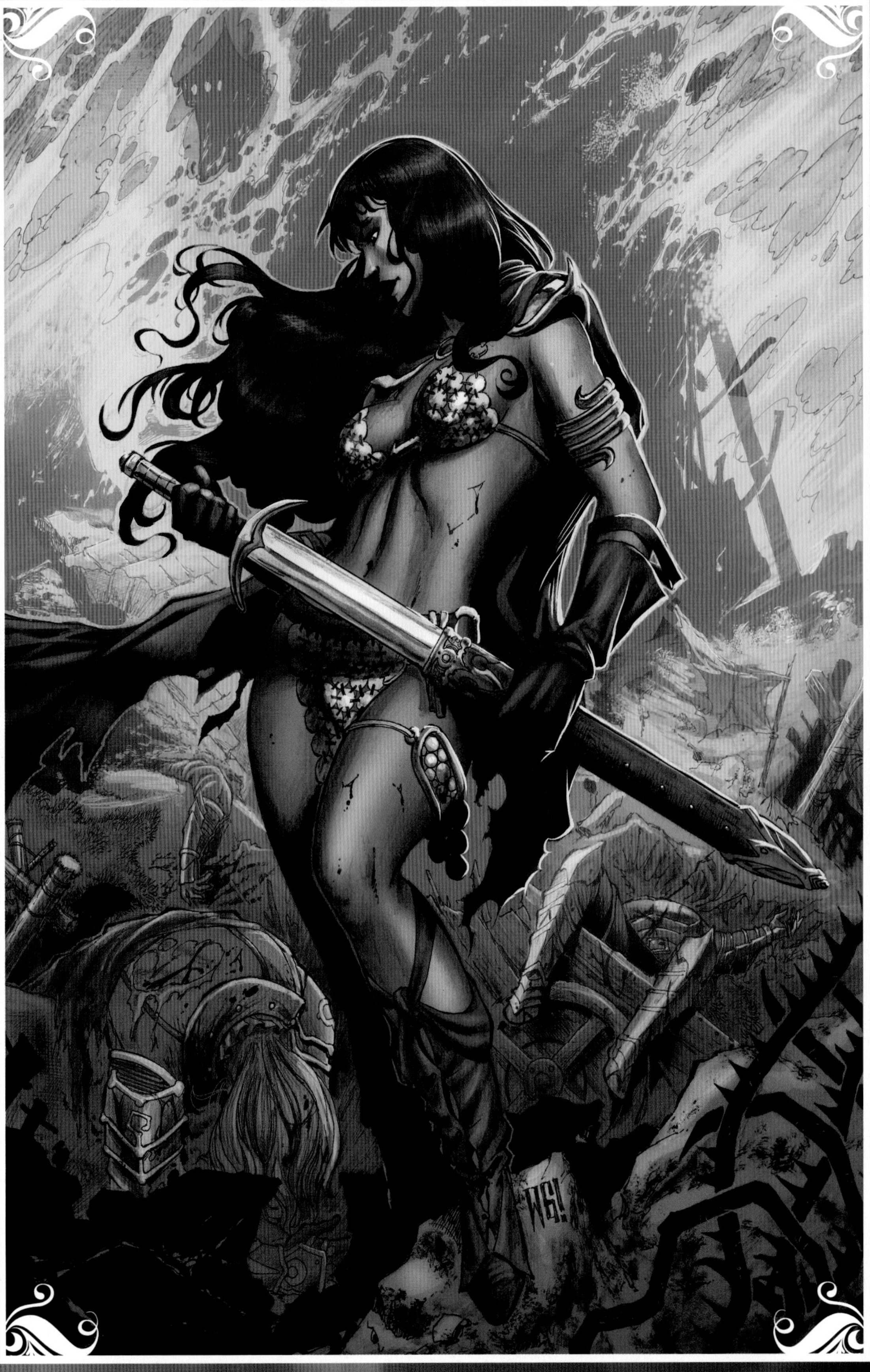

ISSUE ONE

cover art by Walter Geovani and Alex Guimarães

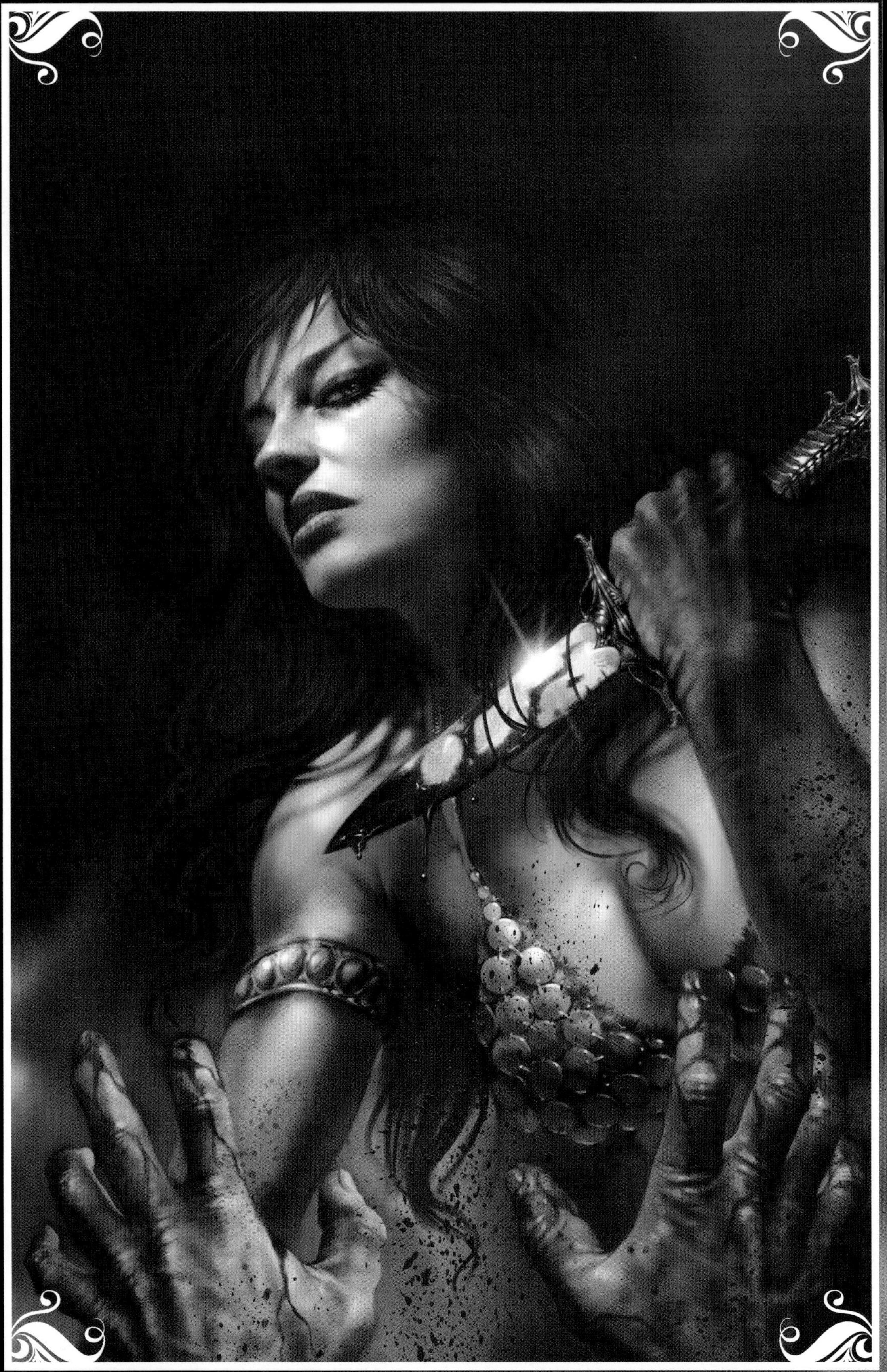

ISSUE ONE

cover art by Lucio Parrillo

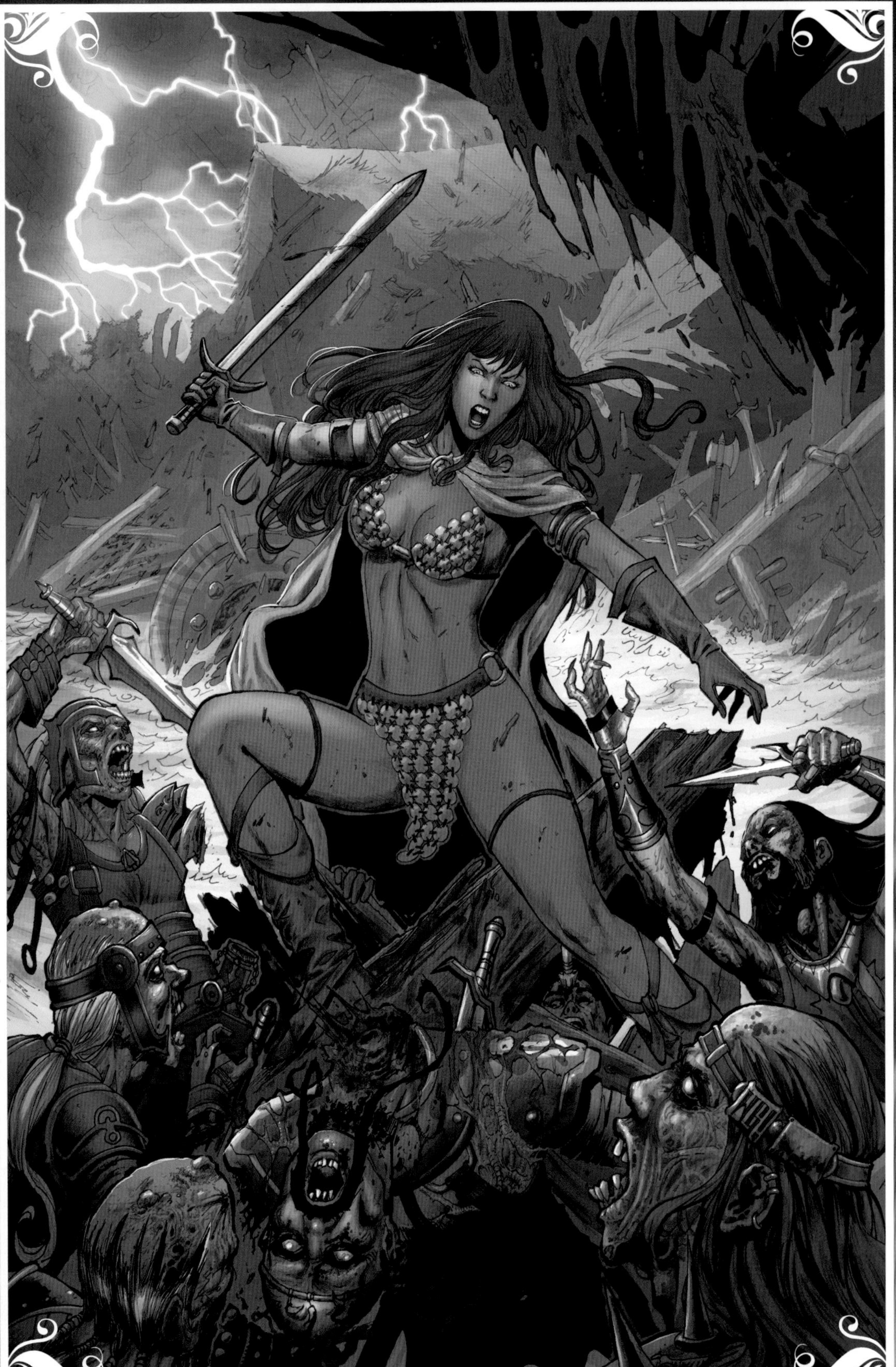

ISSUE TWO

cover art by Walter Geovani and Alex Guimarães

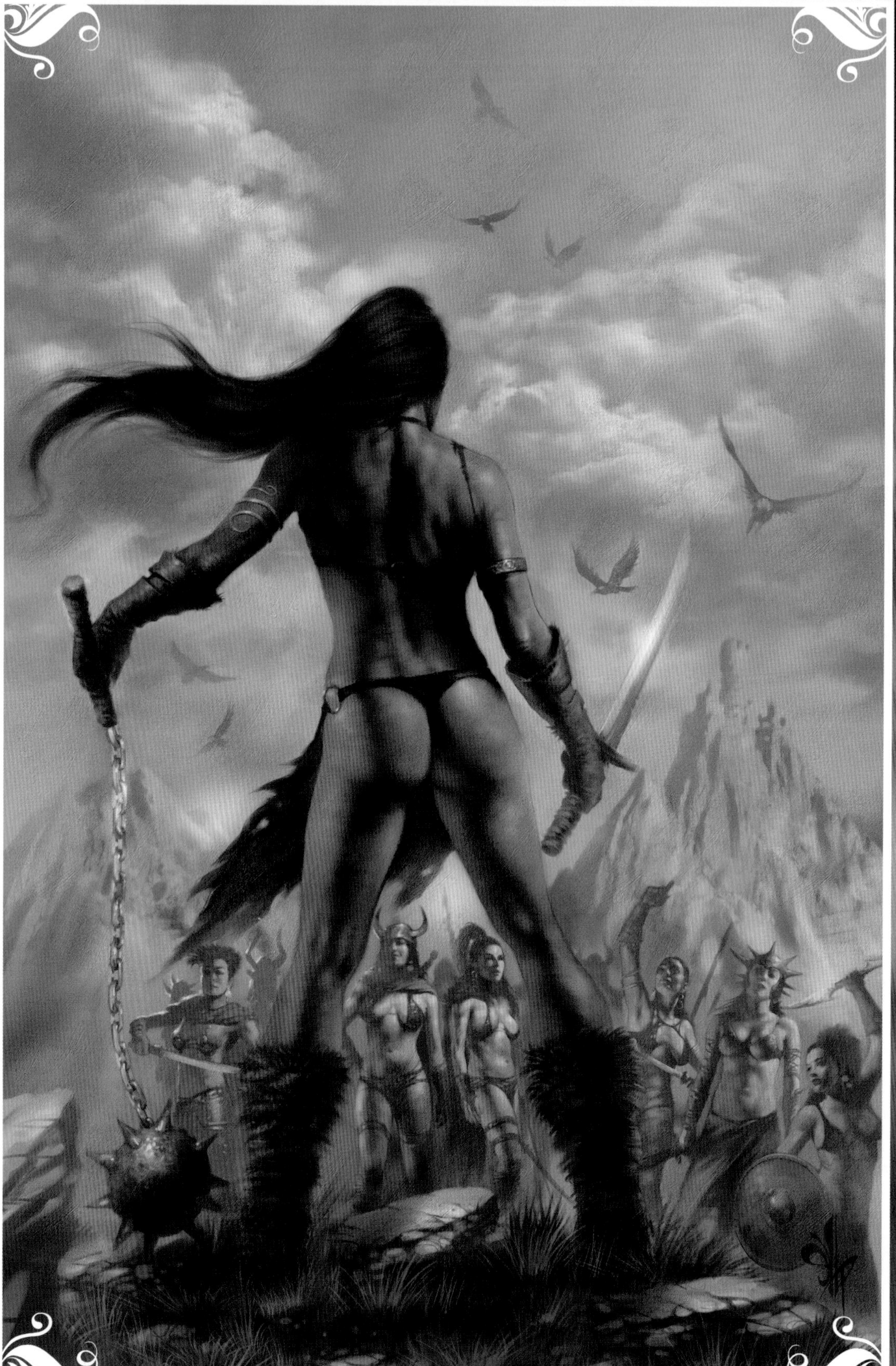

ISSUE TWO
cover art by Lucio Parrillo

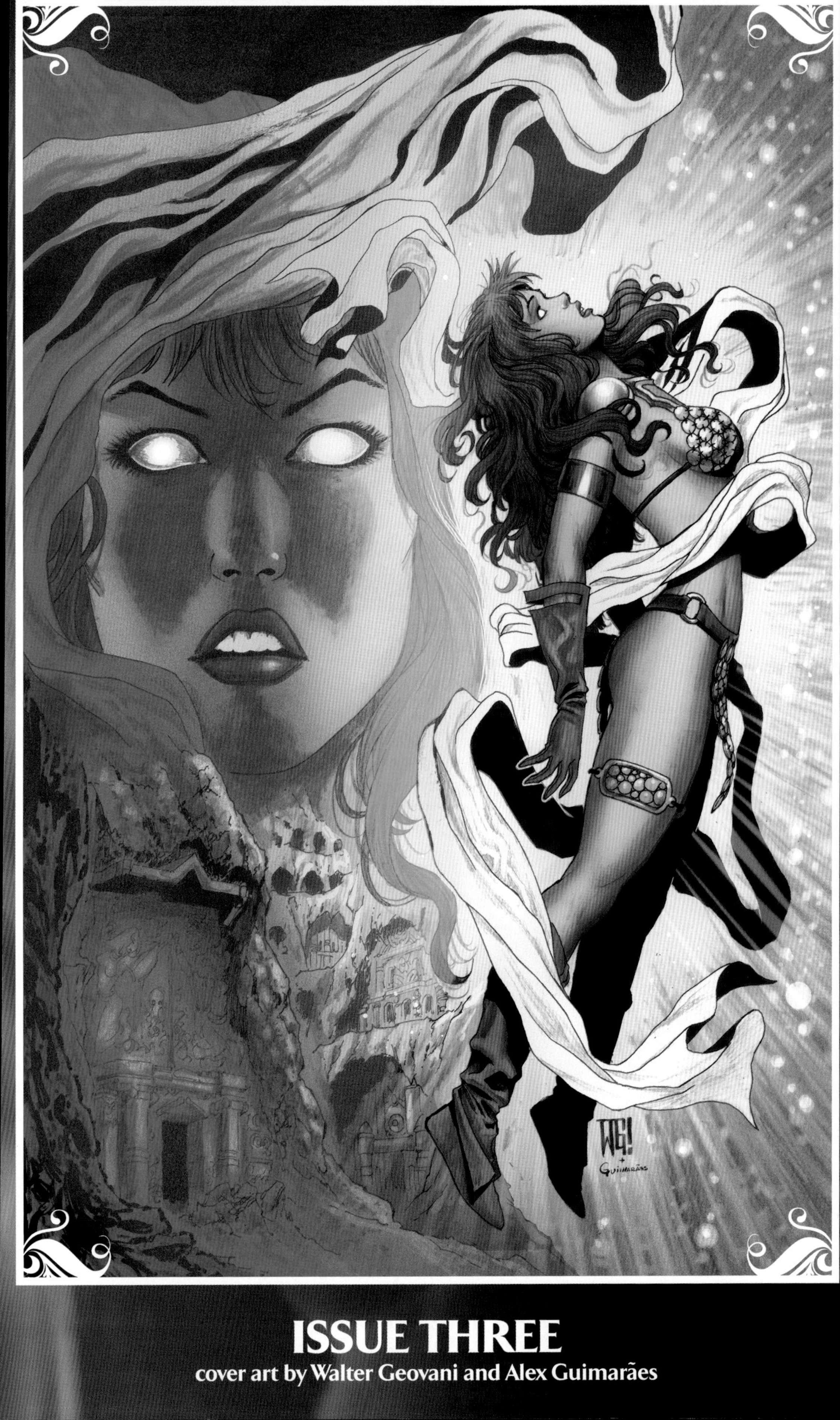

ISSUE THREE

cover art by Walter Geovani and Alex Guimarães

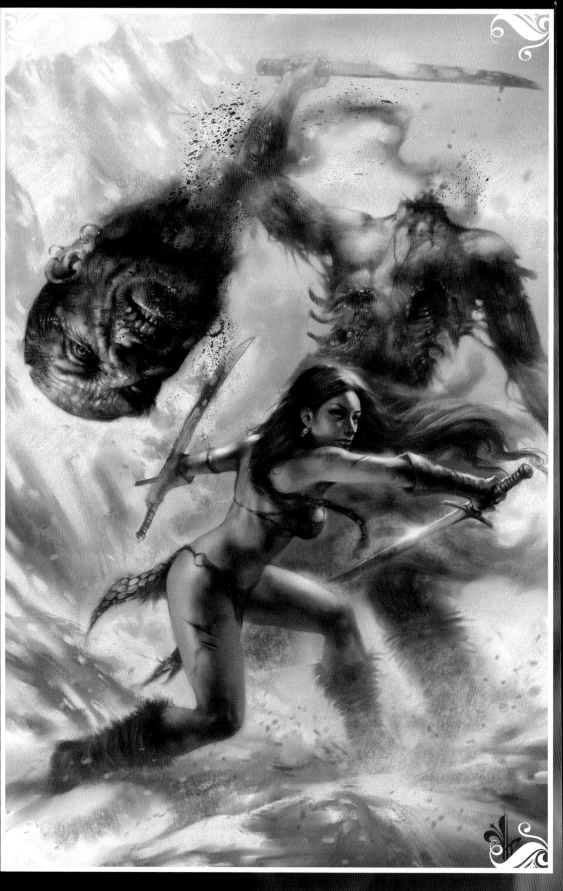

ISSUE THREE
cover art by Lucio Parrillo

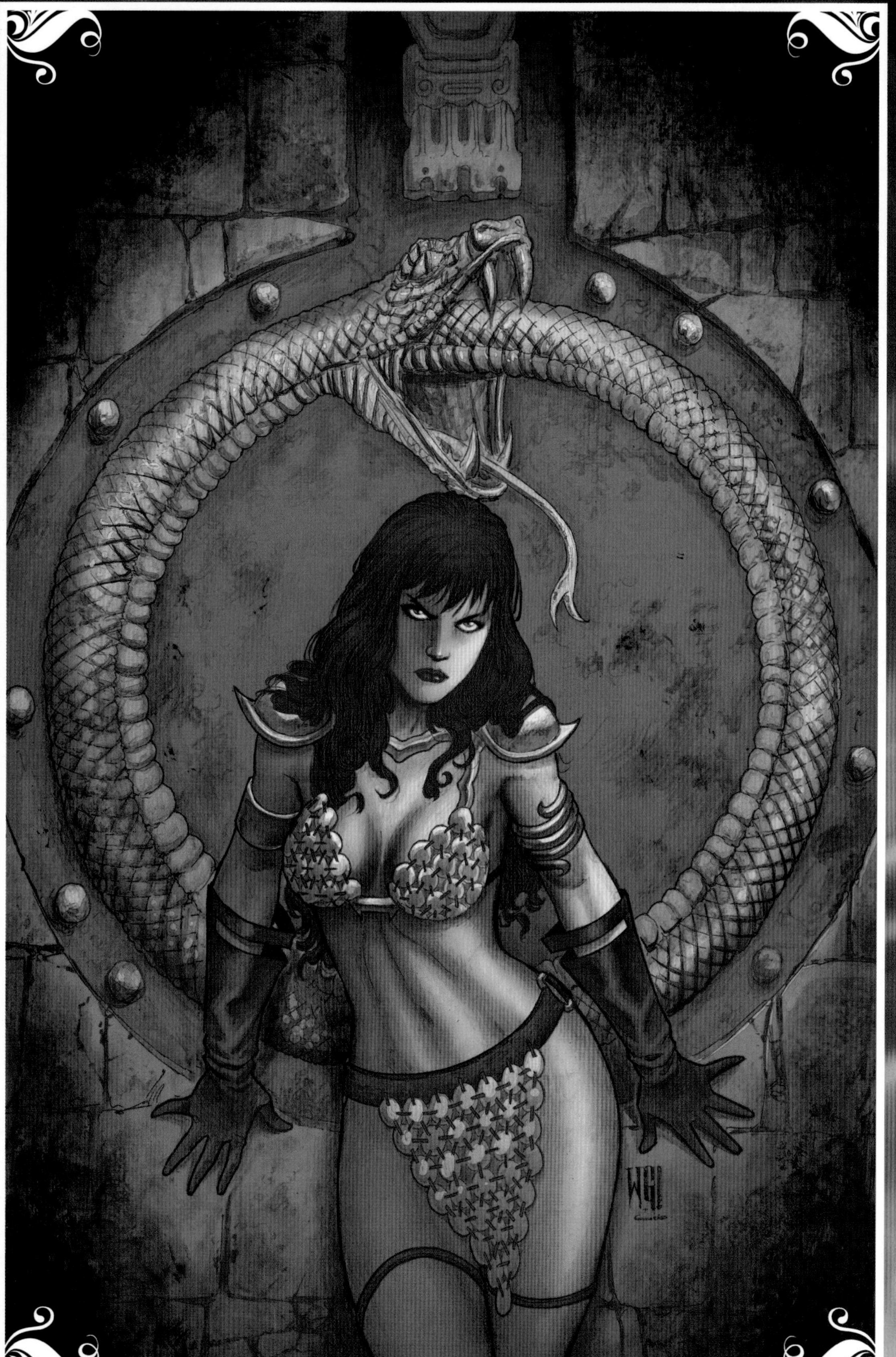

ISSUE FOUR
cover art by Walter Geovani and Alex Guimarães

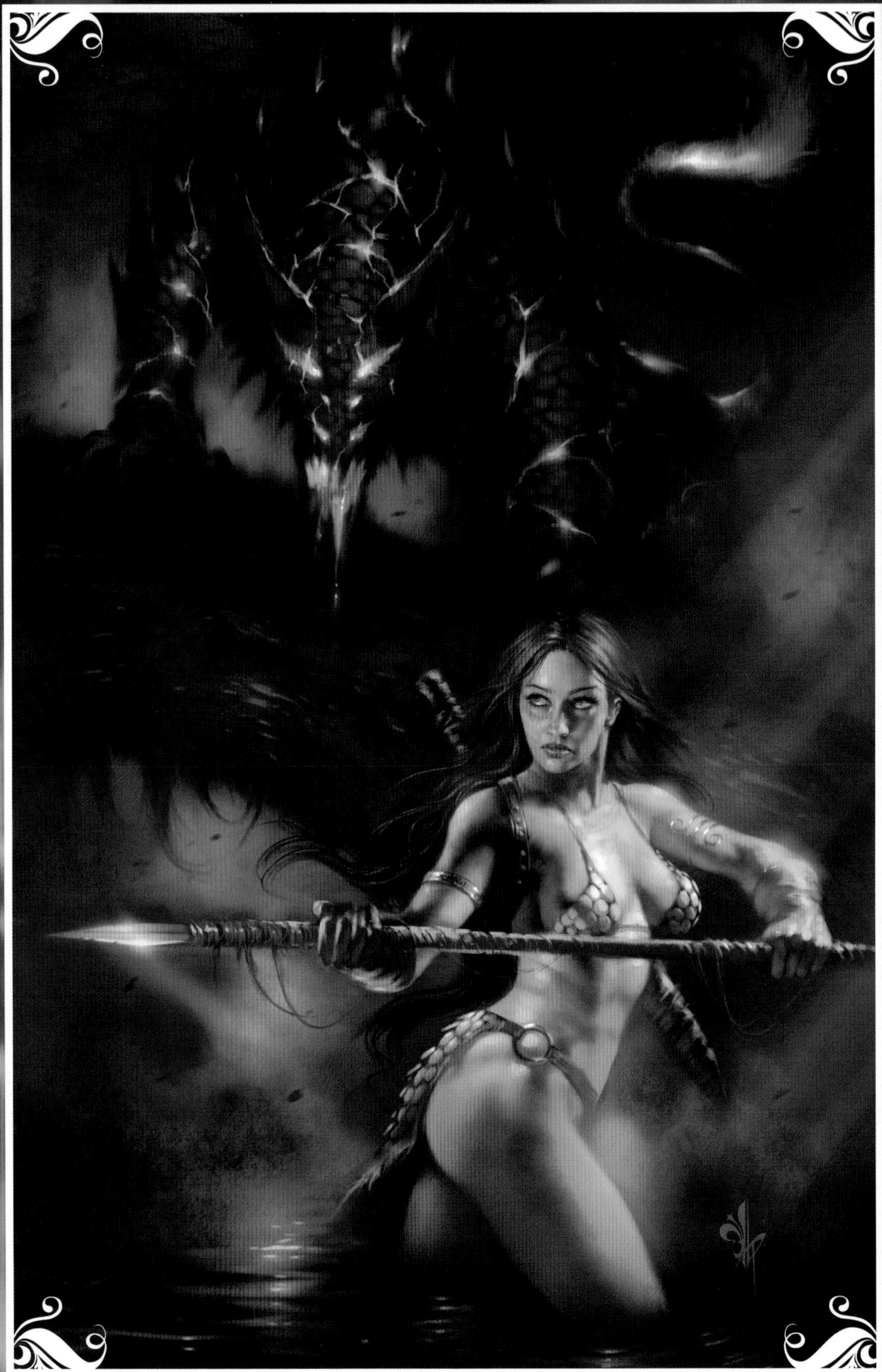

ISSUE FOUR
cover art by Lucio Parrillo

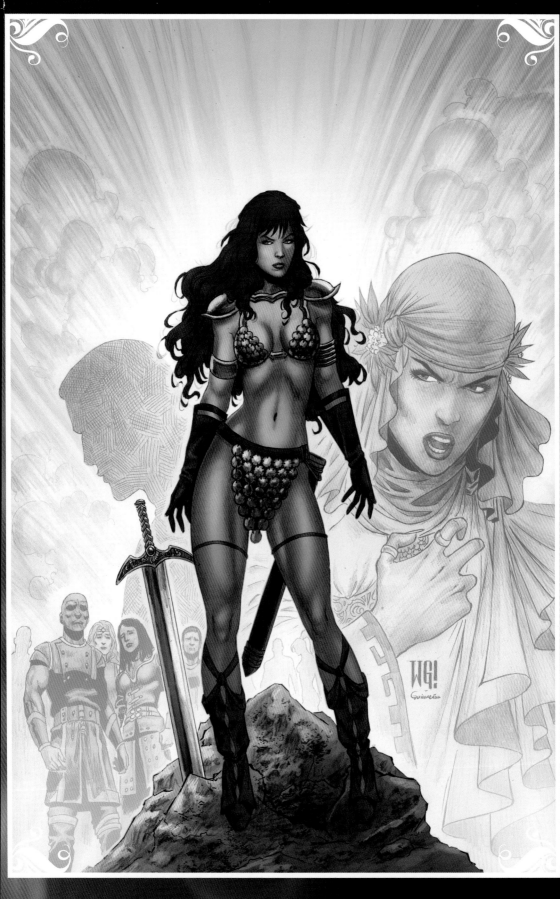

ISSUE FIVE
cover art by Walter Geovani and Alex Guimarães

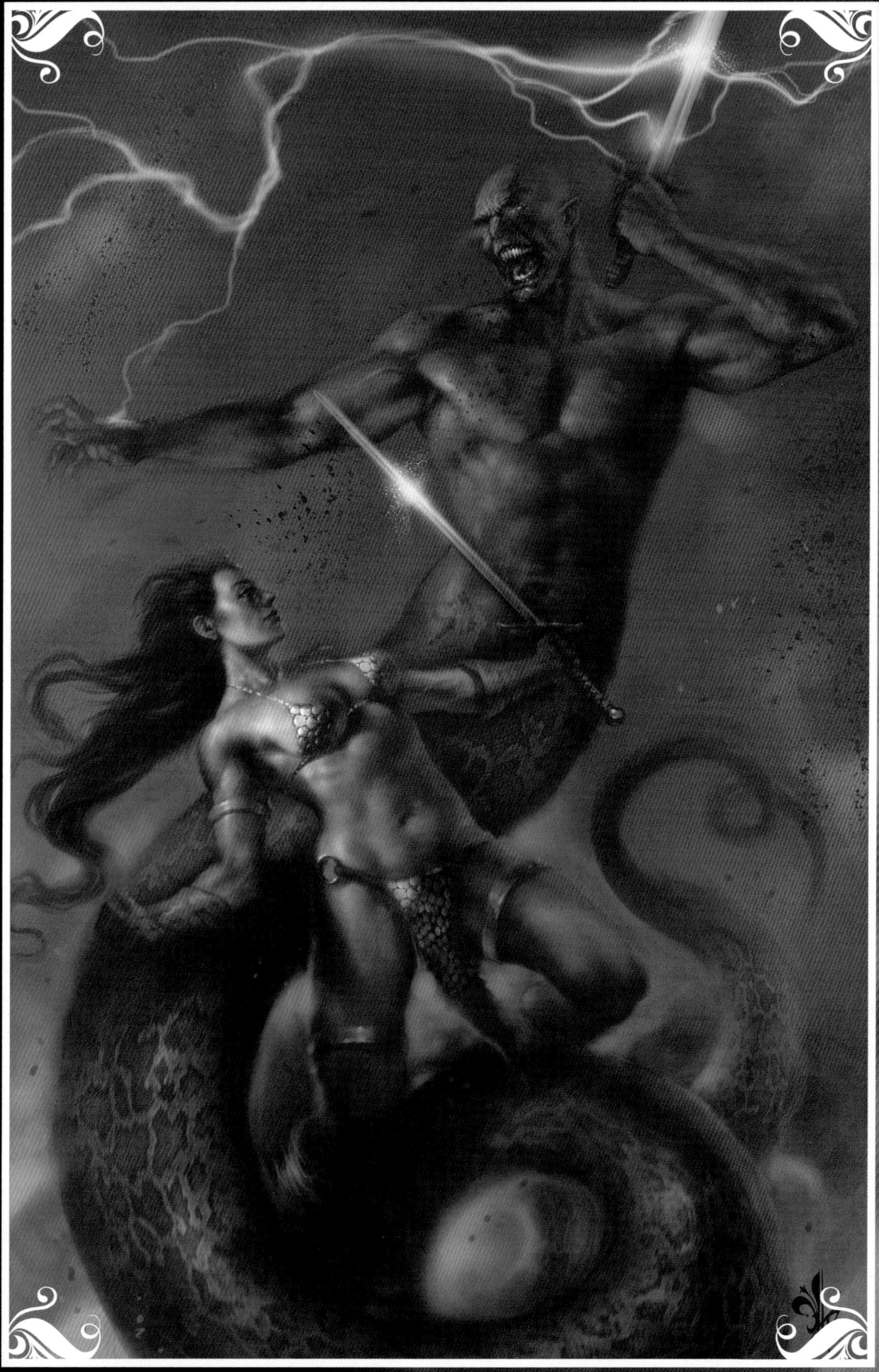

ISSUE FIVE
cover art by Lucio Parrillo

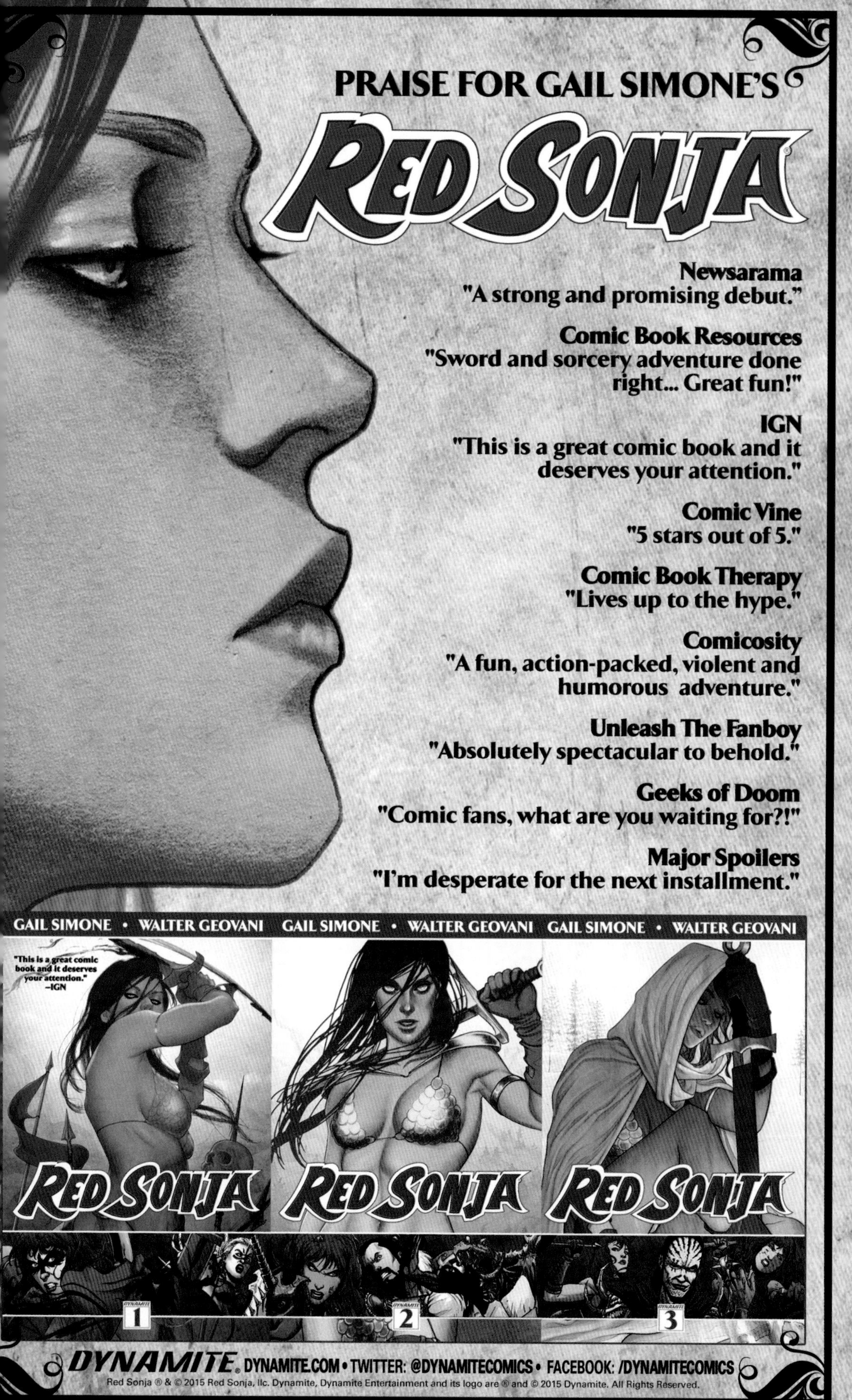
PRAISE FOR GAIL SIMONE'S
RED SONJA®
Newsarama
"A strong and promising debut."
Comic Book Resources
"Sword and sorcery adventure done right... Great fun!"
IGN
"This is a great comic book and it deserves your attention."
Comic Vine
"5 stars out of 5."
Comic Book Therapy
"Lives up to the hype."
Comicosity
"A fun, action-packed, violent and humorous adventure."
Unleash The Fanboy
"Absolutely spectacular to behold."
Geeks of Doom
"Comic fans, what are you waiting for?!"
Major Spoilers
"I'm desperate for the next installment."
GAIL SIMONE • WALTER GEOVANI
"This is a great comic book and it deserves your attention." –IGN
RED SONJA
1
GAIL SIMONE • WALTER GEOVANI
RED SONJA
2
GAIL SIMONE • WALTER GEOVANI
RED SONJA
3
DYNAMITE. DYNAMITE.COM • TWITTER: @DYNAMITECOMICS • FACEBOOK: /DYNAMITECOMICS
Red Sonja ® & © 2015 Red Sonja, llc. Dynamite, Dynamite Entertainment and its logo are ® and © 2015 Dynamite. All Rights Reserved.

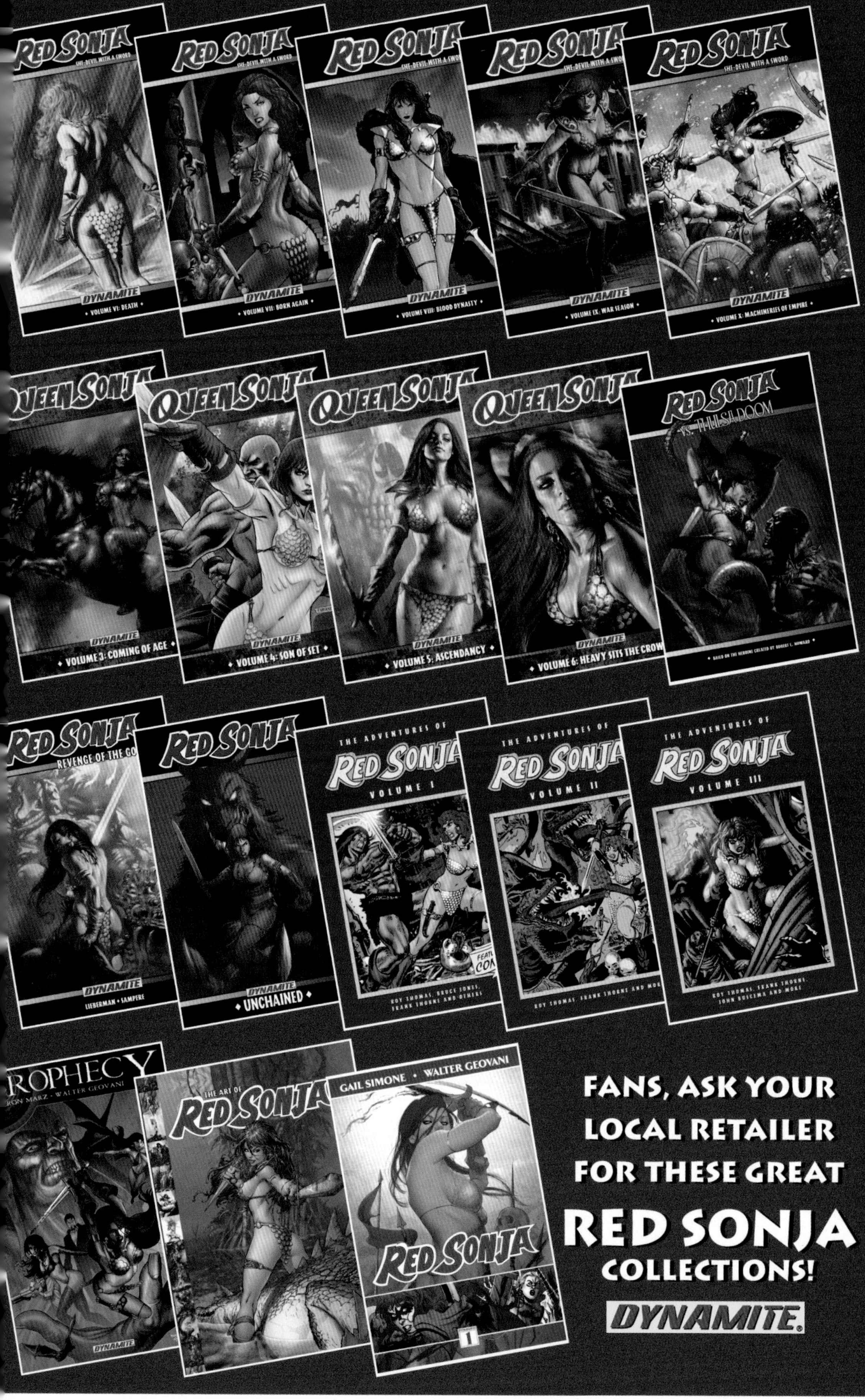
RED SONJA
SHE-DEVIL WITH A SWORD
DYNAMITE
VOLUME VI: DEATH
VOLUME VII: BORN AGAIN
VOLUME VIII: BLOOD DYNASTY
VOLUME IX: WAR SEASON
VOLUME X: MACHINERIES OF EMPIRE
QUEEN SONJA
VOLUME 3: COMING OF AGE
VOLUME 4: SON OF SET
VOLUME 5: ASCENDANCY
VOLUME 6: HEAVY SITS THE CROW
RED SONJA VS. THULSA DOOM
RED SONJA REVENGE OF THE GO
LIEBERMAN • SAMPERE
RED SONJA
UNCHAINED
THE ADVENTURES OF RED SONJA VOLUME I
ROY THOMAS, BRUCE JONES, FRANK THORNE AND OTHERS
THE ADVENTURES OF RED SONJA VOLUME II
ROY THOMAS, FRANK THORNE AND MORE
THE ADVENTURES OF RED SONJA VOLUME III
ROY THOMAS, FRANK THORNE, JOHN BUSCEMA AND MORE
ROPHECY
RON MARZ • WALTER GEOVANI
THE ART OF RED SONJA
GAIL SIMONE • WALTER GEOVANI
RED SONJA
1

RED SONJA

VULTURE'S CIRCLE